# TEASING

# TEASING

## Innocent
## Fun
## or
## Sadistic
## Malice?

## By Linda Sones Feinberg

New Horizon Press                     Far Hills, NJ

Requests for permission should be addressed to:
New Horizon Press
P.O. Box 669
Far Hills, NJ 07931

Sones Feinberg, Linda
        Teasing: Innocent Fun or Sadistic Malice?

Library of Congress Catalog Card Number: Pending

ISBN: 0-88282-145-8

New Horizon Press

Manufactured in the U.S.A.

2000  1999  1998  1997  1996  /  5 4 3 2 1

# *Acknowledgments*

I would like to thank all those who encouraged and inspired me to write this book. I would also like to express my gratitude to those who provided me with resources and suggestions: Betty Sudarsky Bradley, James Callanan, Ellen Cunniff, Phyllis and Clive Dalby, Robert Evans, Leslie Gosule, Diane Gruenewald, Hubert Johnson, Anthony LaVerde, Lois Lang, Larry and Tricia Machado, Nancy Papagno, Mary Margaret Pappas, Karen Pick, Nancy Rhodes, Jeanne Shinto, Pamela Siegle, Nancy Frumer Styron, and Joan Sweeney.

Chapters 16 and 17—Helping Children Cope with Teasing, and Help for Bullies—were largely made possible by interviews with the very dedicated Gayle Macklem, M.Ed., NCSP, President of the Massachusetts School Psychologists Association, coauthor of the Reach Out to Schools: Social Competency Program of the Stone Center at Wellesley College, Wellesley, Massachusetts, Professor at the University of Massachusetts at Boston, and a school psychologist for grades kindergarten through twelve for the Manchester Public Schools, Manchester, Massachusetts.

Thank you to Joan Dunphy at New Horizon Press.

I would like to thank the members of my family who have been infinitely patient with me during the writing of this book. I would like to thank my daughters Marissa and Jennifer for their ideas on teasing and for all their affection. I am most grateful to Alec Feinberg, my husband and my favorite tease, for his continuous support and encouragement.

# Author's Note

This book is based on my research and experience, as well as my clients' own real-life experiences. Fictitious identities and names have been given to some people in order to protect individual privacy. For the purposes of simplifying usage, the pronouns his and her are often used interchangeably.

# Contents

# *Introduction*

Teasing—in its many different forms—is the basis of many psychological problems. Virtually no one escapes the teases in life. We are faced with a continuous series of choices which tease us and tempt us each day as we try to control our lives. It is often difficult for us to stay on our chosen paths because we are constantly confused, sidetracked, manipulated and entertained by various types of teasing which have the potential to take us away from the most important purposes of our lives: devotion to family, country and humanity.

Teasing sometimes hints of the sexual, but it involves much more than sex. This book will show that while some of us are sidetracked by the tease of sex, many more of us are distracted by the teases of money, power, glamour, addictive substances, gossip, or trying to get something for nothing by pursuing a life of gambling or criminal activity. In addition to sexual teasing and flirting, this book will attempt to consider other types of teasing: adults teasing children, children teasing one another, and adults teasing each other in and out of the workplace and in advertising. Teasing in entertainment via the media, literature, suspense, and game playing will also be explored.

# Teasing

I became interested in writing about the subject of teasing when I married a compulsive tease seventeen years ago. I did not realize Alec was a compulsive tease when I married him. I was only aware that he had a wonderful sense of humor. Right after we married, his teasing became relentless. He was at his worst when our oldest daughter Marissa, now fifteen, became seven years old. At that time her father teased her daily. Marissa would get frustrated and angry. Sometimes she would even cry.

Alec's favorite place to tease her was in restaurants where she could not get away from him and he had our undivided attention. I would be yelling, "You two! Cut it out! Behave yourselves!" I felt like I was the mother of them both. I would scold him with, "Grow up!" and he would counter, "Regress!" When we went to places with female servers he would try to get back at me by flirting with every waitress in sight, regardless of her age or appearance.

When Marissa was eleven, she referred to her father as her "brother-father" because her father behaved as she would expect a brother to behave, if she had a brother. We agreed we didn't need a brother in the house. We had Daddy! His teasing was incessant and problematic, a real issue in our family. We eventually got to the point of begging him to desist.

When my husband found out I was pregnant with our second daughter, Jennifer, now seven, his response was, "Oh great! I can't wait until she grows up so I can tease her!" He became quite miserable when I immediately scolded him and yelled, "Over my dead body!" Consequently, Marissa and I became protective of little Jenny. We worked very hard to help Alec lessen his teasing and learn how to communicate in other ways. Jenny can someday thank her sister and me for her "almost normal" childhood because we helped spare her the torture that Marissa tolerated. In the past four years, Alec has really made a sincere effort to mitigate his teasing, and we are grateful that he is now a recovering tease.

Needless to say, my husband and I used to disagree vehemently on the effects of teasing. He would say that teasing is all in fun. I would insist that some kinds of teasing were sadistic and controlling. He would counter with, "You have no sense of humor!" I would then remind him of my academic credentials and training as a professional psychotherapist. He would then challenge me with, "Well then, why don't you go look up a solution?"

I did try to look one up, but there were no books in print on the subject. What was available were mostly articles about children teasing each other written in professional sociological and educational journals, newspapers and popular magazines. None of these articles discussed the problems inherent in adult teasing or compulsive teasing. I was surprised that teasing, an extremely significant and universal form of communication, had never been thoroughly analyzed before. Different types of teasing affect everyone, regardless of age or background. We have all been teasers. We have all been teased. The more I thought about teasing and wrote about it, the more complex and pervasive the subject became.

I believe there are many different kinds of teasing and numerous motivations for teasing behavior. There is teasing and there is TEASING. Teasing can be a very serious problem when it is done by a compulsive or sadistic tease. Teasing can also cause significant difficulties when it leads to, or perpetuates, various self-destructive behaviors such as behavioral and substance abuse addictions.

# I

# *What Is Teasing?*

*Katharina: If I be waspish, best beware my sting.*
*Petruchio: My remedy is then, to pluck it out.*
*Katharina: Ay, if the fool could find it where it lies.[1]*

William Shakespeare, *The Taming of the Shrew*

A universal form of expression, teasing touches all of us. Yet our ability to define the word is as elusive as the definition of the word itself. Teasing is one of those words that we seem to understand intuitively, but not vividly. It's like giving someone directions. You know how to drive somewhere, but you couldn't possibly explain to someone else how to get there because you go by your instincts. Can you put the definition of teasing into words of your own? Our English language contributes to the confusion because we use the one word—teasing—to describe so many different behaviors which have various motivations and consequences. It is no wonder teasing is so difficult to define. The definition of tease teases us! I searched long and hard before I came up with my own personal definition of teasing.

According to the *Barnhart Dictionary of Etymology*, the word tease comes down to us from the Old English word *taesan*

# What Is Teasing?

which was used about the year 1000 to mean "pluck, pull apart."
Three hundred years later the word *tesien* appeared, with the
meaning to "separate the fibers of, shred or card (wool or flax)."
Before 1325 the word had become *tesen*. "The transferred sense of
to vex or worry, annoy, appeared in 1619," and "the sense of one
who teases is first recorded in Dickens's *Bleak House* (1852)."[2]

If "to tease" originally meant to raise the nap, the fibers
on cloth, then when the word was later applied to people, it would
translate into raising our nap, which is the hair on our heads.
This is, of course, the net effect of teasing: it is hair-raising!
Hence, we also developed the expression to "tease the hair" in
hairdressing circles. Used in a sexual way, teasing translates into
any activity designed to make the penis or the clitoris stand on
end.

My favorite dictionary definitions are: "An attempt to
break down one's resistance or to rouse one's wrath"[3] and
"Tempt or entice, esp. sexually, while refusing to satisfy the
desire aroused. . . . Perform a striptease."[4]

A teaser is "a girl or woman who seems to invite a male's
attention and favors, but who does not return them when given;
a cock teaser."[5]

My personal definition of the word tease is any remark,
activity, behavior, or mere presence of a person, place, or a thing,
which promises a shortcut to intimacy but contains a secret message. For example, a little boy teases the pretty new girl in school
who wears glasses by calling her "Four Eyes." She instantly
responds to him, albeit in a negative way, and the boy feels con-
nected to her for this brief time. Her anger causes a temporary
intimacy, a connection between them, because he has succeeded
in getting under her skin. The little girl may think the boy is
being deliberately mean. She may not understand his secret
message which is, "I love you. Pay attention to me. If you can't
love me, then please feel something, anything—even hate! Just
please notice me!"

A bullfighter teases the bull with his red cape. The bull is

promised a quick bodily connection to the matador if he immediately charges into the cape. What could be more intimate than
the horns of the bull mixed with the blood of the matador? The
hidden message from the bullfighter is, "Come closer so I can
stick my weapon in your neck."

The chocolate cake on the counter calls out, "Eat me! Eat
me and you shall be happy!" What is more intimate than putting
something in your mouth? "Wait a minute!" you protest. "Cakes
don't talk." That is ridiculous. Every compulsive eater knows
that cakes do talk. Candy bars and ice cream cartons talk as well.
Unfortunately, the hidden message is, "Eat me and I shall make
you fat!"

Like the chocolate cake, the roulette wheel calls out to the
gambler, "Play me! Play me and I shall make you rich! Put your
money right on me. Touch me!" The secret message here is,
"Sucker!"

The prostitute teases her perspective customer with her
revealing clothes. This is the ultimate promise of a shortcut to
intimacy. "Pick me up and we will make love!" The hidden
message here is, "I really need the money!"

We usually think of teasing as being verbal, but it can also
be nonverbal. A snort, smirk, lifting of the eyebrows, or a shake
of the head can be teasing. Teasing can also be physical, as in
tickling.

Teasing has its benefits. Friendly teasing helps us to alleviate anxiety, cope, play and exercise our wits. Playful teasing can
even improve relationships at work and at home.

Sexual teasing helps to perpetuate our own species, as well
as many other species of the universe. Mating is often initiated
by flirting behavior, another form of teasing, and may be consummated after direct sexual teasing has occurred.

Teasing in advertising is central to our economy.
Advertising tempts the consumer to buy by teasing him.
Advertising promises to deliver something in exchange for a
purchase. The hidden promise of the tease is never spelled out

because it can never be fulfilled. However, it is strongly implied so that people will get the message. "Buy our cosmetics, apply us to your intimate places, and we will give you hope that you will look younger." Perfume ads suggest women will be more sexually desirable. Automobile ads feature lovely female models to coax men into imagining that the models come with the cars. The power of the tease is so strong that the consumer forgets or denies when he makes the purchase that the models are simply being paid and are not truly involved with the purchases. Since the customers who succumb to this kind of advertising will never be satisfied by the potential promises of their products, they will keep buying, hoping the next line of cars or cosmetics will solve their problems. The success of advertising proves that most people can be seduced and controlled by teasing.

Teasing, as a form of humor, entertains us via the most popular situation comedies and talk shows on television. The producer of *Live with Regis & Kathie Lee*, Michael Gelman, has said the secret of the couple's chemistry is affectionate, teasing humor. *People* magazine reported that, "It's the teasing, intimate interplay between Reiser (Paul) and Hunt (Helen) that has helped make *Mad (About You)* not only a Top 30 Nelson hit but a shrewd commentary on yuppie wedlock '90's-style—as well as other states of the union."[6] The success behind the Bundys, in *Married With Children*, is derived from the notorious teasing that goes on among the entire family. Al will tease and insult Peg, and she will just smile and say, "Oh, Al . . ." What makes the Bundys so special is that even though they are so bad that our own families look ideal by comparison, they have the capacity to keep forgiving each other. The forgiveness and the unconditional love they have for one another enables them to stay together. *Married With Children* is a comedy about accepting and forgiving human foibles!

Often, teasing serves to amuse us in our personal, daily lives, especially when we admire the cleverness of a good zinger. Teasing can also entertain us when it appears in the form of suspense. From roller coaster rides to Alfred Hitchcock to modern thriller films, it is the suspense—the tease—which thrills us.

It is a tease for us to be intimate with real people whom we will never meet when we are offered a relationship with them through magazines, or on television. For example, the tease of soap operas is that they offer the viewer, on a daily basis, the false feeling of intimacy with television characters. This occurs to the point where the viewer may feel these characters are his or her actual friends. This kind of tease becomes addictive. Some viewers spend more time with their favorite soap stars than they are able to, or may wish to, with their own family members. It is also a tease when we are offered relationships with fictional characters in literature. There are people who are compulsive readers just as there are people who are compulsive soap opera fans. A compulsive reader, with a good book next to his bed, feels he always has a good friend on standby.

Sports fans respond the most enthusiastically to the tease of relationships with their favorite athletes. When Toronto won the World Series a few years ago, the fans got so excited that they trashed a town. Sports fans, as well as rock groupies, feel they have personal relationships with those they admire, but this is a false intimacy. The citizens of countries with monarchies feel the same way about the members of their royal families.

Movie fans can become obsessed with the tease of the screen relationship and try to force the relationship to become real. Most often this is attempted by writing to the film star, harassing her by taking unwelcome photos, stalking her, invading her home, kidnapping her, or inflicting bodily harm.

The relationship between a patient and his psychotherapist or psychiatrist is another type of tease. The patient and the therapist need to constantly remind themselves that they are not actually friends but involved in a professional, therapeutic relationship. It is not uncommon for a patient to describe his previous therapist to me as his "friend." Perhaps this tease of intimacy that we experience as therapists explains our motivation for choosing our careers. We enjoy the tease of intimacy with others. We thrive on the intimate secrets of others.

The tease of intimacy that people experience with their therapists is not very different from the tease of intimacy which people share with their hairdressers, manicurists, masseuses, personal trainers, housekeepers, home health aides, and other service providers. My manicurist suggests that several of her clients see her as a cheap therapist. She insists she hears as many secrets as I do as a psychotherapist. Perhaps we are so ready to confide in these people because these are relationships that we choose, that we feel in control of. As a result, we do not view these people as part of our daily struggles. We select them for time-limited, specific purposes. If our hairdresser is rude, we just leave and switch to another beauty salon.

We have all heard stories about therapists who sexually abuse their patients. We have also all heard stories of celebrities who have affairs with their hairdressers and who take their manicurists and personal trainers with them on vacations. These types of professional relationships, which later become personal, are often unequal by nature. They are necessary for certain types of insecure people who need to be thoroughly in control of their personal relationships.

The most personal form of verbal teasing occurs between two people who know each other. Every interpersonal tease is an indirect form of communication. Teasing is a way of saying one thing with words or body language, while meaning something else. There is an unspoken, hidden message in every tease. For instance, adult teasing is ambiguous. The person doing the teasing knows what his motivation is, at least unconsciously, while the person being teased attempts to understand the teaser's motivation. Some teases are harder to figure out than others. This leaves the person being teased in the control of the teaser. Many people resent being teased because they like to be in control and hate being manipulated and unsettled by any teaser. Others crave attention and would much prefer to be teased than to be ignored.

# 2

# *Why Tease?*

*It disturbs me to learn I have hurt someone*
*unintentionally. I want all my hurts to be intentional.*[1]

Margaret Atwood, *Cat's Eye*

**M**any people love teasing or being teased because they enjoy having their senses heightened. They love to feel excited. Teasing relieves the boredom and predictability of everyday life by substituting it with the element of surprise. People enjoy being teased by suspenseful films and books. Some like roller coasters. Sex addicts crave the seduction process. Others itch to gamble. Sedgwick wrote, "I like to think I'm simply giving life a little kick in the pants . . . rearranging the universe for a second, turning what is into what is not."[2] A good verbal tease can pull the rug out from under someone who is not even standing on a rug!

Sam, forty years old and married fifteen years, confessed, "I constantly tease my wife. I drive her nuts! I tell her things that aren't true to get her going. We bought a turkey for Thanksgiving. I put it in the freezer and then asked her if she'd seen the turkey. Her response was, 'Oh, Sam. That was a bad one. That wasn't funny.' I really did do it to make her laugh."

Sheila shared, "Once my father and his brothers put a huge serving bowl and a huge spoon at my grandfather's place at the table for breakfast. They always teased him that he ate the same thing for breakfast every day of his life, and they didn't think he would notice the size of the bowl or the silverware. It was their way of teasing him. He never even noticed—that is, he didn't let on anyway."

For many people, teasing is a learned behavior. It seems to run in families. Children learn how to tease from their parents as well as their peers. There also seems to be a tendency for women who grew up with teasing fathers and grandfathers to marry men who are teasers. This should not be surprising considering that teasing is a style of communication and a way of expressing feelings. What we look for as adults is often what we were comfortable with or used to as children, even if what we were used to was a negative influence in our lives.

Teasing is a quick attempt at intimacy or a substitute for intimacy by people who crave it, but are afraid of intimacy or feel unable to express it. People who frequently tease have difficulty handling and expressing their own true feelings. Bruce confided, "I don't have a hard time saying 'I love you,' but in general, I have a hard time expressing myself to anybody. Sometimes I get the feeling that it's too much work or too difficult to explain how I feel or to convey what's in my head, so I keep my mouth shut. It's easier for me just to tease when I want to connect with someone." Instead of being direct, honest and open with their feelings, people like Bruce beat around the bush by teasing.

Because most teasers have difficulty handling and expressing their own personal feelings, they focus on the feelings of others. Thinking about how to tease someone else distracts teasers from thinking about their own feelings. Teasing frees them from having to think about any unpleasant feelings that may preoccupy them, such as feelings of insecurity or loss, or feeling out of control of their lives.

Teasing can also be used to avoid being sentimental or to cover up real feelings of affection. Some people have difficulty speaking to others in an affectionate manner because they did not grow up around people who did this. Nancy, a forty-year-old woman, shared the experience of her wedding rehearsal dinner some fifteen years earlier. "Because my husband's family never said 'I love you' to him, he was incapable of being demonstrative, incapable of saying 'I love you' in a group situation and so his speech at our wedding rehearsal dinner was a teasing speech. All I can remember is he said something about my ability to make eggs. His speech was so painful to me that even though I have an excellent memory, I can't remember what else he said. Although I completely understood why my husband teased me at the rehearsal dinner, I was very disappointed and tried not to make an issue of it. I was too afraid of my own emotions to bring it up. I would say it was a traumatic experience. Since my husband is usually incredibly eloquent, my expectations were very great. My husband is a marketing expert; he is a master of presentation. He had his chance to do his number for me and he blew it. Everyone there thought he was so clever, but I didn't think it was nice. I just didn't want to face my anger."

For some people, teasing is as close as they get to feelings of love and affection. Warm, playful teasing is a form of affection and can enhance friendships and closeness between family members and friends at work or at play. Sybil shared, "My grandfather and my dad were big teasers. My father's sister Ruth was teased the most as a child. She would get a phone call, and her father would answer and say, 'Ruth? Ruth who? Oh, that Ruth! Let me check and see if she is under the bed.'"

Teasing can also be a cowardly way of confronting someone, a way to say, "I don't like what you are doing."

Jerry explained, "Sometimes I've teased people when, deep down, I've wanted them to know they aggravated me. I'm not a confrontational type of person."

Teasing may also serve to totally reject someone, or to expel a person previously included or on the fringes of an intimate circle of friends. Teasing also can be the mode of communication for rejecting an individual who is used as a scapegoat for the problems within a group. In referring to groups run by social workers, Dinkmeyer and Muro state, "The use of a scapegoat is a convenient way for the group members to reduce individual and group anxiety by making the assumption that one or a few individuals are the sole possessors of undesirable trait mannerisms, or behavior."[3] To this Antsey adds, "This frees the group of feelings of inadequacy and guilt, and in a sense performs a useful function in 'freeing' the group to progress with its other tasks."[4]

In this twentieth century, where we are lacking in intimacy, teasing promises a shortcut to intimacy and strong feelings of connectedness. Because our technology offers us seemingly infinite choices, it is hard to select and limit our activities or options or commit to any one person who might offer genuine intimacy. It is difficult to become intimate and confide in others in a world where people often feel the only people they can trust with their secrets are their mothers or their therapists.

There is tremendous pressure in our society to be perfect and jovial—to have it all together.

As a result, too many people in our culture only offer the tease of a fair weather friendship. As I have observed in my work with the newly widowed, many people are terrified of the burden of other people's emotional problems.

A tease is a person who wants to be noticed and valued, not ignored. Through teasing, the teaser gets the attention he craves. Teasing may be the only way he knows to get to center stage. He will try to do this by exercising his wit, intelligence, and imagination, as well as his powers to amuse, flirt, annoy, or insult with clever ad libs.

A compulsive tease is often a multi-talented individual who needs an outlet for her creativity. Therefore, she chooses teasing as her pastime or her hobby, in order to amuse herself and to showcase her talent. She feels the need to show off! A clever line makes the teaser feel smart, self-confident and victorious—all in just a few seconds.

The teasing aspects of certain activities may motivate a person to participate in those activities. For instance, for the addicted golfer, golf is the biggest tease of all games. Golfers say that everyone, even really bad golfers, swings like Jack Nicklaus once in a while. A golfer then assumes, "If I did it once, I can do it again!" That is the tease! Sounds just like the addiction to gambling which occurs after a big win. Crossword puzzle fanatics will tell you a puzzle is an enormous tease because you know the number of spaces for the word, and so you feel you should be able to guess the word. Personally, I feel the game of Scrabble is a much bigger tease than any other game. What could be a bigger tease than having a seven-letter word in the little rack with no available space for it on the board? What about jigsaw puzzles? A difficult jigsaw is like looking for a needle in a haystack when you are sure the needle is there. A terrific tease. Card games are also powerful teasers as you wait and hope your card comes up. I have no doubt that millions of young people would argue and say that video games are the biggest tease and the most addictive of all games. Each person's favorite games are the ones that are addictive, and the ones that are addictive all involve teasing! This is true for the board game of Monopoly as well as those lucky enough to play the real life game of Monopoly. This is true for the surfer who travels the world looking for the perfect wave.

Teasing can be a way to give "affectionate digs. . . . It can also thicken the skin and help us not take ourselves too seriously."[5] In some cases, a playful dig may be a useful way to defuse a difficult situation. For example, my father, who is no longer able to drive himself around due to deteriorating health, is the worst backseat driver in the world. Any ride, even if it is just around the corner, will include at least a dozen complaints about my driving. One day I figured out a way to make him stop. Now when he says, "Why didn't you come to a complete stop at that stop sign and count to three like I taught you?" I smile and reply, "I did it just to aggravate you, Dad." Inevitably, my line puts a smile on his face and calms him down. It helps us avoid getting into an argument and makes me feel less tense.

"Playfulness can also put a lighthearted spin on interchanges between husband and wife. . . . Affirmative playfulness, which includes affectionate teasing, can help couples relax and even resolve disagreements."[6] My husband used to try to resolve our arguments by knocking on our bedroom door, after I had slammed it shut, and then opening the door with a huge marshmallow in his mouth. This would make me explode into laughter, lower my defenses, and help defuse the tension between us.

Unfortunately, the same sort of playful teasing which is welcome in one situation may not be welcome in another arena where it may discourage rather than encourage intimacy. For example, my husband is still trying to learn that if he tells me a joke during sex while I'm aroused, it's a turnoff. He is also still learning not to ruin the climax of every romantic film we see by cracking a joke just when I am about to let the tears flow. For instance, we went to see *Love Affair* with Warren Beatty and Annette Bening, which is a beautiful, old-fashioned movie. At the end, just when he knew I'd be crying, my husband gave me that teasing look of his which said, I knew it would make you cry, you pathetic softie. That look took the edge off my emotional moment, but it was a vast improvement over a joke.

Forty-two-year-old Tommy confessed, "My wife probably wishes I didn't tease. It is a nuisance if she doesn't think it's funny. I really don't like to annoy my wife. I get disappointed if my wife doesn't laugh. Then of course sometimes she laughs and then it's worth it."

Evelyn, Tommy's wife, responded, "It's hard being married to a josher sometimes. Generally speaking, I would say that teasing is a plus in marriage. He will stop when he's driving me nuts. What I don't like is that his teasing makes me the bad guy.

# Teasing

I don't like to be the one to set limits and to say 'Stop.'"

I will tease and make fun of myself as a tension reliever in my marriage. If I set the table for breakfast, for example, for oatmeal, I must put the milk pitcher on the table. Leaving milk outside of the refrigerator for any period of time troubles me for fear the milk will sour. As a result, I will make fun of myself and say to my husband, "Hurry up and pour your milk on your oatmeal. You know I'll have a breakdown if that milk is out for another thirty seconds!" In this way, instead of accusing him of being always so slow to get his act together or his oatmeal ready to eat, I put the blame on myself.

Teasing can also ease the pressures of everyday life. One night when my husband was dressed up to deliver a talk, he asked me how he looked. "You forgot your earring," I joked. The laugh that followed eased the tension he was feeling.

Playful teasing can be a way for couples to compete with each other. For example, my husband asked me to pick up a voter registration form for him when I made my next trip to the library. "It's about time you registered to vote! We've only lived here two years!" I teased him.

"Oh, I don't really want to vote," he replied. "I just want to be registered in case you decide to run for something. Then I can vote against you!"

Unfortunately, there is often a fine line between playful and hurtful teasing. You may feel safe teasing your spouse because you feel you really know your mate and can predict how he will react. In truth, there are too many variables out of your control, such as whether or not your spouse had a bad day. If he had a bad day, he may have temporarily lost his sense of humor, or, at the least, his ability to laugh at himself. Did you have an audience when you teased your partner? What was the reaction of the audience? How your spouse perceived your tone of voice and your facial expression will also affect the response you get. If one partner is hurt by a tease, it is up to the teaser to make amends by explaining the hidden message behind the tease. In order to understand her motivation, the teaser may first have to read this book!

Teasing can be a fun, friendly contest between mates or an unfriendly, painful competition. Some people with deep-seated insecurities feel a desperate need to compete and a constant desire to prove themselves. Even in personal relationships, a compulsive tease needs to feel superior. The relationships of a compulsive tease will not be equal. For a compulsive tease who is not in a position to win at sports, a war of words is enough of a battlefield—if he is victorious. There is also less risk of bodily harm than with other types of aggression. Teasing can be a way of saying, "I'm king here," whether at home or at work.

Sometimes teasing changes from merely unfriendly to downright humiliating. Sometimes this is deliberate. Other times the teaser has merely lost awareness of the feelings of others due to his own self-absorption. A teaser may claim he has the need to break down the pretensions of other people. What the teaser may not understand is that some pretensions are unconscious psychological defense mechanisms that serve to protect a person's ego and that these defenses may be necessary for the survival of the individual.

When you tease someone, you are only telling or giving away part of what you have to offer or to say. You are withholding the other part, so you are in control of the communication and the situation. This is true for strippers in nightclubs and peep shows. They are withholding much more of their sexuality than they are giving away. This is also true of gambling casino owners. They end up withholding much more of the players' money than they will return to the players. Finally, this theory may apply to husbands and wives who tease each other, and school children as well.

The hidden message of any particular tease may be unclear. "Indeed, the ambiguous nature of teasing makes it hard to analyze the true meaning of a specific barb. . . . The very essence of a tease is that its meaning is always open to interpretation, particularly by the person on the receiving end."[7]

June, a forty-five-year-old librarian, complained that the director of her library observed her and a male librarian in an animated discussion. Apparently, the director felt left out of the conversation and jealous and wanted to put in his two cents. "Now you two behave!" He turned to June and added, "We knew where you were in the sixties! Walking around in miniskirts!" June was at a loss to figure out why her boss made that remark. The ambiguous nature of the remark left her feeling out of control and resentful, wondering what he meant.

Why would someone tease another person to humiliate him when he could just insult the person in a straightforward manner? The difference is that an insult is aimed directly at a person. A tease reflects attention back to the teaser who wants to be admired for his clever zinger. This type of teasing serves to elevate the teaser in the eyes of others while putting someone else down. This can be a way for the teaser to get revenge for some perceived wrong done to him or just to reject the other person outright.

A teaser wants to connect with others in a dominant way. The teaser will do this by trying to unsettle others or to elicit a hair-raising type of emotional response. As David, a thirty-eight-year-old compulsive tease, explained to me, "I've been teasing as long as I could talk. It's how I grew up. My family is a bunch of kidders. If you took teasing away from me, I'd die. Teasing is my life."

# 3

# *Compulsive Teasing—*
# *Who Has the Problem?*

*Fremont's ears were much too large for his head. I couldn't*
*help staring at them as we pulled away from the toll plaza. . . .*
*He must've been teased about them when he was little, I*
*thought.*[1]

Scott Smith, *A Simple Plan*

A person who gambles compulsively is not addicted to
gambling per se. He or she is addicted to the high received
from winning or losing or being "in action." Like a gambler, a
compulsive tease is not addicted to teasing per se. This high
comes from being in control of another person, from causing
another person to react, from the power the person feels when he
or she teases.

If a person is a compulsive tease, that means her teasing
is more than simply habitual. It means the person is driven to
tease by forces or reasons she may not understand. She may also
be in a constant state of denial that she teases compulsively, that
she has a problem or that she is doing anything wrong.
Compulsive teasing is a habit that does not show on the outside
of the body, like an addiction to food, and so it is easy to deny. A

# Teasing

compulsive tease will not lose her home or go bankrupt like a compulsive gambler and will not be arrested for driving under the influence like a compulsive alcoholic. A compulsive tease will, however, create serious problems in her relationships at home, at work, and in the community. If her victims are lacking in assertiveness, she may have an uninterrupted teasing career which could last a lifetime.

In trying to understand the denial of someone who teases, the concept of "Whose Problem is Whose?" becomes important. As a psychotherapist, I can assure you that if a person is unaware or unwilling to admit that she has a problem, then, for all practical purposes, she doesn't have one, even if everyone around her has a problem because of her.

Here is an example to help explain the concept of "Whose Problem Is Whose?" Loretta is the wife of a typical couch potato who loves to watch sports on television. She comes to see me for counseling and complains that her husband has a serious problem which is: wasting his life in front of the television set. She claims that as a result of his problem, he refuses to take her anywhere. She feels grossly neglected, and the marriage is going downhill. Things are in crisis as football season is in high gear. Loretta is threatening him with "No sex until football season is over!"

Through therapy, Loretta is helped to understand that when her husband watches sports shows on television he is doing exactly what he wants to do and he is thoroughly enjoying himself. Therefore, he does not have the problem. Loretta has the problem, because she does not approve of his obsession with spectator sports. Loretta is advised that she will either have to accept him for who he is and find some new companions who share her own interests, or she will have to divorce him. He is not going to change!

What about teasing? Who has the problem? Most teasers are aware they are teasing. What a teaser may be in denial about is his motivation and the reasons for his continuous need to tease.

# Compulsive Teasing

A tease will often insist his motivation is harmless, and if you cannot take his teasing you have the problem. He is right! You do have the problem! You are a "teasee."

Teasing requires at least two people, the teaser and the teasee. Generally, the teaser is teasing for the effect it has on the teasee. Sometimes the teaser is teasing for the effect it has on an audience of one or more people surrounding the teasee. The teaser may also have a sidekick or accomplice who urges him on. Sometimes the teaser merely plays to the audience or tries to impress his accomplice, succumbing to peer pressure. At times like these, the identity of the teasee or his feelings may be of absolutely no consequence to the teaser.

Understanding the motivations of the teaser is helpful to the teasee in handling his feelings about being teased. (See Chapter 2: Why Tease and Chapter 4: The Personalities of Teasers.) For example, if the person teasing merely plays to his surrounding audience, it is easier not to take his teasing personally. The teaser gets his high from controlling his audience, and the victim is merely the convenient scapegoat. He is just in the wrong place at the wrong time.

It is the teasee who always defines what type of tease is taking place by her own reaction to the tease. If the teasee is enjoying the tease, then the tease is a benign or friendly tease and does not present a threat. To withstand the negative effects of teasing, a person must have a certain amount of self-confidence and the ability to laugh at herself. It also helps if a person has a life history where she connects teasing, in her own mind, with playful pranks and good times. When a person is teased, she is put in a situation where she may be temporarily out of control in an unexpected and unpredictable situation. Therefore, easy going and flexible people who are able to adapt to new circumstances are generally able to withstand the negative effects of teasing better than anxious and rigid people who need to feel in control at all times.

If the teasee does not enjoy the tease, then the tease is a

problem for the teasee. In this case, whatever purpose the teaser might have in his own mind is not important. Good intentions mean nothing in teasing. It is only how the teasee feels that matters. For example, people who were overweight as children and who were teased may also have low self-esteem. Being fat may have been associated with being unintelligent. As adults, they may still suffer from the inability to cope with early teasing. When teased they find it painful, and such remarks can cause long term suffering. Because feelings are not necessarily rational or predictable, it is impossible to guess with absolute certainty how any individual will react when teased.

It is also impossible to predict with absolute certainty who will be teased and who will not be teased. Anyone can be a teasee, the victim or the target of teasing behavior. While some vulnerable and sensitive people who are lacking in assertiveness may find themselves frequently teased, some self-confident types will also get their share.

The only person who will not be teased by a particular teaser is an individual who intimidates the teaser. Intimidation is a very personal feeling based on one's past history; consequently, it is impossible to predict which person will intimidate another. It is interesting that *The Synonym Finder* lists the following as synonyms for intimidate:

1. Overawe, awe, cow, subdue, daunt; domineer, bully, bullyrag, browbeat, buffalo, push around; terrify, petrify, frighten, affright, scare; dismay, appal, alarm, abash.

2. Tyrannize, terrorize, threaten, coerce, compel, twist arm, bulldoze; extort, pressure, rough up, lean on, bear down on.

3. Dishearten, deter, discourage, dispirit, psycho out, one-up.[2]

What this means is that a person will not tease someone he fears. (See Chapters 14 and 15 on how to cope with unwanted teasing.)

Some teasers will avoid teasing people who are sensitive, unpredictable, or people they don't know well. They may fear their teasing remarks will be unwelcome or misinterpreted. Often teasers will not tease someone upon first meeting her but will wait until they get to know the person better.

People are often teased because of identifiable or distinguishable features or behaviors. People are teased because of their accents, backgrounds, age, extremes in weight or height, hair colors or styles, types and styles of clothing or jewelry, appetites, level of sexual attractiveness, size of sex characteristics such as breast sizes and sexual preferences, high or low I.Q., facial features especially noses, males with long eyelashes, skin eruptions or scars, those with unusual occupations, even those with Ph.D. degrees!

Children who look, talk, or behave differently and those who are overweight, stutter, or wear glasses can be prime targets. The new child on the block—to whom no one owes any loyalty—may also suffer. Children with learning disabilities or physical handicaps as well as those who suffer chronic illnesses may be the subjects of teasing. (See Chapter 19: Children with Disabilities and Teasing.)

People may be teased about any unusual devices they utilize from canes, crutches and wheelchairs, to hearing aids, large briefcases, or small lunch boxes. People may be teased for having unusual pets or unusual taste in art or architecture, or even food.

People can also be teased for their intense passions, likes and dislikes. Bookworms, addicted sports enthusiasts, compulsive shoppers and house cleaners may all be teased. People whose passions deviate from the norm such as gay people or very religious people may be teased as well.

In some closed environments, such as a family, classroom, work environment, prison, or even a group therapy session, one particular person may be scapegoated. In a discussion of social work with groups, Ansley cites Heap's observation "that the central processes involved in scapegoating are those of projection and expiation. In essence, group members finding themselves to possess feelings and characteristics they do not wish to, ascribe these to a particular individual who is then isolated and rejected for possessing them."[3]

People may also be teased for their close association with a scapegoat. The sibling, parent, or boss of a scapegoat may be teased. In the same way, a relative or friend of a person who has done something shameful, such as having engaged in criminal activity, or a relative of someone who has committed suicide, will suffer for the sins of his associate. Sometimes, children whose parents have died, whatever the reason, are teased unmercifully.

Any eccentricity or idiosyncrasy is fair game for teasing in our culture. We live in a conformist society which means that people feel safest around what they can control and predict. If a person represents something the majority of people around him don't understand, the majority may feel threatened. They then pick on the person to get rid of negative feelings and then blame the person for causing them. This is why it is so important to educate young children from the earliest grades in school about the validity of individual differences regarding race, culture, religion, and sexual preference. When people understand each other's differences, they are able to tolerate them much better.

Can a person be addicted to being a teasee? For some people, getting negative attention is better than getting no attention at all. If a teasee allows herself to be teased continually by constantly exposing herself to the teasing and by failing to change her reaction, the teasing may become more than habitual; it may actually become traditional and expected within the person's community.

Can a teasee ever be blamed for the tease? No. This is similar to blaming the victim of a rape for wearing a short skirt. It is possible for a person to knowingly or unknowingly set himself up for a tease (like the time I asked a mechanic if he'd mind checking my fluids), but it is the teaser who makes the conscious decision to make the teasing remark. A compulsive tease can never resist a good zinger. She will never censor her impulse to tease. She will tease whenever the opportunity presents itself, because she needs the high she gets from being in control.

Theoretically, it is possible to say that the teasee has a masochistic need for punishment, but this is probably incorrect. It is much more probable that due to a limited intellect, inexperience, cultural differences, or just plain fear, a person may be unable to change his reactions to the teasing remarks, thereby unwittingly perpetuating the remarks. There may also be peer pressure not to confess that the teasing is upsetting, thereby forcing the teasee to pretend he is ignoring the teasing. In most instances, the teasee is nevertheless feeling its effects, and not actually fooling anyone.

Can the teasee be guilty of being too supersensitive or hypersensitive to teasing remarks? Obviously, some people are more sensitive to teasing than others, given their own personalities and life histories. What if the teasee was hardly teased as a child and does not understand the joking meaning of the tease? What if the teasee was tortured with teasing by older brothers and sisters and every tease he experiences as an adult reminds him of those past bad experiences? In this case, the individual may experience a negative transference reaction, which means he may react inappropriately by overreacting or misinterpreting a current mild tease. However, accusing someone of being supersensitive puts the blame on the teasee instead of on the teaser who, in fact, should be held totally responsible for the effects of his words. If you don't know a person's life history, how can you tease him and be guaranteed he will not get upset? You cannot.

Twenty-seven-year-old Emily shares this episode. "My husband will say, 'Do you think I would say something to hurt your feelings? No. Teasing is just my way of making contact. If I choose the wrong way to do it, don't hang me for that!' However, this is a rationalization by Bob. If he's smart enough to succeed in a difficult business, he's smart enough to speak in an unambiguous way." Teasing is ambiguous. A tease is either trying to convey a good message or a bad message. Teasing is a double-edged sword. The question is, can the teasee get beyond her sensitivity to figure it out or will she take it to heart? Often, the teasee can't get beyond her sensitivity.

Even though we should not blame the teasee for the tease, we can still say it is the teasee who has the problem, because it is the teasee who reacts. By their reactions, some people will stimulate repeat performances by the teaser. The people who are teased are not necessarily the weakest people or the easiest to pick on, but they are usually supersensitive and less able to tolerate being made fun of. Some may blush, while others may cry. In the 1994 television production of *Scarlett*, a beautiful belle asks Rhett Butler why he teased her so. "Because of the delicious way you respond!" confessed Rhett.[4]

For some teasees, being teased is a major problem. For others, it is only a minor issue. How big an issue it is depends on many factors. Who is the perpetrator of the teasing remarks? What kind of relationship exists between the teaser and the teasee? Where is the tease taking place? Is there an audience to witness the tease and further humiliate the teasee? How frequent is the teasing? Does it vary or is it repetitive? What about the personality of the teasee? How comfortable is the teasee with his own self image? What if the teasee just had a very bad day? Because of these many variables, no two people will react in exactly the same way to a particular teasing remark.

This brings up the issue of submission to teasing. Who allows teasing and by whom? Thirty-five-year-old Diana confessed, "I wouldn't have complained to my grandfather or my father about their teasing. They were too important to me. Anger has its potential outcome—loss. And certain people I shield from my anger. I feel that few people are in control of their anger enough to do it in an unemotional way. I don't shield my husband from my anger. I have a different relationship to him than I have had to any other man in my life. I have an angry response to his teasing. I have had a lifetime of being teased, and I can

# Compulsive Teasing

finally say, 'I don't like it.'"

Can a teasee be in a total state of denial about the tease and not react at all? It would certainly be possible for a teaser's remarks to go in one ear and out the other of a potential teasee, without that person reacting. However, if that happened, then no tease took place. This is similar to the old question, If a tree falls in a forest, did it make any noise if there is no one there to hear it? Is it a tease if there is no one there to be teased? No. Someone has to react for there to be a valid tease.

Sometimes a person will try to hide or mask his feelings of shame, humiliation and anger to being teased, taunted or bullied. Sometimes reactions are involuntary, such as blushing. Sometimes a teasee feels such a strong emotional reaction that he may get extremely angry or annoyed immediately. Should a teasee feel guilty for showing strong feelings to a teaser, for allowing the teaser to get his goat, to pull his chain? What does this say about him? By reacting strongly to the tease, is the teasee allowing someone to get control of him? Does this mean that he is easily influenced or vulnerable to someone else's power or control? In my opinion, no. It means he is a human being. If this human being wants the teasing to stop, he should try controlling his reactions. If he gets very upset, the teaser will be pleased and the teasing will continue.

There are other major reactions which will be dealt with later in this book. How should the teasee react to the teaser? How can a teasee honestly deal with his emotions while being teased and afterwards? How can the teasee save face? How can he recoup after a tease and recover his equilibrium? Can he ever put the relationship back on an equal footing? Can he ever come out on top? How should the teasee deal with a compulsive tease who is in a state of denial about a significant behavior that is affecting everyone around the tease whether at home, at work, at school, or at play?

Susan, a forty-three-year-old homemaker who has been teased all her life, insists, "When I'm teased, I can take it pretty well. You need to learn to take it. It's part of maturing. You learn that most teasing is not true, not important. It is just a joke. You shouldn't take it seriously or personally."

# 4

# *The Personalities of Teasers*

> *Gilbert reached across the aisle, picked up the end of Anne's long red braid, held it out at arm's length and said in a piercing whisper: "Carrots! Carrots!" . . . And then—thwack! Anne had brought her slate down on Gilbert's head and cracked it—slate, not head, clear across.[1]*

> L.M. Montgomery, *Anne of Green Gables*

The following are twenty-seven different teasing personalities.

1. *THE STRATEGIST.* This is the person who uses teasing the way a checkers player uses the double-jump strategy. The strategist recognizes when another teaser is trying to get "the jump" on him, yet he allows it. However, he then quickly teases that person in order to come back on top. A good example of this occurs in the film *The Bridges of Madison County.* Clint Eastwood surprises Meryl Streep by picking some wildflowers for her, thereby changing the tone of their relationship. Meryl appears to be flattered and then quickly tells him the wildflowers are poisonous, when in fact they are not. This totally unsettles Clint. Meryl then laughs, embarrassed, and denies knowing why

she said the flowers are poisonous. In essence, Meryl "double-jumps" Clint so that she can regain both her control and the advantage in the relationship.

2. *THE SPY.* The spy loves to secretly uncover the vulnerabilities of another and then expose him or her by teasing. Ross Benson tells us in his biography of Prince Charles that Queen Elizabeth is a "spy." Benson says, "There was the Queen's trick of leaving her chocolates out on the grand piano in the salon by the front entrance at Sandringham and then peering down unseen from the window in the corridor overhead to see who would filch one. She took a great delight in teasing the embarrassed culprits who could not work out how they had been found out."[2]

3. *THE BUG.* This person is annoying, like a fly. You keep swatting her and she keeps coming back for more. The bug is not very clever and will repeat the same unfunny, irritating remarks. The bug will commonly use name-calling which attempts to reduce a whole person to one particular trait or symbol. This is the type of individual who calls all tall men "Shorty," all fat people "Skinny," all those who wear braces "Tinsel Tooth," and all eyeglass wearers "Four Eyes." The bug thinks she is funny, but no one else agrees with her. The bug will tease the woman named Olive Green about her name and think she is original when it is actually a very old joke. This person is often anxious and miserable—and misery loves company. She likes to annoy people in order to pass her own frustrations onto others and make herself feel in control of the smallest things. This is the only way she knows how to get attention. The bug gets no respect.

4. *THE ATTENTION GETTER.* The attention getter feels attention of any kind is better than none and will settle for teasing as a way to get it from the teasee. He is often very childish

and immature and has not developed the conversational or social skills necessary to gain attention in other ways. This individual has a relatively harmless teasing personality.

5. *THE HAM.* The ham merely plays to the audience which passively surrounds the teasee. The teasee is of no real consequence to her and just happens to be in the wrong place at the wrong time. This person wants to put on a show, be the center of attention, and uses teasing as her instrument. The ham wants to elevate herself in the eyes of others by putting other people down. This teaser can be dangerous as she may not see the teasee as an individual.

6. *THE ROASTER.* This individual plays to the audience but, in this instance, the teasee is a very significant person in his life. The roaster will tease in order to avoid showing real love and sentiment in public. The roaster grew up without seeing affection displayed openly, and it is impossible for him to be demonstrative in front of others. Roasting behavior is called for and expected at events like the Hollywood roasts. This is enjoyable for the roastee when he has been warned in advance that he is about to be roasted.

7. *THE SIDEKICK (THE ACCOMPLICE).* The sidekick gives the teaser permission to tease by urging her on and encouraging her. Unlike a passive audience, the sidekick takes an active role in the tease and may even criticize the teasee for being so sensitive. Ed McMahon, of Johnny Carson's *The Tonight Show*, was the ideal sidekick.

8. *THE HOMOPHOBE.* Although it can be true of the female sex, this is usually a man who is uncomfortable speaking to almost any other man on any real or emotional level for fear he will be perceived as feminine. The homophobe continuously chuckles nervously during his conversations with other men and

can only communicate with them by teasing. This person may be a closet homosexual.

9. *THE MOUSE.* This is the man who is terrified of women (or the woman who is terrified of men) and the power which they perceive the other sex has over them. They cannot speak in a straightforward manner to women (or men) and are forced by their own insecurities to tease if they wish to communicate with a member of the opposite sex. They lack confidence in their sexual performance and may never marry.

10. *THE MOCKER.* The mocker views teasing as a sport, and he thoroughly enjoys it. He will try to elevate himself in the eyes of others by putting people down. He feels genuinely superior to others. This type of teasing can be very competitive, especially when done in the locker room or the boardroom. Sometimes athletes in high school or college are very aggressive, and they will act in packs and attack someone. People vying for promotions at work may try to knock down the competition in this manner as well.

11. *THE BIG BULLY.* This individual usually has a particular scapegoat who serves as the object of her teasing. The scapegoat is usually perceived by the big bully as a very vulnerable, non-assertive person. The big bully tries to win by intimidation. She may be a confident, aggressive person with no conscience or she may actually be a very secure person who needs to feel there is someone worse off than herself. She may be unhappy and wanting to discharge her unhappiness onto another. The big bully may have been the victim of another big bully herself in the past, and she has learned this behavior. This type of individual would rather be a big bully than run the risk of being the teasee again. This is the type of teaser one usually associates with children teasing one another. This person never grew up.

**12. *THE LITTLE GUY (OR GAL).*** Like the small man who obsessively works out in the gym to develop oversized muscles to make up for his compact stature, the little guy teaser uses words to overcome or to overcompensate for his or her size. He tries to be the wittiest and the fastest. The little guy tries to put people off balance in order to display his sense of humor and to distract himself and others from the inadequacies he perceives regarding his physique. The little guy does this on an unconscious level, not intentionally. This type of tease is very intelligent, and it would be too painful to his consciousness to admit that his small stature bothers him to any great degree. He prefers to think that his personality and wit more than make up for his lack of height or strength.

**13. *THE SARCAZZER.*** This person uses sarcasm, either in a friendly or unfriendly way to tease others and get his points across. Sarcazzers have an especially hard time dealing with their feelings. Sarcasm is a form of passive-aggressive behavior, a way of being very aggressive in a passive way. These people will often engage in sarcastic teasing in the workplace.

Today's most famous sarcazzer is Roseanne of the hit television show. Here is an example of Roseanne's wit.

*Darlene:* Why can't I go to some stupid party?

*Roseanne:* 'Cause you're going to do the stupid dishes.

*Darlene:* That's why I don't get invited to parties. 'Cause I have dishpan hands!

*Roseanne:* Well, now, you're only thirteen, honey. Did you think your looks would last forever?[2]

A child psychologist confessed to me that she was addicted to her own sarcastic humor. This makes her feel guilty because she knows that sarcasm can have a negative impact and that it can be taken in two ways. "When I feel comfortable with someone, I assume they feel comfortable with me, and this frees me to be sarcastic. My problem is that I should never assume that someone is comfortable with me, but I keep doing it anyway. I worry that I should know better. One colleague at work got very angry at one of my sarcastic remarks. I became very apologetic. I said, 'Oh, God, talk to me. I didn't mean it. I presumed you'd know I'm always kidding.' I did feel she overreacted, and that wasn't good."

I suggested to her that perhaps being occasionally offensive is the price she has to pay for her joy in making funny, sarcastic remarks. It was interesting to me that this child psychologist, a single woman in her early forties, enjoyed sarcasm to the extent that she did. My gut reaction was that perhaps this woman was a bit tired of being nice and giving all the time, with no one at home to give anything back to her, and so she enjoyed getting in her share of sarcastic digs as a release of tension, anger and frustration.

14. *THE JOSHER.* This teaser is a frustrated, would-be stand-up comic. The josher likes to make fun of himself as well as others. He is the funniest kind of tease. This teasing can sometimes be friendly and playful while at other times annoying, especially if he repeats the same line several times. The josher also loves to tell jokes.

One josher explained himself to me this way: "I love to tease. I'm an intelligent guy, but I don't think you have to be intelligent to pick on other people's imperfections. I was never the big bully type. I never pick on the little guy. I'm constantly trying to find something funny in a situation. I definitely see teasing as interconnected with humor. I'll often be the first one in our group at work to notice something funny going on and the first one to notice the opportunity for a tease. People will say about me, 'Oh, he's got an incredible sense of humor. He's such a tease!' I love to laugh and tell jokes. I'd do almost anything to make other people laugh."

# The Personalities of Teasers

**15. *THE GAME PLAYER*.** The game player will be the first teaser to stop at the first sign of discomfort or at the request of the teasee. He also has the ability to apologize for his behavior. "Sometimes I'm going to tease and upset someone, but I've learned to live with that," the game player says. "If I find out they don't like it, I try to stop or change the way I tease and use more self-deprecating humor."

**16. *THE PRANKSTER*.** He thinks it is fun to turn the world upside down on occasion, just to see what will happen. The prankster enjoys playing tricks on people or teasing them in a physical way. This individual may use events or the threat of impending doom to tease people. He will tell you that your toilet is overflowing when it is not. When we were first married, my husband would answer the phone on a Sunday morning and inevitably it would be my mother who would ask for me. He'd say, "Linda? Okay, just a minute. I have to untie her!"

**17. *THE PRACTICAL JOKER*.** This is a person who wants to act out his teasing in the form of a little play. He is in a world of his own. What is funny to him may cause the rest of us to think the practical joker has a warped sense of humor. Tony, thirty-five years old, trashed his parents' condo while they were away on vacation and pretended burglars had been there. Tony thought that was hysterical. His parents, who had to hire a service to clean up the mess and had to buy new furniture, failed to see the humor of it.

**18. *THE RUG PULLER*.** This person gets her kicks from unsettling others, especially those people whose self-confidence she envies. This is the formally dressed woman who tells another formally dressed woman in the powder room that she has a run in her black stocking when there is no run. This person enjoys cutting through another's defenses. She will say she hates pretense and is a lover of the truth. In actuality, she is a very jealous person. The rug puller is power hungry and a control freak.

**19.** *THE MIMIC.* Like a talented cartoonist, the mimic is actually a very talented person who is capable of distinguishing a person's most salient characteristics and imitating them. The mimic can copy voices, posture, ways of walking and talking, as well as the attitudes of others. The best mimics get paid for doing this and often work as comedians. It is very flattering when Rich Little mimics you, but it may not be so flattering when done by your coworkers.

**20.** *THE COPYCAT.* This is the type of mimic who copies whatever you do or say at the same time as you do or say it, just to drive you crazy. This is a popular game among school children who enjoy keeping it up for great lengths of time.

**21.** *THE INTELLECTUAL.* This is the intelligent tease who gives himself points for his comeback lines. He prides himself on being gifted with words, double entendres and puns. He would like to elevate the status of teasing to a fine art. This person is a competitive tease. He wants to be admired for his wit. Barbara, a thirty-five-year-old wife, discussed her husband's affinity for teasing. "There is no question that my husband is a genius, but feelings are not part of his repertoire. It is much easier for him to be intellectual than emotional. My husband is a professional strategist. Everything is a game to him. He loves to display his intellect by teasing."

**22.** *PETER PAN.* This tease is a person who prides himself on his inventive name-calling. In Steven Spielberg's movie *Hook*, Peter Pan and his rival Rufio engage in a verbal duel with Tinkerbell as Pan's sidekick. When Peter finally becomes creative with his name-calling, he is recognized as the one and only Pan and the true leader of the Lost Boys.[3]

# The Personalities of Teasers

**23. THE FLIRT.** Teasing can be a form of emotional or sexual attention getting. Flirting behavior is teasing because it attempts to attract the attention of a prospective partner. Flirting can also be an invitation for an action. Serious flirting may offer a promise of future sexual play. It may also relieve tension between unavailable people who are attracted to one another but want to show respect for their sexual partners. Some married people are outrageous flirts. They regard flirting as Safe Sex. (See Chapter 5: Flirting.)

**24. THE SEXUAL TEASE.** This person uses teasing to captivate another person and, in turn, gets sexual attention. Some sexual teasing can be harmful to the psyche of the teasee. (See Chapter 6: Sexual Teasing.)

**25. THE DRILL SERGEANT.** This person is an actual drill sergeant, sports coach, or parent who uses the tease of humiliation to attempt to motivate others. Her intentions may be good but her actions are extremely difficult to tolerate. In the armed forces, the purpose of humiliating a new recruit is to destroy the recruit's ego and his psychological defense mechanisms so he will be able to be reconditioned to follow orders. These orders may, in the end, save his own life and the lives of his comrades. In sports, a coach might use humiliation as a dare, to make his team prove him wrong and to spur the athletes on to better performances. A parent might also try to motivate her child through the use of humiliation. Unfortunately, a person who uses humiliation in this way may simply be a big bully in disguise with the actual intention of elevating himself by putting others down.

**26. THE SADIST.** This is the most malicious type of teasing personality. This person exhibits truly aggressive behavior and thoroughly enjoys inflicting emotional pain and tormenting others. Teasing is used in this way as a form of torture, and it is destructive in nature. The sadist inflicts cruelty. He is much worse than a big bully. He does not need a scapegoat, an audience, or a sidekick to perform. This type of teasing among children definitely calls for adult intervention.

One study from Finland discusses the origins of sadism. "Pathological pleasure from inflicting as in sadism towards an animal or individual, may develop in extreme conditions of rejection and punitiveness. Blanchard and Blanchard also suggested that the conceptualization of one's prerogatives may become abnormal or defective as the result of certain life experiences. . . . It is typical of bullies to pick on other boys with minimal provocation. They have unloving and punitive parents, which has produced a defective view of their prerogatives and their challenges."[4]

27. *THE COMPULSIVE TEASE.* This person is addicted to any number of the above types of teasing and cannot control his own teasing behavior. He is in denial concerning his motivations for teasing and will not admit he has a problem. Living with such a person can be very difficult. (See Chapter 3: Compulsive Teasing—Who Has the Problem?)

# 5

# *Flirting*

*Richard Krebs, the sixth-grade bully, tells her he can see
her when she takes a shower. Although she knows this is
impossible, she thinks he may have some apparatus, the kind
boys invent and girls don't, that will allow him to see her, so
she takes faster and faster showers.[1]*

Lynn Luria-Suknick
*Do You Know the Facts of Life? (Quiz)*

Remember when Jessica Lange confided in Dustin Hoffman
(dressed up as a woman in the film Tootsie) her fantasy of
meeting an honest man? "You know what I wish, just once? That
a guy could be honest enough just to walk up to me and say, 'Hey,
listen! You know. I'm confused about this too. I could lay a big
line on you. We could do a lot of role playing. The simple truth
is, I find you very interesting, and I'd really like to make love with
you.' Wouldn't that be a relief?"[2] Dustin, later dressed as a man,
approached Jessica at a party with her fantasy opening line, and
she tossed the wine from her glass in his face!

When a new man approaches a new woman, or vice versa,
the situation is so sensitive that direct communication may be too

strong and potentially offensive. Some people give subtle hints about their interest in a light, indirect, teasing manner until they can be sure the other person shares their interest. This is one form of flirting.

Flirting is a type of teasing, as well as a form of communication. Flirting is also about playing a game where the goal is to make a quick connection with another person, to find a shortcut to intimacy. Rabin explains what happens: "Flirting is a process through which we explore increasing levels of intimacy. At first you engage another person with your eyes, from across the room. When your interest is acknowledged, perhaps with a smile or a gesture, you are permitted to come closer and begin a conversation. But how close is too close for a first encounter? How close you should get depends on how intimate you want to become."[3]

And Barrows confirms, "Flirtation starts off as impersonal, or fake-personal (via teasing and mock insult), and only progresses to the truly personal with both partners' consent."[4]

Flirting transmits a hidden message the same as other types of teasing. The underlying communication is to find out how intimate a person wants to become or if she wants to become intimate at all. Some flirts are so dedicated to the process that they have no interest in going beyond the flirting stage. These are people who get high emotionally, or aroused physically, by the process and see it as an end in itself. Some flirts merely have a need to lift their egos by confirming their attractiveness to others. Some people fear intimacy and commitment. Flirting is as close as they get to genuine intimacy. Others have no sexual experience or sexual self-confidence and feel limited to flirting as a way of relating to the opposite sex. Some view flirting as the ultimate form of Safe Sex.

Some flirts are married or involved and do not wish to complicate their lives with additional affairs. "No matter how happily married a woman may be, it always pleases her to discover that there is a nice man who wishes she were not."[5]

# Flirting

"I'm monogamous, but I couldn't live without some sexual connection with other women. . . . To some, flirting is the paprika of existence. Eye-lock, the sexy smile, the brushing touch on the arm: it makes them feel good."[6]

The most accomplished flirts are the ones who know flirting takes practice. They have the most open minds, the most adventuresome spirits, and they are able to imagine infinite opportunities from the most casual of meetings. Such flirts would never intimidate others with their aggressiveness. That would be such obvious behavior that it could not even be labeled flirting. Flirting is light and subtle. It does not call attention to itself, but has as its goal "to pass that sense of well-being on to others, to make human contact without saying a word, and to send this message of friendliness and warmth: 'I may not know you well, but I like you. I'm making this first gesture in the hope that you'll let me know you better.'"[7]

"Flirting is much like a good joke. Just as a good joke depends on the element of surprise, so flirting surprises both the person you have chosen to flirt with—and you."[8]

Flirting evokes images of Scarlett O'Hara before she was seduced by Rhett Butler in *Gone With the Wind*. Of course, Scarlett possessed a perfect profile and a tiny waist, but those physical advantages alone could not account for her enormous success with men. Scarlett enjoyed the flirting game as she strutted, blinked, smiled, and strutted. Scarlett was a consummate flirt who used every inch of herself, from her eyelids to her shoulders, to engage the interest of men. Most of all, however, she was attentive and flattered them. Scarlett's flirting made men feel desirable. It was only Rhett who saw through her hidden message and knew that behind her flirtatious teasing was a skilled manipulator whose motives were nowhere near as pure as they seemed.

The question is whether or not Scarlett gave flirting a negative connotation. If someone called you a flirt, would you feel insulted or complimented? That would probably depend on whether you see a flirt as a manipulating, role-playing, insincere person or as a friendly, playful, charming, sexual soul.

Psychologist Monica Moore, Associate Professor at Webster University in St. Louis, has studied flirting over the past twenty years. According to Dr. Moore, these are the ten most popular techniques for the use of body language in flirting:

1. SMILE. A beautiful smile is often hard for any man or woman to resist.

2. OCCASIONAL GLANCE. A common practice in flirting, the occasional glance is used to convey a message of interest.

3. HAIR TOSS. Often, a person's hair is one of his or her most attractive assets. By playing with one's hair, a man or woman draws attention to him or herself.

4. LICKING ONE'S LIPS. A suggestive come-on which makes one's lips appear ready for a kiss.

5. THE FIXED GLAZE. Unwavering eye contact is a very direct means of communication.

6. PARADE. This is when a man or woman walks seductively past the person they are trying to attract.

7. SELF-TOUCH. This is a subtle way of drawing attention to parts of the body, and of suggesting sensual energy.

8. GIGGLE. A giggle erases any nervousness a man or woman may feel. It also makes a person seem attainable.

9. DANCING ALONE. Dancing alone is an invitation to romance.

10. THE BRUSH. When a man or woman brushes up against a person, it establishes direct physical contact without seeming to do so on purpose.[9]

If you decide that flirting is a positive rather than a negative trait, you may wish to try it. Once you get a person's attention, what do you say? Jillian suggests, "Adjust your opening line to your flirtatious body language. If you are an outrageous flirt, your opening lines must compensate for this, so make them especially low key. If you are a low-key flirt, you can be a little more outrageous with your lines. Still, the more conservative you can be, the better."[10] The point is not to intimidate your partner.

Remember, in sex play, the most important part of the body is the brain; in flirting, the most important part of your body is the eyes. To establish the first level of intimacy and connect with another human being, look at him or her. In flirting, one looks at another with admiration and respect. You are not supposed to undress a person with your eyes in flirting. That would be intimidating, unfriendly, and definitely not flirting. (See Chapter 9: Sexual Harassment.)

What about "the stare" tactic in flirting? There is a debate over this! Rabin suggests it is less aggressive to look at all parts of someone's face, not just the eyes: "The object is to catch the gaze of a man or woman you find interesting, linger a while, then look away. Do this once and you will establish your identity in your partner's mind. Do it several times and your new acquaintance will begin to think of you as a friendly, familiar, and intriguing face in the crowd."[11]

Jillson recommends, "Try this: throw a glance to a person, and then, as soon as your flirting partner turns to meet your gaze, immediately lower your eyes."[12]

Gelman tells women to be more aggressive: "Let the guy know you are interested. Look directly at him. . . . Smile at him. Once you get the guy's attention and you are talking to him, there are a few things to keep in mind. You should keep eye contact while you are talking to the guy. Don't look around or you'll seem uninterested."[13]

My own suggestion is to trust your own flirting instincts and do what you feel comfortable with. What works for one flirt may not work for another, and what captures the attention of one person may not capture the attention of another. The strength of the initial eye contact will put you at a certain level of intimacy, and each person has to begin a new relationship at his or her own pace.

# Teasing

Another tip is, when you've captured the person's attention with your eyes, smile when you say hello. "No one can resist a cheerful, gregarious flirt."[14]

Jillson recommends something stronger than a smile. "When you say hello, pretend that there is an electrical current pulsating through your body. It is brief, like turning on a light bulb for just a second. Remember that what follows from an introduction or meeting depends on how your new acquaintance perceives your hello."[15]

To flirt effectively, be imaginative and original with your words. Never settle for any opening line that you have used before or heard someone else use before, especially in a book or a film. Your partner may have read or seen it too. If you are lucky, your flirting partner will be wearing an unusual article of clothing or jewelry or carrying an unusual prop for you to comment on. If the person is walking his dog, so much the better. Flatter the person or the dog. Be sincere. Giving an unexpected compliment works wonders. Telling a beautiful woman you like her smile, her teeth, or her humor will surprise a woman who is used to more general compliments.

If a person carrying an unusual prop makes it easier for you to open a conversation with that person, remember that you can do the same thing for others. When you are in the mood to flirt or attract attention, you may wish to wear something remarkable or carry something unusual with you such as an antique pocketbook or a hand painted scarf or a novelty tie.

My husband and I met while we were both trying to park our cars. I was pulling up behind him in my car, while he was parking his. I yelled out my window, "Would you mind moving up a bit? You're taking up two spaces!"

He pulled up, came out of his car, and watched me park mine. His opening line to me was, "You know, you are the best parker I have ever seen! I never thought you would get your car into that space." He recovered nicely from my negative criticism of his parking and turned it around and complimented me. He must also be a good parker because our cars have been parked together now for eighteen years!

What really works best is an open-ended question or a statement about your own feelings of the moment which calls for more than a yes-or-no response. It is hard work to begin a conversation with a person you don't know, especially one you are attracted to. It helps to remember that everyone is a bit shy with strangers. Some people in the media, who entertain us with their sparkling dialogue on their radio and television shows, are among the shyest people in the world in their own personal lives.

A few words must now be said about first impressions. Basically, first impressions are often false. Consequently, you should approach new people and allow new people to approach you with an open mind.

When I lecture on this subject, I love to entertain my audience by breaking down their first impression of me. I acknowledge that I appear to be a competent professional and a fairly attractive person. Then I confess to them that my fingernails are not really my fingernails and that it took three nose jobs for me to look the way I look. (The first nose job was to make me prettier. The second was to fix the breathing problem the first doctor caused by trying to make me prettier. The third was for free by the second doctor who forgot to fix my breathing and finally succeeded in making me prettier. I still can't breathe!) I admit to the audience that I color over the gray in my black hair, brighten my hazel eyes with green contacts, and that I just lost ten pounds. I also confess I have terrible allergies and absolutely no balance on the left side of my body so I can't ski, have any pets, or tolerate dust! I admit that while I seem so competent professionally, beneath the surface I am actually a harried housewife with two children, one of whom got her first bra on the same day that the other one got her first pair of panties! My oldest is now fifteen and constantly reminds me when I am too controlling with her (why I taught her what the word controlling means I'll never know) and a seven-year-old who controls me.

# Teasing

I go on and explain to the audience that things are not always what they appear to be. Some people are just better at hiding their flaws than others. The point is not to make up your mind about people until you can peel away their layers of defenses and get to know them.

I also like to share with my lecture audience an anecdote about a young widowed woman named Sophie, a lovely fortyish woman with a thick Russian accent. Sophie had a buxom appearance and wore very colorful blouses and scarfs. She was very excited on this particular evening at the support group I was running for young widowed people. She said she was so happy because her friends had found a nice Russian man for her to date and she was going to meet him the next evening. The following week she came to our support group profoundly depressed. "Do you know what happened?" she questioned us. "I opened ze door, and there was a short, fat, bald man. Is that all my friends think of me? That I am only worth a short, fat, bald man?" Clearly Sophie was distraught. For two weeks she did not show up for her support group meetings. On the third week she returned, looking extremely happy. We asked her what had transpired over the last few weeks to account for her newfound happiness. Sophie confessed she had fallen in love since she last saw us. When we asked her who was the lucky man, she replied, "Do you remember ze short, fat, bald man? He turned out to be ze best lover in America!" The lesson here is, never say never.

A great idea, if you wish to enhance your flirting, is to practice your conversational skills with children. If you don't have any children of your own to talk to, borrow one from a friend. Children are notoriously difficult to open up, especially young children. A typical exchange might go, "How was school today?"

"Fine."

"How was the ball game?"

"Great."

This is not how to talk to children. You must ask a question which demands more than a one word answer. The following are better openers:

"Tell me what story your teacher read to you today."

"Tell me what games you play outside at recess."

"Tell me about your best friend."

One of the reasons adults tease children is because teasing is another way to make contact with a child, and it is easier for many adults to tease a child than to figure out how to talk to one. If you can make conversation with a child, trust me, you can talk to anyone.

With a flirting partner, the best openers show how clever or funny you are. You can ask, "Are you feeling in control of your life tonight?" Or you can confess, "I don't know a soul here. How about you?"

If your flirting partner tells you, "No one ever asked me that before," you know you are talk show host material. An advantage to asking questions is that it gives you the feeling that you are in control of the conversation. In turn, this will be good for your self-confidence and help you to relax. The easiest approach is just to comment upon the situation you both find yourselves in because it is the only guaranteed thing you have in common. Don't be afraid to reveal a vulnerability because it will make you seem more believable and approachable. If you share something personal before you ask a question, your question will seem less threatening, and the person will be more honest with you.

Most people love to talk about themselves. People especially love to talk to someone who is really interesting. It is very hard to pay attention to what an attractive stranger is actually saying if you are thinking, "Does he like me? Do I have too much lipstick on? Is my skirt all wrinkled?" In order to concentrate, try to put all your energy onto the other person. Pretend the other person has a serious problem, and you are trying to help him by getting him to talk about himself. This will help you to feel less self-conscious.

# Teasing

Once the conversation gets going, it helps to have something to say. Sometimes it is easier to talk about other people or things than it is to talk about yourself. Because of this, people in the flirting arena should read a daily newspaper or at least a weekly news magazine. Of course, it helps if you've seen the latest film or read the latest book.

There is a temptation to agree with everything your flirting partner says. Let's be honest. There is a strong temptation to lie to your flirting partner. "Oh, you like to sail? I love sailing!" is not the best thing to say when, in truth, you get seasick. It would be better to explore what sailing means to your flirting partner.

If someone says, "I love sailing," you can respond, "Who taught you to sail?" Or, "Do you like to race?" Or, "How often do you get to sail?" If he just won the America's Cup Race at Newport, maybe he isn't the man for you—even if he does have Paul Newman eyes.

People need to feel appreciated and are entitled to their own feelings about things. You must remember that feelings aren't rational. They're just feelings. Therefore, it is important to try to be nonjudgmental and have an open mind about the view of others. You can't understand people or how they think until you get to know their histories.

To get to know a person it helps to use listening techniques. Psychotherapists are trained to reflect ideas back to their patients and to rephrase their patients' ideas in such a way as to assure their patients of empathy and understanding. There is no reason you cannot use these techniques in your personal life. If a person says, "It's hard to juggle my work life with my social life and my family life," you can respond with, "It's really rough trying to juggle all aspects of your life and keep everybody happy at the same time, isn't it?" The person will look at you with amazement as though you truly understand her. If a young widower is complaining about the unfairness of life because his lovely wife died so young, you can empathize, "Yes, life can be the pits."

48

# Flirting

In addition to reflecting and rephrasing techniques, there is another technique called mirroring, which is "matching or mimicking another's gestures, stance, or facial expression. . . . If you can subtly match the timbre and tone of another's voice, flow into the rhythm of her speech pattern, speed or slow your pace according to his, talk loudly or softly as she does, you can show the person that you are in synch and on their wavelength."[16]

Your opening line may depend on how confined you and your partner are. If you want to flirt with the woman sitting next to you on the plane or the train or the bus, a good idea is to take mints, gum and a current magazine with you to offer her. If you have a crossword puzzle, you can lean over and ask if she knows a three-letter word for a "Company VIP." Answer: CEO!

In flirting, there is also the issue of playing hard to get. Mosbacher advises, "Never play hard to get unless there's a very good reason for it. Be available and supportive."[17]

Jillson disagrees: "People want what it appears they cannot have. . . . Leave the second you know you're hitting off fabulously with someone and you're sure you'll see or hear from him again."[18]

Rabin agrees with this: "When you become a little mysterious, slightly distant, and have less time for someone than he or she desires, you add a certain extra appeal to your assets."[19]

O'Connor advises the female flirt that she "may want to play the mystery woman. Every time he turns the conversation to specific questions about where you live or work, be politely vague and redirect the conversation. This provides you with an intriguing image."[20] While that may be true for hardcore playboy types, my suggestion is that only very secure people will want to chase those who play very hard to get. Since most people have their share of insecurities, an honest, interested approach works best.

Next to playing hard to get, the biggest tease in flirting is called intermittent reinforcement, which is to give "constant praise or constant criticism, but to *intermittently* give rewards. . . . A man flirts with you for a while, and then pays *no attention to you* at all. . . . This is a fabulous, albeit a bit calculating, technique for making someone start worrying about your opinion."[21]

Whispering is also an effective technique in flirting. Lovers whisper. Children like to whisper. Whispering connotes innocence, playfulness, and the language of lovers. Whispering is a tease. It can be light, airy, and seductive.

So you know how to flirt, and you know how to dress. Next step is to figure out where to go: anywhere the people are who you are trying to attract! To find a man to flirt with try the health club, driving range, bakery, bookstore, auto-supply store, hobby store, pharmacy, computer store, pier, supermarket, restaurant, pet store, hardware store, airport, library, post office, video rental store, cleaners, medical waiting room, electronics store, bank, health food store, shopping mall, as well as organized activities for singles. Check with the reference librarian at your local public library for the addresses and phone numbers of organizations for single people in your area.

When you are in the mood to go out to flirt, go alone if possible. You are so much more approachable when you are by yourself. You will also feel more adventurous when you go somewhere alone. There will be no obligation for you to rejoin someone at a specified time. There will also be no competition with friends about which one of you had the most successful evening. If you do go alone, do not appear to be too busy, or someone important may be afraid to interrupt you. If you feel uncomfortable going places alone for safety reasons, at least agree to separate from your friends for periods of time in order to be open to the approaches of others. Sit by yourself. Take a walk outside during intermission.

Here are some suggested rules if you decide to try the tease of flirting:

*Rule No. 1.* Don't flirt with people whose spouses or significant others are nearby. It doesn't make sense.

My husband and I were once seated at a family wedding

with some of the bride's friends whom we didn't know. My husband Alec soon found another person suffering from a bad back at our table, a single woman named Liz. Alec generously and innocently offered to share with her all the information he had acquired over the years about the care of the back. We saw this woman again when the bride's sister got married. Liz came right up to my husband and said, "Oh, hi! I remember you! I think of you whenever I lie in bed at night and put a pillow between my legs!"

The tastelessness of this remark coupled with Liz's disregard for my presence puts her action into the category of harmful sexual teasing.

*Rule No. 2.* Don't even try to flirt with anyone who intimidates you. Perhaps your unconscious is trying to warn you away from the person. A relationship should be between peers.

*Rule No. 3.* Don't wait to be introduced by a third party. If you could always depend on third parties to help you, you wouldn't need to flirt in the first place.

*Rule No. 4.* Don't cling to the same person all night. You may miss some fabulous opportunities, and you may find out too late that you were stuck with a person who just didn't have the nerve to walk away.

*Rule No. 5.* If you sense that your attention is unwanted, for example, your would-be flirting partner keeps glancing at his watch, back off and move on. Flirting should be a soft sell. You shouldn't have to strain yourself.

*Rule No. 6.* If the object of your attention does not seem to reflect the same interest in you, do not take this personally. She didn't even take the time to know you. Maybe she disliked you right off because of your name or because you look like her father or her ex-husband. Maybe you are better off without her!

*Rule No. 7.* Take a conscious break from flirting once in awhile. It takes an incredible amount of energy to keep up a flirting mentality. You have to be energized and directed toward noticing everything and everyone around you while the rest of us are just going through the motions. If you don't take an occasional break from flirting, you may find that flirting is addictive! Indeed it can be. Flirting gives you feelings of self-confidence and control while rewarding you with some very playful feedback. Like any other addiction, compulsive flirting is just a tease. People who get addicted to flirting have difficulty in the commitment area. They never seem to get much more intimate than the flirting stage with a would-be partner. Antoine de Saint-Exupery wrote, "Whoever loves above all the approach of love will never know the joy of attaining it."[22]

*Rule No. 8.* Remember to be generous when you flirt. Effective flirts can develop a vast social and professional network. If he's really nice, but not quite your type, play matchmaker! Introduce him to a grateful friend.

*Rule No. 9.* Don't take flirting too seriously. If you flirt for the sheer pleasure of flirting, even if nothing comes of it, chances are you've enjoyed it and so has the other person. Sydney Biddle Barrows suggests, "Flirting can be an end in itself, and would-be flirts are cautioned not to impute too much meaning to a partner's words and manner. It is not bad manners to flirt for hours and then refuse to take it any further. But it is disingenuous to pretend not to know that much flirting does, in fact, lead to more physical forms of expression. It's important, therefore, to try to gauge a person's ultimate intentions, lest you say or do something inappropriately leading."[23]

*Rule No. 10.* Never confuse flirting with sexual teasing. You are

# Flirting

just playing a friendly game while trying to make friends and expand your social circle at the same time. If you touch someone while you are flirting, make sure it is in a friendly, caring way and not on an erogenous zone.

*Rule No. 11.* Don't bother to flirt with anyone who is on drugs or intoxicated.

When I was in college, I had what I thought was the evening of my life flirting with one of the most handsome men I had ever seen. I thought this was true love at first sight, and, after we kissed good night, I flew up the escalator to my dorm room to share the great news with my roommate. Unbeknownst to me, my roommate had been watching us in the dormitory lobby. After I told her the news, she sadly advised me, "Linda, I hate to tell you, but he's never going to call you. He was stoned. He won't even remember you in the morning. You're still so naive about drugs, you can't even tell when they're stoned!" She was right on both counts. I was very naive, and he never did call.

*Rule No. 12.* Make sure you flirt in safe, public areas. Even if you never confuse flirting with sexual teasing, there is the danger that your flirting partner might. Some men will assume that if a woman flirts with them, especially one who is dressed seductively, that she wants sex. They may not realize that a woman may consider dressing suggestively a matter of style. She may do this for attention, not as an invitation for sex.

*Rule No. 13.* Never sit by the phone. The traditional follow-up promise to flirting, "I'll call you," is one of the worst teases. Don't fall for it. Get an answering machine or pick up the phone and call the other person yourself. Instead of waiting for the phone to ring, go out and flirt some more.

*Rule No. 14.* Enjoy yourself!

# 6

## Sexual Teasing

*When he raised his eyes, Erin flashed her million-dollar smile. . . . The congressman's neck went limp, and his body swayed. Scary, Erin thought. . . . She liked the rush on nights like this, when the dancing was so good. The feeling of control was indescribable.[1]*

Carl Hiaasen, *Strip Tease*

A tease enjoys controlling the reactions of another person. We sexually tease by the way we dress and undress, walk, wiggle, dance, sway, talk, whisper, smell, smile, and use our eyelashes. We also sexually tease by our behavior and our attitudes, and by what we say.

Sexual teasing is a deliberate attempt to increase the appetite for sexual pleasure. This category of teasing is not to be confused with sexual harassment or flirting. Both males and females conduct sexual teasing: we all know the stereotypes of the coed who has a reputation on campus as "a tease" and the baseball player who makes a bet with his teammates that he will "steal home" on the first date. Individual personalities and the kind of give-and-take that exists in the partnership determine if teasing will occur, and by whom, how much, and what kind it will be. The sexual teaser does not have to consummate the teasing: he or she merely has to hold out a perceived promise or a distant promise to do so. This is the secret message in sexual teasing— will the tease be consummated or not? Sexual teasing is, in essence, a type of foreplay.

Sexual teasing can be playful and romantic when engaged in by an affectionate couple, or it can be harmful and dangerous when one partner tries to dominate the other. What is important is the acceptance and respect for the taste of the individual and his or her fantasies and a willingness to try to participate in what pleases the mate, short of any physical violence.

Succumbing to sexual teasing is risky, because you never know what kind of relationship or even disease you might encounter or whether or when your new partner will start to become a fatal attraction. It is important to distinguish a playful slap on the buttocks, which both parties might agree on, from being tied up or engaging in any other form of restraint or violence which might lead to dangerous consequences.

Victims of unwanted sexual teasing can explore different remedies to get the teaser to stop. In a dating situation, the victim is usually well advised to refuse to date the teaser again, since the teasing may escalate to violence and bodily harm. Even in an established relationship, the victim who has had enough can choose to become disinvolved with the abusive partner when he or she realizes the inequality of the relationship and the absence of genuine love. In a marriage, discussing the problem with the teaser in a calm way often helps, or the couple may seek counseling from a therapist who specializes in marital problems. (See Chapter 14: Coping with Adult Teasing.)

Sexual teasing between agreeing partners often calls for compromise. Women who are looking for romance and dinner by candlelight may not understand the men who want them to dine in a babydoll negligee. If both parties attempt to understand their mates and are willing to bend a little they may be

# *Teasing*

rewarded by a more satisfying relationship.

Rules in sexual teasing must be spelled out. When a woman says no, or when a man says no, it means no. It does not mean yes or "maybe." What is not okay is to force a woman or man to do anything he or she is uncomfortable with, including but not limited to: have sex or oral sex, have sex in public, have sex with friends, have sex for money with friends or acquaintances, or physical assault.

Playful sexual teasing requires an active imagination and the willingness of both partners to pretend. While harmful teasing is often unexpected, unpredictable and cruel, playful teasing tends to be creative, surprising, and fun and is always kept within bounds which are acceptable to both partners. Playful sexual teasing can be a matter of trial and error: what "turns on" one person may be a "turnoff" to someone else. How does one know which is which? You have to ask.

If you do not know or if you are not sure which moves please or displease your mate, just ask. It is never too late to learn how to sexually please someone. It is also important to realize that what your partner loved five years ago may strike her as boring today. Remember, too, that a lover who is considered wonderful by one person might be considered out of line by another. A playful sexual teaser needs to be curious, flexible and responsive to the teasee's negative reactions should they occur.

Those married readers who remember the backseat petting days of their youth will recall that there is no greater tease than foreplay without consummation, better known as "sex with your clothes on." In the days of the "double standard" (which in many places is still today's standard), it was the female's role to say no and the male's role to try to coax a yes. I believe the combination of this double standard and the teasing nature of sexual foreplay is the reason why some men mistakenly think that no means yes. While sexual teasing can be fun and can even be considered a game, it is also a very serious tactic that can have devastating consequences for those who feel violated by it.

# Sexual Teasing

It is not uncommon for women to complain that, after they first had intercourse with their mates, their sexual lives went downhill. At that point their mates expected to be allowed to consummate each sexual experience, and the men felt they no longer had to put forth any special seductive effort to do so. In other words, sexual intercourse often puts an end to foreplay. Women are slower to become sexually aroused than men and need more teasing foreplay than do men. While for men the primary organ for sexual excitement is the penis, for a woman the primary organ might be her clitoris, lips, or breasts, or even her brain.

Aromatherapy can be an enticing sexual tease. Perfumes and aftershave lotions are turn-ons for many people. When I was young, English Leather was fashionable and I loved the smell of it, so my then boyfriend used to sprinkle it around his car before he picked me up for a date. Some men like women to smell like roses or cinnamon. Some even like Vicks Vapo-Rub!

Sexual teasing may involve the use of other aids such as sex toys, suggestive or submissive costumes, and erotic films and books.

What about erotic films when it comes to sexual teasing? What is an "erotic film" to one person may very well be a "disgusting porno movie" to someone else. This is often a very difficult decision even for some married couples to make. There are some women who feel that any erotic film is an exploitation of women. However, there are many women who enjoy "naughty" films. Some feel the films also exploit men. Most of the early erotic films were made by men for men and were originally shown in movie theaters in the seedy parts of town to an all-male or a gay male audience. Now the majority of erotic films are rented from video stores and intended for home use. Most of the erotic films available at the family-oriented video stores are R-rated rather than X-rated because the producers know that soft porn is generally more appealing and less offensive to women and community standards.

Sexual violence has become a horrifying trend in American society today. Spouse abuse (usually male to female but also female to male) and the sexual abuse of children are acknowledged more openly now than in the past. Child victims are often too frightened to report what has happened to them, and women victims often lack the financial means or family support to leave an abusing partner. Only recently have local police forces begun to train their personnel how to respond effectively in these cases.

Sexual teasing in which the teaser dominates the teasee and/or inflicts pain on the teasee or on him or herself is a form of violence, and is never acceptable, even if both parties seem to consent. The practices of sadism, masochism, and sadomasochism are aberrations from the normal. Even though some practitioners may find these sexual teases "divinely degrading,"[2] they are in fact not normal, and treatment in therapy is usually recommended.

For some people, erotic literature is a turn-on. Some couples read the sexy parts of erotic poems or novels to each other. This dramatically illustrates that the most powerful sexual organ is the brain.

This is why telephone sex sells. Telephone sex panders to those who are aroused by explicit sex talk and four letter words, and who masturbate to the faces and bodies of their imaginations. It may be that their partners are not aroused by such talk or it may be that their partners do not even know they become aroused by it. The people who enjoy explicit talk may be embarrassed to admit it to their spouses. Telephone sex also services the sexual addict, the person who feels the need to stay anonymous, and those who wish a safe approach to sex with those of the same sex.

Sex talk between lovers can be an enormous sexual tease, but it can also serve as comic relief during sex play that turns silly. As Zilbergeld writes in *The New Male Sexuality*, "My girlfriend and I were in bed one afternoon. . . . She came out with phrases she had gotten from a book of pornography she had looked at earlier that day. . . . We both broke out into gales of laughter. . . . There was no intercourse. . . . But it was an incredibly wonderful experience that I recall vividly and lovingly over twenty years later."[3]

For many people, the greatest sexual tease is whatever society deems forbidden. This may be due to early life experiences and conditioning. The little boy whose bare butt is smacked by his pretty mother or nanny may grow up with an attraction to sadomasochistic sex practices. What is more common are the sexual experiments of teenagers, who don't have the luxury of privacy, in the backseats of cars and in houses, where the parents aren't home. These early backseat sexual adventures are so highly charged sexually that they imprint on our psyches the association between intense sex and doing what is forbidden. These attitudes often persist long after those teenagers marry and become parents themselves. In other words, many married people still love to do it in the backseats of cars.

Fantasies can be another form of sexual teasing. In light of the threat of AIDS, fantasies about sexual orgies are physically much safer than actual orgies. As Freud said, "The wish is not the same as the deed." Personally, I always thought actual orgies were for people lacking in imagination. Do not make the mistake of sharing all of your sexual fantasies with your partner or think you have to act them out in reality. If your partner is horrified by your fantasy, his reaction may take away all your future fun in thinking about it.

What about sex shows and the tease of a stripper? Gypsy Rose Lee, the famous stripper, figured out that the reason a partially clad female is far more exciting to a male than a nude body is the tease factor! Too much nudity is actually capable of desensitizing people to sex. A brilliant biology professor once confided to me that the reason he never applied to medical school was because he was afraid that after looking at all those naked bodies, he would not be able to perform when he went to bed with his wife. This reportedly also happens to bartenders who work in strip clubs. After awhile, they totally lose interest in what is happening on stage.

# Teasing

What is sexy in a man or woman? Some women and men believe that whatever they don't have, but the opposite sex does have, is sexy and vice versa. Those women will love deep voices, beards, mustaches, hairy chests and hairy backs on men. Such men will love large breasts, long hair, and shapely legs on women. However, as we've said earlier, a "turn-on" to one person is a "turnoff" to another. I have heard many women say that they hate men with hairy chests and backs—that they resemble other types of animals. And then there are those women who think a hairless chest on a man looks like the flat chest of a female. There is obviously no right and no wrong answer here. In the same way, some men prefer petite women with big breasts while other men will argue that big breasts make a woman look matronly and remind them of cows.

The point is that, in playful sexual teasing, looks are almost irrelevant. It is how one acts that is significant. When I was so very heavy while pregnant I was constantly amazed that my husband was still able to become so easily aroused. Creativity and attitude are the most important elements in playful sexual teasing.

The tease factor is why the conquest is far more fun to some than the satisfaction. This accounts for most one-night stands. "You see a pretty woman and you say, 'I'd like to spend the night with her,' and you start making moves and it's a challenge. . . . Once the conquest occurs with this type of guy—a guy like me—the relationship ends because it's no more magic than the last. The race was more important than the finish line."[4] People who fall for the sexual tease of the one-night stand are choosing a situation with no intimacy, a situation where they will not have to connect except physically.

What does it take for a monogamous man or woman to succumb to the tease of adultery—sexual intimacy with another person? There is the temptation of availability. Some people have jobs or lifestyles where they are highly visible and are exposed to many attractive strangers. If a monogamous person travels on business for prolonged periods or is in a time in the relationship where his emotional and sexual needs are not being met, the person is more susceptible to an outside sexual tease. If the third party is very aggressive sexually, the monogamous person may feel less guilty and less responsible for the new sexual relationship having occurred. Sometimes a person succumbs merely because she is curious, bored, needs a boost for her ego, and/or she is in a very demanding environment either at home or at work or both and is looking for an escape hatch, even if it only lasts for twenty minutes. The third party typically takes the pressure off the previously monogamous person, if only momentarily. Some men and women use beautiful or handsome "trophy" women and men as symbols of success, like other material props. Some people are willing to risk a lot for momentary acceptance and recognition via the tease of adultery, but not as many as we used to think. According to the latest sex study at the University of Chicago, "Adultery is the exception in America, not the rule. Nearly 75 percent of married men and 85 percent of married women say they have never been unfaithful."[5]

A man or woman may have a tendency to confuse emotional intimacy with dependence and vulnerability. Rather than feel dependent and vulnerable, he or she may wish to exercise their sexuality outside of their primary relationship to illustrate that she or he is not dependent on the primary partner to fill all needs. Such people want to prove to themselves that they can take care of some needs on their own, even if those needs are merely sexual.

The greatest problem for monogamous relationships is that the infatuation stage of being in love, that glorious high we feel when our lovers can do no wrong, is a terrible tease. It definitely seems as though we should be able to maintain that high state forever with our chosen partners. We get terribly disillusioned when we cannot maintain that state, especially when the characters in every romantic movie, television program and novel are able to maintain it. This makes us angry at ourselves and even more angry at our mates for not trying harder. Of course when we mature we realize that fairy tale romances are just stories, and real life, while it can be magical from time to time, cannot sustain that magic on a continuous, daily basis forever due to the demands of the workaday world and the distractions of everyday living. People who will not accept that some of the petals will eventually fall off the marital rose are doomed to numerous divorces or a continuous stream of adulterous relationships. Such individuals become so addicted to sexual teasing that an obsession with sex or a particular sexual obsession with an individual can rule or ruin relationships, marriages and lives. (See Sex Addiction in Chapter 11: Teasing, Perfection, and Addiction.)

Playful sexual teasing in a good relationship can add spice to life. For me, some of the most fun occurs when I don't really want sex, but I want to remind my husband that I think he's the sexiest man in the world. Last week my husband came home from work completely and utterly drained. He didn't get the contract he'd worked so hard to obtain so he hated his job, his commute, and his life. When he lay down in bed after his hard day, I teased, "I know you want me!"

He laughed and said, "Touch me and you die!" When I tried to seduce him, he said, "I'd love to, but I don't know if I can because I'm so tired."

I responded with, "That's what you always say but then you keep me up all night."

It was silly playful teasing but it lightened the mood and made us feel good about each other.

# 7

# Teasing at the Workplace

*I said to Polen, "What's this about a med student who irons
your shirts and picks you up every night? What's her address?
I want to send her my women's lib book. . . ."*
*"You wouldn't."*
*"Oh, yes, I would."*
*"She doesn't believe in that stuff."*
*"She will after she marries you."[1]*

Peggy Anderson, *Nurse*

We have all heard the old adage, "Don't mix business with
pleasure." This need to keep business and pleasure separate at the workplace often reinforces teasing at the workplace as
coworkers are prevented from genuine intimacy. Teasing guards
against meaningful dialogue. Teasing guards against coworkers
getting too friendly.

In offices, especially small ones, people are often in close
contact. They feel the need to establish some sort of personal
relationships with their coworkers. Many people spend more time
with coworkers than they do with their own families. However,
though relationships need to be cordial for people to work effec-

tively, employees are afraid to get too friendly with people at work fearing they may be targets of office gossip, or fearing their coworkers may confuse their friendship with romantic interest. Therefore, some may consciously decide to keep their relationships at work superficial by teasing.

From the managerial viewpoint, teasing may have the advantage of guarding against people developing the kinds of close relationships which would enable them to form unions, conspire against the company to steal equipment or ideas, or start a competing business.

Playful teasing can serve as a tension reliever and a way to strike a common ground. A school principal confides, "I will send cartoons to the assistant superintendent because she says she has no sense of humor. This is my way of getting close."

Brian describes what he will and will not do: "People I would never tease at work are those I don't have a good relationship with. I have to have a strong bond with someone, a strong personal relationship, for me to tease. If I don't have a strong bond, I'd be afraid the person would take my remarks the wrong way and that wouldn't be appropriate at work."

Often, it is those people within the most serious of professions who are the greatest teasers. They do this in order to lighten their loads. Medical professionals use crude jokes and teasing remarks, especially while working on cadavers. Some medical professionals also enjoy playing practical jokes that at first glance may seem disrespectful to the deceased, but actually serve a purpose. As Peggy Anderson writes, "Four or five of my friends were working the night shift on a floor when an old man died. They all went in to do postmortem care together. They got to joking around and manipulated the man's finger into an obscene gesture. Then, because rigor mortis had started to set in, they had trouble getting the finger out of the position. . . . 'Oh, God, what kind of nurses are they? How could they do that to another human being? That's horrible.' That's just how I felt at the time, I was so shocked. Now when I look back, I don't consider the incident so disrespectful. My friends were upset about the man dying. He was the first person they had ever taken care of who died. They were so afraid that they could hardly look at the body. They did what they did for comic relief."[2]

Law enforcement personnel are also notorious teasers. The medical examiner "didn't mind having medical students as observers because they were always so solemn during an autopsy. Cops were something else: one dumb joke after another. Dr. Allen had never figured out why cops get so silly in a morgue."[3]

Partly due to their continuous exposure to nudity, sexuality and death, medical professionals and police personnel are desensitized to the kinds of remarks that might strike lay people as shocking.

Teasing can also help relieve monotony. Teasing at the workplace can thus serve as a form of entertainment. "The more monotonous the job, the more likely it is that horseplay will take place. . . . It is usually defined as 'rude, boisterous play' and runs the 'gamut from relatively harmless teasing, clowning, and poking fun in a rumpus room environment to acts involving some physical touching and also involving a high risk of serious injury or property damage.'"[4]

As Davis and Jennings point out in *Labor Law Journal*, horseplay can cover "a wide variety of activities such as 'mooning,' squirting water on a fellow employee, giving coworkers laxative gum, pulling a chair out from under a supervisor, and putting lit cigarettes in coworkers' pants."[5]

Some of the more intense instances of horseplay, which have led to discharge of the offending employees, included rather deranged practical jokes. According to the Davis and Jennings article, such bizarre practices included: exploding a cherry bomb in the employees' locker and shower room and causing damage to another employee's eye. Another incident occurred when an employee threw a long, gasoline-soaked strip of cloth across a sleeping employee's leg and lit the cloth as the employee was awakening, causing serious burns of the body. A person threw fireworks in his work facility where workers were already performing dangerous tasks. In a similar case, an employee placed lighted cigarette butts in the back pockets of other employees who were operating machines with moving blades causing serious injury.[6]

Not all instances of intense horseplay on the job result in dismissal. Arbitrators, using their own judgment, may reinstate employees found guilty of conducting relatively harmless pranks such as those equal to the ones played in a grade school classroom. If the employee has a long, unblemished work record or if he apologizes to the victim and/or has remained friends with the victim after the incident, the employee has a better chance of being reinstated. It is still recommended that employees "should exercise self-control, even under provocation and refrain from practical jokes or horseplay. Experience shows that boisterous and disorderly conduct tends to 'get out of hand' and frequently has serious consequences: damage to company property or product, physical injury, even death."[7]

Jimmy, a forty-five-year-old male josher, explains, "I like to kid around and tease at work. To me teasing is making fun of something I do or someone else does. I tease myself a lot in conversation, sort of like self-deprecating behavior. I like to acknowledge when I screw up while I'm talking in a professional setting. I feel more comfortable if I let them know how I screwed up. If I acknowledge when I screw up with a joke at myself, then I am in control. This is a lot better than being criticized by others."

Timothy, a forty-eight-year-old scientist, shared, "I love kidding around and joking at work. What I can't tolerate is being teased about my actual professional credibility. I feel this could have a damaging effect on my reputation. One day, at a large meeting, a coworker made some crack like, 'Well, if that's Tim's data, we don't know if we can trust it!' Everybody laughed, and I felt totally humiliated. I didn't think it was funny at all. I think that coworker just put me down to make himself look good to the company directors who were present at our meeting, to put

himself in a better position. I never could stomach the guy afterwards. That's the danger of teasing or messing around at the
workplace. You're stuck with these people afterwards. You just
can't walk away."

Certain kinds of work environments provide maximum
opportunities for teasing, such as jobs where employees must live
together as well as work together. In work situations where
employees spend the night—such as the military or long shifts at
the hospital or fire department, or those who must travel while
on the job—people will be more vulnerable to one another. Their
knowledge of each other's personal habits and weaknesses
increases due to the amount of time they spend together. This
knowledge gives teasers more material for clever remarks and
more time to create and deliver them.

We live in a very mobile society. People move from place
to place and job to job. Teasing provides a feeling of quick intimacy between people who do not know each other well. Yet it is
risky to tease people you do not know well, especially at work,
because you cannot tell whether or not a teasing remark will
offend someone. For example, "Janet, a book editor, is leaving
the office an hour earlier than usual. She tells Bob, her boss,
she's going. Bob glances at his watch and cracks, 'Half day
today?' If Janet enjoys a comfortable working relationship with
Bob and he is an inveterate tease, she might parry the thrust
with, 'Just going out to a late lunch.' If coworkers are within
earshot and they too laugh at her comeback, the tease isn't at
anyone's expense, and no one walks away wounded. On the other
hand, if Janet is new on the job or running late with her work,
her retort might be defensive: 'Oh, but I came in early.' Or, if she
comes from a family in which teasing is rare or where teasing is
torment, she might miss the joke and interpret Bob's remark as
pressure to work harder."[8]

In the workplace, a person's rung on the corporate ladder
also affects whether they will be teased or not. "Sociologist Rose
Coser . . . observed teasing practices among the staff members at

# *Teasing*

a Boston hospital. Those with the most power—the male senior psychiatrists—did the most teasing, almost always targeting their arrows at workers lower in the hierarchy. It's usually the boss who does the teasing and not the employees. 'If a lower status person makes a joke upward, it can be quite risky.'"[9]

It is easy to see how teasing at work often becomes competitive as some people will try to prove just how clever they can be with words. In competitive teasing, a teasee can either rebound with a clever comeback on his own, or get on the offensive by being the first to make a teasing remark. This competitive teasing reinforces the vicious circle at work of relationships based solely on teasing.

# 8

# *The Male Aspects of Teasing*

*I know better than to speak to my brother during these times, or to call his or any boy's attention to me. Boys get teased for having young sisters or sisters of any kind, or mothers; it's like having new clothes.*[1]

Margaret Atwood, *Cat's Eye*

Some believe males dominate the world of teasing at work and at home and at play. Is it because the male has a keener sense of humor? Certainly most of our stand-up comedians in nightclubs are males, but that is probably because of the risks of the profession. The things that happen when one hangs around bars late at night with a bunch of drunks do not appeal to many women except perhaps those with the guts of a Rosie O'Donnell.

Most males enjoy teasing as a way to communicate in a dominant way. All teasing attempts to elicit a particular emotional response in another, to control another person. For centuries, men were used to being in charge at the workplace and in the home. We must remind ourselves that women only obtained the right to vote in the twentieth century.

# Teasing

For men who are not adept at expressing their feelings or communicating directly, or for those who are uncomfortable with their own feelings, teasing offers an alternative, an indirect way of communicating, and another way to assert their dominance.

I believe men dominate teasing at the workplace for several reasons, the most obvious being that they have had more practice. There is a tradition of male teasing which probably stems from the earliest soldiers who were forced to live and band together, to the first company that was formed with only male employees. Women have only in recent history joined with males in the workplace, the armed forces, and team sports. Women are still feeling their way and continually redefining themselves and their roles. I believe women may become more expert at teasing over time as they assume more leadership positions.

The bigger the prize, whether it's a contract to be signed, a country to be conquered or a gold medal to win, the bigger is the tease to accomplish the goal. Many men have become quite superstitious in going after the reward which teases them. Men in sports have traditionally associated a ritual with a reward. If a man wore a particular pair of socks when he won the trophy, he may wear the same pair of socks each and every time he competes, and he may not change for fear of becoming unlucky. The bigger the tease, the more likelihood there will be rituals.

Some men look upon teasing as their armor, their protective shield against the world, a type of defense mechanism. Most importantly, teasing guards men against becoming too close to other men. Why are males so resistant to forming direct, close verbal relationships with other men? I believe it is because homophobia is widespread. Men who are straight and unrelated are not supposed to love one another in our culture.

Frankly, I believe it all starts with those damned locker rooms and communal showers that males grow up with in gym class and summer camp. Without meaning to sound too Freudian, I believe that because adolescent males are so highly sexed and preoccupied with sexual thoughts, and because they are not supposed to be modest around the other guys, young men may have severe conscious or unconscious fears of getting an involuntary erection in the communal shower in the presence of male witnesses. Since this is such an excruciating fear, I feel these adolescents are then very intolerant of those gay men who dare act out the adolescent's own worst fears and that this intolerance stays with them as adults. When I discussed the idea of this fear with a male patient, he exclaimed to me, "I can't believe you figured that out! I have been married for twenty years, and I never even discussed that with my wife!"

Another aspect of male domination in teasing is that teasing is a form of risk-taking, and males are more risk-oriented than females, e.g., there are many more male compulsive gamblers than female compulsive gamblers. (See Chapter 11: Teasing, Perfection, and Addiction.) Certainly, verbal teasing is risky because you can never predict with absolute certainty how any individual will react when teased.

Do males and females tease differently? Dr. Cheryl Pawluk, Professor of Psychology at Western Nevada Community College in Carson City is quoted as saying: "Women tend to be merely playful in their teasing. . . . Boys, by contrast, go for the jugular, challenging each other's masculinity."[2]

John Friel says this about men: "As you begin to learn about yourself as a man, you will notice that men have certain ways of communicating that are different from women's. Men have some unique ways of honoring one another." He goes on to mention examples of men honoring and supporting each other in the movies *Field of Dreams* and *Dances with Wolves*. "Men communicate a lot with each other," Friel says. "We just need a man to teach us how, by his example."[3] It is interesting that he puts down some notorious male sex addicts in his book and then praises two Kevin Costner movies in which sex plays a dominant role.

Kathryn Borman, Associate Dean of Research and Development at the University of Cincinnati, found that "playful

# Teasing

behavior creates solidarity among young men, whereas it often denigrates young women."[4]

Do male and female children taunt and bully differently? Traditionally, boys use physical aggression such as tripping, pushing, elbowing, shoving, refusing to let another child physically pass, wrecking other children's possessions, and stealing. Girls use intimidation, gossip, social alienation, and circulating nasty notes during class. Some girls will deliberately ignore other kids or not include them in their circle at recess or in the cafeteria by pushing away the extra chair. In one northeastern town, a bolder reaction occurs when an unwanted girl sits down in the cafeteria and the rest of the girls at the table will get up and move away! These girls will do the same thing when an unwanted girl walks over to them to join in conversation. They will move away. The girl, not understanding, will move with them. They move again. When the outsider catches on, it is an incredibly humiliating experience.

John Sedgwick reassures us about males that "teasing has other, more benign uses than as a subtle way to convey criticism. It can also be a . . . way of getting close without having to own up to some treacly sentiment. . . . It would never occur to a woman to greet her oldest and best friend by shouting out, 'Hey, Pizzaface, I thought I smelled you around here someplace.' But guy pals do that all the time, and it never fails to bring a smile."[5] He shows that teasing can also be viewed as verbal horseplay.

Sometimes racial and ethnic teasing between males who genuinely like each other conveys a special intimacy as shown in Hiaasen's novel *Skin Tight*. "'Now, there's something you don't see every day,' Stranahan announced, pretty loud. 'Two Cubans in a boat, and no beer.' Luis Cordova grinned. The other man climbed noisily up on the dock and said, 'And here's something else you don't see every day: an Irishman up before noon, and still sober.'"[6]

While men dominate the teasing industry, a synonym dictionary lists synonyms for "teaser" which are all sexually

# The Male Aspects of Teasing

alluring females: "stripteaser, ecdysiast, peeler, stripper, strip-teuse."[7]

In the same vein, *The Dictionary of American Slang* defines a teaser as, "A girl or woman who seems to invite a male's attention and favors, but who does not return them when given; a cock teaser (taboo)."[8]

The only sexually alluring male animal to provide a definition for tease is, "An inferior stallion or ram used to excite mares or ewes before serving by the stud animal."[9]

It is interesting that a stud is never the teaser. Note Helen Lerner's observation in *The Dance of Anger*: "It is an interesting sidelight that our language—created and codified by men—does not have one unflattering term to describe men who vent their anger at women. Even such epithets as 'bastard' and 'son of a bitch' do not condemn the man but place the blame on a woman, his mother!"[10]

These contradictions and definitions seem to back up a male assertion to me that, women tease with their bodies; men tease with their brains.

To some men, teasing is synonymous with masculinity. When I told my accountant that my new book was about teasing, his comment was, "I don't think you can be a man without the ability to tease."

It may well be that nature gave many males an innate drive or reflex to tease and to respond to teasing, to lure as well as to automatically reach out and grab whatever passes by, a sort of hunting instinct, in order to outwit and capture food. This grab-it-or-lose-it response, if we might give it a name, is not so very different from holding up a peekaboo toy to a baby who tries to grab it. Unfortunately, this response often translates into the sexual arena where some men merely view women as Playboy bunnies to be outwitted, seduced, captured and eaten for dinner.

# 9

# *Sexual Harassment*

> *He had the feeling as he lay on his back that he was somehow agreeing to a situation that he did not understand fully, that was not fully recognized. There would be trouble later. He did not want to go to Malaysia with her. He did not want an affair with his boss.[1]*

Michael Crichton, *Disclosure*

In attempting to define what something is, it is also helpful to define what it is not. Sexual harassment is not good natured teasing, it's not flattery, it's not flirting, it's not funny, and it's not uncommon. There are still those harassers who try to use the excuse that they were "just teasing" in defense of their behavior, but this is untrue.

Sexual harassment carries teasing to a malicious, and degrading, extreme. It is to teasing what rape is to sex. Sex is just the means the rapist uses, like a weapon, to gain power, to control and to use violence over another human being. In the exact same way, sexual harassment is just the means the harasser uses, a verbal and sometimes a physical weapon, to gain power, to control, and to be verbally or physically violent to another human being.

# Sexual Harassment

Sexual harassment makes people feel violated just as rape does. Like rape, sexual harassment is an enormous personal invasion and makes women or men who experience it feel they have totally lost their privacy and that someone is trying to steal their souls. Sexual harassment makes the victim feel physically dirty, so dirty that twenty hot showers cannot get them clean enough. As a result of sexual harassment, victims may suffer severe symptoms of anxiety and depression as well as physical problems, such as fatigue caused by stress or insomnia, eating disorders, headaches, and other bodily aches and stress. This suffering also translates into dollars when you consider the cost of missed days at work as well as therapy and medical bills which may be incurred.

A sexual harasser is someone who enjoys making other people miserable by using crude sexual remarks. A male sexual harasser may pretend that he likes women and that he simply enjoys kidding around with them. In fact, he is a misogynist, a woman hater who has no respect for women. He is using sexual remarks to try to control a woman—either to force her to have sex with him or just to make her feel uncomfortable. He probably has a history of poor relationships with women, of distrusting and resenting them as mothers, sisters, nannies, girlfriends or wives. He is probably a very insecure person who resents that the sexual revolution ever took place, and that women ever entered the job market. "In the end, sexual harassment serves to remind women of their historically inferior status as primarily lower echelon employees. When they do manage to enter fields traditionally reserved to men, harassment makes women realize they are unwelcome equals."[2]

Sexual harassment is not limited to attacks on women. There are women who sexually harass men. You do not have to be bigger and stronger than someone else to sexually harass him. Some gay people, both men and women, attempt to sexually harass each other as well as members of the straight community. However, there are far more members of the straight community who attempt to harass members of the gay community.

If you are a victim of sexual harassment at work or in your community, it is not your fault. You are not being overly sensitive. You do not deserve to be sexually harassed. Sexual harassment is not a response to anything personal about you. It is not about the way you present yourself or the way you behave. It has nothing to do with your clothes, your makeup or the way you walk or talk. Sexual harassment has nothing to do with your age or marital status or your job status. It happens to all kinds of people, in every job and at every level of employment.

No one is automatically exempt from sexual harassment. "The most comprehensive study of the problem . . . by the Merit Systems Protection Board, found that 42 percent of the female workers and 15 percent of the male workers among the 20,000 government employees surveyed had been victims of sexual harassment during the preceding two years. . . . Other studies demonstrate that the percentage of victims climbs even higher when those surveyed are predominantly female. Of the 9000 women who participated in a recent survey by *Redbook* magazine, 88 percent reported harassment."[3]

Sexual harassment is not limited to the workplace. I have had my own worst experiences in doctors' offices. My former obstetrician and gynecologist (who has since lost his license for sexually abusing his patients) once told me, while I was lying flat on my back with my feet in the stirrups, "I always enjoy putting my hands inside of you, Linda." Why I paid his bill, I'll never know. At a visit to a dermatologist for a rash on my hands, the doctor sat down in a chair and told me to pull down my pants and turn around. My buttocks would have been at the level of his face. I told him I had no rash on my buttocks and had no intention of pulling down my pants. He became furious and yelled at me and said he never had a patient who refused to be examined before! At that point I walked out of his office. Another gynecologist once gave me the longest breast exam on record, with no nurse present. That bill I refused to pay.

Due to the terrible effects of sexual harassment, laws have been formulated against it. In 1980 the Equal Employment Opportunity Commission (EEOC) issued guidelines on sexual harassment. In 1986 the United States Supreme Court heard its first case of sexual harassment in the workplace, *Meritor Savings Bank, FSB v. Vinson.* "The Court observed that Title VII guarantees employees the right to work in an environment free from discriminatory intimidation, ridicule and insult."[4]

There are two kinds of sexual harassment under Title VII. The first kind is called "Quid pro quo" which means "this for that." Quid pro quo is used when someone is attempting sexual blackmail. This occurs if a supervisor threatens that you will lose your job, never get a raise or promotion, or be transferred if you do not sexually perform for him or allow him to flirt with you or touch you. Even if the supervisor's threats are not specifically stated, if the victim understands the consequences and does not wish to comply, this is sexual harassment.

The second type of sexual harassment claim is called "Hostile Environment." This is when the harassers' behavior creates a hostile environment where it is extremely uncomfortable, difficult or impossible to continue to work. "Conduct that might be harmless or even enjoyable in a social situation can be upsetting at work. Sexual behavior that is repeated, unwanted and interferes with your job has crossed the line. It is not only inappropriate, *it is illegal.*"[5]

Specifically, the types of sexual behavior that victims have encountered include:

*   The supposedly accidental brushing up against the body, done repeatedly
*   A refusal to move out of the way when a woman wishes to pass by
*   Spreading rumors about a person's sex life
*   Attempting to have conversations about sex in the work place

# Teasing

- Leering or unwelcome staring at physical attributes
- Repeated comments about a person's physical attributes
- Requiring women to wear sexually revealing clothes
- Requiring the use of safety equipment designed for the other sex
- Boasting of one's own physical attributes
- Making unnecessary physical contact or physical assault
- Subtle requests or obvious requests for sexual favors
- Pinching or fondling
- Rape or the threat of rape or assault
- Tactics which humiliate a person because of his or her sex
- The posting of lewd photographs
- The drawing of lewd pictures or cartoons
- Diagrams of hypothetical sexual acts
- Repeated sexually derogatory remarks insulting to a person's sex
- The continual stream of dirty jokes told directly to an individual or told in the individual's general vicinity
- Repeated invitations to date at work or repeated phone calls at home for dates
- Repeated writing of lewd or romantic or inappropriate letters or notes
- Uninvited knocks on a person's hotel room door while on out-of-town business
- Stalking: following someone around at work or after hours
- Unwelcome attention paid to a person that focuses on his or her sex instead of his or her job.

At the workplace, where sexual harassment most commonly occurs and where it receives the most publicity, penalties for the harasser can range from verbal reprimands on the job to steep monetary damages from the offender as well as the offender's employer. The Supreme Court ruled in November 1993 that a woman who claimed she was sexually harassed at work does not need to show psychological harm to win monetary damages.[6]

# Sexual Harassment

"Most victims ultimately pay economically, too," say Beier and Greenberger. "The Working Women's Institute has found that 24 percent of the women it surveyed were fired and an additional 42 percent resigned when the pressure of continuing harassment or retaliation because of their complaints made work intolerable."[7]

Because the penalties for sexual harassment can be so severe, an actual claim or a threat of a claim of sexual harassment becomes a very powerful weapon. Therefore, the problem is double-sided. We need to protect those who are actually sexually harassed, as well as those who may be accused falsely of sexual harassment.

The key word in sexual harassment is "unwelcome." Just because an advance was welcomed in the past, does not mean an advance is welcome today. Attorney Segal advises, "There is a simple rule which avoids confusion: Employees don't ask for it unless they ask for it."[8]

However, flirtatious advances sometimes are welcome in the workplace! About this, Singer and Hustead say, "The important thing to keep in mind is that harassment is illegal; advances that are welcome, personal flirtations or relationships occurring between two willing participants are not [illegal]. The purpose of the legal proscription against sexual harassment is to eradicate unwanted sex-based behavior that has a detrimental impact on employees, not to require that workplaces be asexual or to prohibit all personal relationships between employees."[9]

## HOW TO HANDLE SEXUAL HARASSMENT

Many women have serious problems with trying to handle sexual harassment in the workplace. They are scared of making waves. Marian Horoskip, writing for *Dance Magazine*, explains that, among dancers, "Women tend to deal with harassment by men in several ways: detachment . . . ; denial . . . ; by rebelling

. . . ; by attributing harassment to performing attire, or by suffering in silence through fear of retaliation, blame, embarrassment, or believing that no one will help."[10] But the problem with ignoring sexual harassment is that "75 percent of the time, harassment grows worse when it is ignored."[11]

What about stopping sexual harassment outside of the work environment? What if you're on a crowded train and a man is pressing his body up against yours? Should you speak up? Experts say it is important to say something if you feel uncomfortable. Trust your instincts in this situation. If you don't say anything, you will feel helpless, which will result in feelings of depression. "You don't have to interpret a man's behavior or decide his motives. . . . Just act. A firm request, 'Please move back from me,' for example, addresses the behavior and not the intent."[12]

What if you are sexually harassed as I was in a doctor's office? Every state government has a Board of Registration of Physicians. Write a detailed letter of complaint and keep a copy. It will be investigated. Maybe nothing will happen with one letter, but if they get a dozen similar letters, you can be sure some action will be taken.

What if you are sexually harassed by one of your teachers or university professors? Many colleges already have laws banning sexual contact between faculty and students, especially when the faculty member has professional responsibility for the student and there is an imbalance of power between student and teacher. This is much like the laws against psychiatrists and psychotherapists having sexual contact with their patients. If you are a target of sexual harassment by a professor, discuss your concerns with a dean of students.

Ideally, the best way to prevent sexual harassment is through education. Many companies do run required in-service training programs for their employees. The Equal Employment Opportunity Commission requires in their Guidelines on

# Sexual Harassment

Discrimination Because of Sex that it is the legal obligation of every employer to provide a work environment free from sexual harassment. As a result, many companies have extensive policies and procedures to cover sexual harassment.

In an article titled, "It's Not Just Teasing," *U.S. News & World Report* reported, "In a widely quoted survey . . . by the American Association of University Women, 81 percent of students in grades 8 through 11 said they had been sexually harassed at least once. Of those, 76 percent of girls and 56 percent of boys reported that, on at least one occasion, they had been targets of sexual comments, jokes, gestures or looks; 65 percent of girls and 42 percent of boys said they had been touched, grabbed or pinched in a sexual way."[13]

Schools deal with the problem in two ways. Individual states have already passed laws against sexual harassment in the schools. In addition, some schools require courses concerning sexual harassment and sex education to teach children what the consequences of improper behavior can be. California passed a law in 1993 to curtail sexual harassment by children in the fourth grade and up by allowing school administrators to expel offenders. Minnesota's law covers kindergartners. "During the 1991-92 school year, more than 1000 children in Minneapolis alone were suspended or expelled on charges related to sexual harassment."[14]

Many experts say children should be informed about sexual harassment before the kindergarten age. "The need for early intervention is critical," says the *Ladies Home Journal.* "That's when the seeds of gender bias and violence take root."[15]

As with sexual harassment of adults, the key word here is "unwelcome." Parents should teach their children the difference between flirting and sexual harassment. This is the point of "Flirting or Hurting," a sexual harassment curriculum from the Wellesley College Center for Research on women co-authored by Nan Stein. When the high school in Mills, Massachusetts banned hand holding, hugging and other forms of touching in school,

# Teasing

*The Boston Globe* reported it with this comment by Stein: "There's not enough hand holding in high school. But there are all these other assaultive behaviors that are basically sanctioned: butt-grabbing, bra-snapping, pants-pulling-down. We need to promote kinder gestures in high schools; we need to err on the side of affection."[16]

Flirting is fun. Sexual harassment is unwelcome—it is not fun. It isn't funny, and it isn't teasing. Sexual harassment means any kind of unwanted sexual advance or request, or any other unwanted verbal or physical sexual contact. Teach your children to speak up if they are harassed. Tell them to give a warning to the offender not to repeat the behavior. Let them know that no matter what happens, they can share their experiences with you. Make sure they understand that you will believe them and help them get through their experiences so they can exist in safe and non-threatening environments.

Parents should teach their children the difference between respect and admiration, and disrespect and harassment. Boys and girls should learn to treat other children the way they would want their little brothers and sisters to be treated. They should be helped with their self-confidence so they can resist peer pressure to join in on a sexual harassment attack.

Thankfully, the sexual harassment that many of us took for granted growing up is now both unacceptable and illegal. "Reformers like Sattel see acts of sexual violence, a term that encompasses ogling and grabbing, along a single continuum of oppression. 'Serial killers tell interviewers they started sexually harassing at age ten, and got away with it,' says Sattel."[17]

No longer will the world tolerate such lame excuses as "I was only teasing."

# 10

# *Gossip is a Tease*

*Ah, gossip: the junk food of conversation, the cocaine of*
*"interpersonal communication." It's bad for you, it's not nice,*
*you feel slightly guilty, but everybody does it, and you want*
*more.[1]*

Sydney Biddle Barrows,
*Mayflower Manners*

G ossip is a tease. We are tempted and teased to participate in
gossip just as we are tempted and teased by seduction. Like
teasing, gossip is a titillating form of communication.

We have all observed people who seem to either live to
gossip or gossip to live. These people are compulsive gossips.
Compulsive means the person has a continuous need to gossip.
This need is out of his or her control for reasons she or he may
not understand.

As we have all teased and been teased, we have all gossiped
and been gossiped about. Like teasing, gossip has a negative
connotation. A person may not wish to admit being a gossip any
more than a person may not like to admit being a tease. Similar
to teasing, people will either claim to love or hate participating in

gossip. However, even people who say they hate gossip will, at times, still find themselves participating in it, which shows just how strong the tease factor is. Anybody who says he never gossips is lying. The French philosopher Blaise Pascal once said, "I maintain that, if everyone knew what others said about them, there would not be four friends in the world."[2]

Are you a gossip? Are you a "blabbermouth, flibbertigibbet, newsmonger, poll-parrot, tattletale or a wagtongue?"[3] Obviously, gossip means many different things to many people. The equation for gossip is most often one plus one against a third. Just like teasing, gossip takes at least two people. Somebody provides the information (the teller) about a third party (such as a celebrity), while somebody else absorbs it (the listener). Do we think of the gossip as the teller? What about the listener? A gossip can be either a compulsive teller or a compulsive listener. After all, without listening, where would the stories we tell come from?

"Some have suggested in order to be 'admitted' to a gossiping group, one must add a new item of one's own about the subject at hand. Must one? . . . While new members of the group will always be welcome if they present a fresh item at the door, all that's really needed is something to heighten everyone else's Level of Titillation. And all that takes is an expression or comment that emphasizes the titillating aspect of whatever is already under discussion. Phrases like 'You're kidding!' and 'I don't believe it!' . . . serve this purpose admirably."[4]

When the listener becomes the teller to the next listener, a communication chain is formed, and a rumor may begin. Remember the telephone game from childhood birthday parties? Everybody sat in a circle. The birthday child whispered something in the ear of the person sitting next to her and that person was supposed to repeat what was told to the next person, and so on. At the end the story was always drastically different from what was originally told. Gossip and rumor have similar ends. The information is based on something solid, but the result is just not true.

# Gossip is a Tease

Why does the content of a rumor keep changing as the rumor circulates? Is it because people have poor memories for unwritten facts? Is it because people who love gossip are intelligent and imaginative story tellers with the ability to embellish and exaggerate? A gossip will say he hates pretension and yet it is pretentious for him to say his own gossip is true. How truthful is gossip? Or perhaps it is true that "Man's mind is so formed that it is far more susceptible to falsehood than to truth."[5]

Like teasing, which plays off the truth but isn't supposed to be true, gossip is a tease. It pretends to be true, but it often isn't. It can't be. The teller of the gossip wasn't there. How one person perceives a situation is not the way another person perceives the situation.

Does gossip merely improve upon the truth? Are we desensitized to truth? Is the truth not good enough because the truth is dull and boring? Do we lie or exaggerate the truth to impress others with how much we know? Is the need to lie unconscious due to the state of denial in which teasers and gossips find themselves? Do good intentions mean anything in the world of gossip?

Should there be any boundaries or rules for gossip? Should anyone be exempt from gossip or teasing? Or is it a free-for-all? Do you believe in publishing the diaries of a deceased person with the approval of the executor of the deceased's estate? Would you read your best friend's diary without permission if you knew you wouldn't get caught? Can you say one thing over the phone that would not be considered apropos in a restaurant or at a private dinner party? Is it merely the juicier the better? Should we always tell everything we know? If your husband was cheating on you, would you want to know? If you did, would you want to be told by a friend or a stranger? Why do we choose not to protect the privacy of our friends, families, and celebrities?

Is it jealousy that makes people tease and gossip about more negative things than positive ones? Why does gossip accentuate the bad and the shocking: kinky sex, money lost, or crime?

# *Teasing*

We say we want our newspapers to report more good news, but if they did, would we continue to buy them? Is good news too dull? Patrick Spacks writes, "People enjoy knowing other people's weaknesses, not their strengths. Happy endings, assurances of respectability resolve novels but supply no compelling interest."[6] Gossips and teasers are most expert at discovering and exposing the vulnerabilities of other people. That is their business.

Do people really enjoy the company of compulsive gossips who often bring bad news with them? Are compulsive teasers and compulsive gossips regarded as good conversationalists? Do compulsive gossips and teasers receive social invitations just for the promise of what they will reveal or their witty one-liners, or does the hostess wish to make friends with them to avoid being the target of their gossip and teasing in the future?

The tease of gossip is hard to resist for the teller because he is addicted to the high he gets from controlling the emotions of the listener. This is similar to the high experienced by the teaser in controlling the emotions of the teasee. The major difference between teasing and gossip is that with teasing, the teasee is reacting to criticism of himself; with gossip, the person is reacting to the criticism and secrets of others.

A compulsive teller, like a compulsive teaser, may also be addicted to the attention she gets from gossiping. Gossiping makes her feel good. Like the teaser, the teller may be lonely, and gossiping or teasing makes her feel close and bonded to the listener. Gossiping or teasing therefore gives the teller an opportunity for intimacy with the listener, an intimacy which may be lacking in the personal life of the tease or the teller of gossip. The teller may be bored and, as with teasing, gossip becomes a form of entertainment or a pastime. In addition to being a compulsive gossip or a compulsive tease, perhaps the gossip or the teaser just likes to hear herself talk. When people gossip they are distracted from the humdrum quality of their daily, ordinary lives and are able to temporarily escape. Just like teasing, when one thinks about the behavior of others, one can avoid thinking about one's own behavior. Not unlike teasing, gossip helps people avoid change.

Why do some people love to sit in judgment upon others and gossip about them or tease them? Gossiping makes people feel superior to others. When a person spreads gossip or teases, he or she is in control because the gossip is actively doing something. It makes the person feel important. He or she feels knowledgeable and powerful and in control of another, able to divulge his secrets or get his goat. Of course, the ultimate secret is to know what another is like in bed, which once again ties gossip to the tease factor. The reality is that we can never know such information in a vicarious fashion. "Perhaps the urge to participate in gossip comes from knowledge of the impossibility of knowing. We continue to talk about others precisely because we cannot finally understand them, defying possibility."[7]

Like the teaser, the compulsive gossip may be in denial about her need to gossip and her reasons for doing it. It would be easy to deny because, after all, doesn't everybody do it? Depending on the life history of the gossip, the gossip might view gossiping as normal conversation. Also like teasing, compulsive gossiping may run in her family, and often begins in early childhood. Spacks quotes Brownstein, "Gossip, like novels, is a way of turning life into a story. Good gossip approximates art."[8]

Perhaps gossip approaches an art form when it occurs in a novel, but I feel oral gossip is competitive, aggressive and sometimes hostile in nature. Both teasing and gossiping are like fencing. The words are weapons. It is best to be "on guard." Who is capable of the best zinger? Who has the juiciest secret? Gossip is intrusive. We are trying to climb into bed with someone just to learn his innermost secrets. We are deliberately invading the privacy of another person. Someone might become hurt in the telling. People routinely get injured playing sports. It is rare when someone is injured creating art.

Gossip is safer for the teller than teasing. There is not usually a confrontation with the victim as there is in teasing. We tease people we know. We often gossip about people we have never met and never will meet. We tease down the chain of command, but we gossip all the way up to the President of the United States. While the boss teases, his workers get revenge by gossiping in secret, allowing them to release their anger, frustration and resentment about the boss in a socially acceptable way.

A gossip can humiliate a teaser. A gossip has the ability to destroy someone's reputation and honor and make his life feel worthless. In a way, one who teases may be braver than one who gossips because the teaser humiliates openly. A gossip usually does it behind the victim's back. Both crave attention, but a teaser wants to show off in front of the teasee while a gossip often tries to hide from his victim. Gossip is less immediately threatening than teasing, but every gossip lives with the fear of wondering when it will be his turn to be gossiped about. A gossip knows he may be judged for himself as well as the quality of his gossip.

The teaser needs the emotional connection with the teasee, his audience, or his accomplice. A gossip is much less discriminatory. While some gossip goes on in intimate circles, most gossips repeatedly share their information with anyone who will listen to them.

The teller of gossip creates an illusion of intimacy with the listener as well as with his victims. This is why those gossiped about in the tabloids actually feel undressed by the media. Isn't this the very definition of humiliation: feeling naked and vulnerable before the vultures? The person who is gossiped about may feel shame and humiliation, as may the person who is teased.

Does gossip only happen when both people recognize the person whose secrets are being shared? Is this why celebrity gossip is an international pastime—because celebrities are the only people who everybody recognizes? Or is it because ordinary people cannot afford press agents to leak their secrets to the world? Perhaps we prefer celebrity gossip because it is safer to dissect a strange cadaver than the body of a friend. We feel superior to

# Gossip is a Tease

those we gossip about because we know their secrets; they don't know ours. We feel in control of others when we are able to divulge the intimate details of their lives. Perhaps we gossip about the beautiful, the wealthy, and the talented because the gossip is as close as we're ever going to get to being beautiful, wealthy, and talented ourselves.

Is gossip immoral? "The very way we describe and talk about gossip, the whole atmosphere in which it is conveyed, suggests something wicked or forbidden. . . . Where not-niceness fits on a scale of morality is for everyone to decide for himself."[9]

Why do we get such vicarious teasing thrills from the lives of others? Why do we even care? If we are unwilling or unable to act on our feelings or impulses, at least we can get turned on by obsessing and talking about those brave enough to act on theirs. Why do we have such a desperate need to share such personal information? Are we all just Peeping Toms, responding to the tease of the media to climb into bed with strangers on soap operas and in courtrooms? Why do we perceive that the lives of others must be more interesting than our own?

Do we gossip and tease because misery loves company and only the miserable gossip and tease, or is it only when we're miserable that we gossip and tease? I believe that misery likes to be outdone!

The media coverage of the O.J. Simpson trial brings up the difference between news and gossip. The difference between news and gossip is, when I tell it, it's news; when you tell it, it's gossip. That's easy. What about when the media tells it? Is it news or gossip? It is both. Never before in the history of the world have people gossiped so openly without guilt or shame and in such intimate detail as they have with Mr. Simpson. Who can resist the tease?

Because so few can resist the powerful pull of the tease factor, gossip translates into money. One photo of Princess Di will earn thousands of dollars. Patricia Spacks feels that, "Real gossip (i.e., oral gossip) rests on shared group assumptions, but

# *Teasing*

it also provides opportunity to test, clarify and interpret those assumptions, partly by bringing them into conjunction with various individual moral positions."[10] Spacks does not include journalistic gossip as having the same value: "Journalistic gossip, making public what it insists is private, promulgates the illusion of being in the know, declares the universal comprehensibility of other people's lives. It both imitates and debases social functions of oral gossip. Often, it usurps the place of real news, as information about the personal lives of people involved in important events substitutes for attempts to comprehend the events themselves."[11] Spacks offers further criticism of journalistic gossip. "Such gossip exists because it sells; it sells brief illusions of intimacy and power. It thus corresponds rather precisely to prostitution."[12] It also corresponds exactly to teasing.

Malicious gossip or slander is different from, and should not be confused with, routine or compulsive gossiping. Slander is the making of malicious and false oral statements about an individual or group of individuals. Like sadistic teasing, malicious gossip is a way of being aggressive with minimal risk of bodily harm—that is, of course, unless you get caught. One can be sued for slander because it is against the law. Lawsuits for slander are difficult to win and the ensuing publicity further spreads the slander.

If the defamation is written down, it is called libel. "American libel laws make it hard to win a judgment against a publication that prints something untrue. Among other things, you as plaintiff have to prove it is not true. The paper or magazine does not have to prove that it is true."[13]

Should we feel guilty for gossiping? Weren't we all raised with "If you can't say anything nice about someone, don't say anything at all?" Should there be a punishment for gossiping? Is it more than embarrassing to be caught? Society treats stolen property much more seriously than reputations. Can we rationalize gossip as mere curiosity about the psychology of others?

I believe that our society's obsession with gossip and teasing

# Gossip is a Tease

is one of the reasons that the business of psychotherapy is booming. People would prefer to pay professional secret keepers rather than risk being gossiped or teased about their shortcomings and vulnerabilities.

But how truly confidential is psychotherapy today when insurance companies want to know what your problems are before they are willing to pay to treat them, and when the courts can subpoena your records just as they can any other medical record?

The opposite of gossip is professional confidentiality and secret keeping, but that can also be a tease. I know a prominent psychiatrist who apparently treats many famous people. I found out about the status of his clients when the psychiatrist's wife, who does her husband's bookkeeping, phoned my mother years ago and bragged, "You'd never believe the names that I write on the envelopes!" My late mother, who loved celebrities, thought it was the worst tease she had ever been offered. She tried desperately to coax the name of just one famous person out of the psychiatrist's wife, to no avail.

One of my friends teases me that I routinely tease her with, "I've got this great idea! No. I'm not ready to tell you about it yet. I shouldn't say anything yet until I've worked it out." My friend is then dying to know what's on my mind. Finally I give in with, "Okay. I'll tell you, but promise you won't tell anybody!" She wants to inscribe on my tombstone: "Don't tell anybody!" My friend suggests that when you ask someone not to repeat some information, the value of the gossip immediately goes up in price and increases the chance that your information will be circulated. Sometimes I advise a friend to give me a nickel as a token therapist payment for listening to her secrets if she wants to make sure I won't tell anybody. If I take the nickel and tell, she can sue me!

Is gossip totally bad or does it have its redeeming features, as does some teasing? Can any good come out of gossip? Can we learn from the lives and mistakes of others how to better understand ourselves? Can the sharing of gossip, like the sharing of teasing, create intimacy and solidarity? Gossip can bring people together, socially, politically, and morally. Gossip, like teasing, becomes a punishment for bad behavior and therefore reinforces our impulse controls and aids in maintaining law and order. Gossip, as a form of history in the making, can sometimes spread knowledge faster than newspapers.

I feel that gossip is a process of democratization. When we gossip, we most often choose to gossip up the social scale. We like to look for inadequacies in the people we admire and depend on or those we are jealous of because they have something that we wish we had. Their inadequacies make those people seem more human, more like us. If they are more like us, then we are more like them, which is how we would like to be and what we should strive for, if we could. We idealize our heroes and subsequently tear them down in order to make us all equal.

# II

# Teasing, Perfection, and Addiction

*The nature of my compulsion was such that I danced in my sleep. The entire household was sometimes awakened by loud thumping sounds coming from my room. . . . Even in my sleep, I was struggling to perfect the technical execution of the step.[1]*

Gelsey Kirkland,
*Dancing on My Grave*

What all addictions have in common is the tease factor. An addiction promises a quick fix by connecting to something or someone to end emotional or physical pain. Addictions give immediate gratification, a short cut to problem solving, and a short cut to intimacy but with a hidden message. The hidden message is that every addiction is a tease because addiction just doesn't work. It's not an answer. It never solves a problem. The addiction, which starts out as the quick solution to a problem, soon becomes a much greater problem than whatever emotional or physical pain the addict was originally trying to escape from. Sooner or later, the addiction makes it difficult, if not impossible, for the addict to function or maintain his personal relationships.

# Teasing

Another teasing aspect of addictions is the tease of being in control. Like the man who smokes three cigarettes in a row and says, "I can quit anytime I want," many of us really do feel that we can control our addictions. The reason we feel this way is because we can control them at times. Control, like perfection, is elusive. The biggest problem in treating addiction is breaking through an individual's denial to get him to admit that, while he may be able to control his addiction some of the time, he cannot control his addiction all the time. As a result, he gets into trouble because of it.

Most people think of drug addicts when they think of addiction, but there are many other kinds of addictions. In addition to illegal street drugs, people become addicted to prescription drugs, alcohol, caffeine, nicotine and certain foods. There are also behavioral addictions such as overeating, sex and love, shopping, and gambling. There are those who exercise compulsively instead of exercising to keep fit and have fun. Some people are addicted to using rage as a mood changer and a way of releasing inner tension. Others may become workaholics if work offers them an opportunity to feel in control when they feel out of control in other areas of their lives. Some will use religion or social causes in order to compulsively structure their lives, because they feel out of control otherwise. As Carl Jung wrote, "Every form of addiction is bad, no matter whether the narcotic be alcohol or morphine or idealism."[2]

Behavioral addictions also occur. "There are the swelling ranks of scalpel slaves, those addicted to altering their looks with serial plastic surgery. Such people use tucks, lifts, and other procedures the way an addict uses a drug: they get a temporary high, but can never get enough. Then they keep coming back for more, trying to make themselves feel better."[3]

Some people are teased into the addiction of participating in cyberspace technology. According to *Time*, "The vast majority of people who troll the Internet's byways are there in search of social interaction, not just sterile information. An estimated 80 percent of all users are looking for contact and commonality, companionship and community." In other words, these surfers on the Internet are searching for intimacy in a roundabout way, which is a profound tease. It is the tease of the search which is addicting! *Time* also quotes Mitch Kapor, cofounder of the Electronic Frontier Foundation: "We could collectively invent a new entertainment medium, one that taps the creative energies of a nation of midnight scribblers and camcorder video artists. 'In the worst case we could wind up with networks that have the principal effect of fostering addiction to a new generation of electronic narcotics.'" The article mentions a female freelance writer, shy and wary of emotional encounters who "became addicted to this constant stream of approval. It was like a big co-dependency machine."[4] Meeting people through electronic communities involves participating in the blindest of blind dates. Cyberspace connections dramatically illustrate the lengths to which people will go to achieve intimate relationships.

Some people are "cross-addicted" which means they suffer several addictions at the same time. An alcoholic might also be addicted to gambling and drugs while a compulsive shopper might also overeat and have an obsession with gambling. At Alcoholics Anonymous meetings, there are always many people smoking, drinking coffee, and eating candy bars. Sometimes, when a person tries very hard to overcome one addiction, another type of addiction will take its place. "Use of any substance, activity, or person that you use to anesthetize your feelings is a relapse, whether you've had a problem with that particular mood changer in the past or not."[5]

While there are a number of people who are cross-addicted, it would be a mistake to talk about only one type of addictive personality. The personality of the gambler is different from the personality of an alcoholic or a drug addict.

Addicts grow up without intimacy. Addicts are afraid of intimacy, and yet they crave it. People who grow up without intimacy suffer low self-esteem. People with low self-esteem or false egos (false senses of themselves) are very susceptible to the tease of addiction because they don't have the self-confidence to defend themselves against the teasing which constantly surrounds them.

Low resistance to teasing in childhood may create a susceptibility to being teased into addictive patterns in adulthood. Perhaps Mack had a need to reenact his earlier humiliating childhood experiences caused by teasing: "There was no glamour at the end of my gambling career," he confessed. "Just a sniveling, scared child. I was humiliated over and over again—every time I started gambling."

Marilyn, a shopping addict, recalls: "In second grade there was a group of girls who made me their scapegoat, I think because I wore thick glasses. They'd call me all kinds of names and be really cruel. I was miserable, but I had to keep it inside. I felt that I couldn't tell my father; he was even meaner than the girls. And it seemed hopeless to tell my mother. She couldn't stand up for herself, so how could she help me?"[6]

When problems seem insurmountable and there is no one to turn to, life is a "Catch-22"—you're damned if you do and damned if you don't. Repressed anger turned inward creates low self-esteem and depression. Thus addiction, a quick fix to end emotional pain, seems attractive.

There is obviously nothing inherently wrong with shopping, sex, or eating. It is not even the amount or how often a person engages in these activities that counts, but how these activities affect a person. Generally, a person is considered to be an addict if his or her use of a drug, a person, or an activity is getting the person into trouble and making life unmanageable, but the person keeps doing it anyway. If an individual uses alcohol to change a mood because of tension, the person is not merely a "social drinker." "When the behavior begins to take control—causing the person to act inappropriately, deny and try to escape from problems, and go against personal values—it should be considered an addiction."[7]

Every addiction begins with a particular tease, "trigger," or "cue" to which the individual is susceptible. Rosalind, a beautiful and expressive young woman in her twenties, advised me at a meeting of Sex and Love Addicts Anonymous that the biggest tease for her is when a man compliments her—gives her emotional strokes. She confessed she never felt truly confident inside. Her self-esteem is so low she needs outside reinforcement to feel good about herself and to alleviate her loneliness and feelings of depression. Rosalind is seduced by the tease of flattery in order to wipe out her emotional pain. What she gets from her sexual response is just an illusion of intimacy, a quick fix. She ends up feeling even more emotionally unsatisfied and lonely when she realizes the intimacy was false and the relationship will not progress past the point of a sexual encounter. After the sex, she feels guilty about her lack of self-control. The guilt causes Rosalind to feel even more pain—to feel even worse about herself. This additional pain can only be alleviated by an even greater dose of the drug: more compliments and more sex from another man. A different man will solve her problems. Her obsession with sex and love is seen as the cause of her problems as well as the solution. This is the vicious circle of all addictive behavior.

Like Rosalind, the addict is often an intelligent person with high standards and big dreams. The person also craves control and wants immediate gratification. Control freaks often suffer deep insecurity and anxiety because, inside, they feel unacceptable and unworthy. It is difficult for them to feel unconditional love for themselves and others and to feel that they are valuable. People who long for control will often try to cover up their feelings of inadequacy by striving for perfection.

Perfection is the greatest tease of all. Perfection seems like it would be possible to achieve, but it never is. Look at Princess Diana who seemed to have it all and yet was miserable. Individuals who strive for perfection will be continually disappointed and frustrated and will continue to look outside themselves for a quick solution. When they can't reach perfection, they are unable to forgive themselves, and their despair becomes addiction. One of the goals of the various twelve step programs

# Teasing

is to turn it over to God or a higher power instead of addiction.

Some perfectionists were pressured by their parents as children to present a perfect image—a perfect body and "A" grades. These children may seek an outlet for their frustrations in addiction. The addiction is an attempt to mask fears that they are not worthy of unconditional love from the parents, others, or themselves. Where does this idea of the perfect image come from?

The media—television, radio, magazines, and newspapers— presents the greatest tease of perfection to the public by displaying a series of false images for us to covet. The media constantly bombards us with unrealistic role models who tease us into wanting to emulate them. Although supermodel Cindy Crawford has admitted that even she doesn't look like Cindy Crawford when she wakes up in the morning, the fact that these images presented by the media are not totally real seems to escape the consumer.

At one time, Debbie, a twenty-five-year-old alcoholic, was convinced that *The Cosby Show* on television was about an actual family and that their problems were real. She complained that she was at a loss to understand why her family was not more like that make-believe family she admired. Debbie was a television addict, the way others are movie addicts. Television teases us into believing that "problems could be solved in easy, magical ways within half hour segments."[8] Like drugs, television is also used to alter one's mood. Television provides immediate distraction from one's problems and feelings, as well as entertainment and baby-sitting—all at no cost.

No cost? The cost is a willingness by the consumer to allow him or herself and his or her children to be influenced by the advertisers in exchange for watching their favorite programs. Because many of us are too busy to spend more of our time with our children and teach them about important values, we allow them to be teased by the commercials on television. Television may coax our children to buy violent toys and junk food, as well as expose them to violence and sex. That cost is steep indeed! We all used to say, "My mother made me do it." Now the modern day defense it, "He was influenced by the violent movie or cartoon he watched that day."

Thousands of creative advertising people try to convince us that we want things we do not need. We are being brainwashed, and it is perfectly legal. The goal of advertising is to tease us into believing that if we use a particular perfume, we will have both spectacular sex and the glamour of Elizabeth Taylor. We'll be popular if we wear certain labels. If we buy a special liquor, we'll be grownups. The promise of the tease that can never be fulfilled is that we will immediately achieve our goals of being successful, wealthy, sexy, popular, beautiful, young forever, and happy—if we keep buying.

## COMPULSIVE SHOPPING

The tease of compulsive shopping is that it is the treasure hunt to intimacy. A woman who does not get love and emotional intimacy from her husband may unconsciously try to buy herself some love in the stores and get revenge by spending money at the same time. Some women go shopping directly after fights with their husbands. Unhappy childhoods can cause people to develop narcissistic feelings of entitlement, which means they feel they deserve everything they want right now and should not have to work or save for it. This kind of thinking can also lead to compulsive shopping.

Shopping is one of the most powerful teases we face, and compulsive shopping is a growing addiction. We are constantly being offered an infinite range of things to buy which compete for our attention by teasing us. Before we even get to the stores, we are teased by billboards and impressive looking catalogs sent in the mail. Newspaper and television ads exert their powerful influence. Once we get to the stores, the merchandisers tease us with fabulous window displays. They know exactly what colors will attract us and where to place certain items to get our attention when we walk around the aisles.

The biggest tease in shopping is a sale. Bargain hunting, the idea that a person can buy something for practically nothing, is a great tease. The logic the merchandisers use is, tease them into the store with a lead item which is practically being given away. Once the shoppers are in the store, they will purchase higher priced items, and the store will more than recover the loss of the lead items. A friend of mine once had a cabinet full of canned carrots and peas. I told her I didn't know she liked carrots and peas so much. She said she didn't, but they were on sale. She couldn't resist the pull of the tease.

Bargain hunting can cause frenzied panics. Many years ago I was in Filene's Basement in Boston during a cloth coat sale. People were grabbing the coats out of each other's arms. It was frightening to see these shoppers so "high" with the excitement of a bargain that they were actually violent with each other.

There are also coupons with expiration dates to tease us into taking them to the supermarket in a hurry. The discounted price is the tease.

Another powerful tease that contributes to compulsive shopping is a wallet full of credit cards. The idea of "Buy now, pay later" puts the compulsive shopper in a state of denial that he or she is spending real money. Applications for credit cards are offered everywhere.

In the nineties, we have the new tease of home shopping networks on cable television. People have been known to go bankrupt from compulsive shopping without even leaving their homes.

Why do some people "shop till they drop" while others become compulsive shoppers? Janet Damon writes, "There is a high correlation between sexual abuse and compulsive shopping. In my treatment of addicted spenders, there has been an unusually high percentage of women who have been abused.'" We know that some victims of childhood sexual abuse do not blame the abuser, but will blame themselves. Even in adulthood, they feel out of control, ashamed, and guilty. This contributes to very low self-esteem and the susceptibility to the tease of addiction.

Another teasing aspect of compulsive shopping is that each purchase may represent love to the point where it doesn't matter what is bought. "The objects they purchase are an attempt to regain the security they yearn for, the security that is lacking inside them."[10]

To feel more secure, the compulsive shopper is teased by the perfect image in ads and displays for all the latest clothing, state-of-the-art electronic gadgets, and items for the home. People can never be comfortable with themselves if they have to change every time the styles change. They will be forced to keep shopping instead of trying to accomplish something worthwhile. "Many people today are not conscious of the fact that fulfillment comes not just from making money, but from accomplishment. This attitude can lead to misplaced values and confusion. The dollar is often worshiped for its own sake, so people want to appear rich even when they are not—so they overspend."[11]

People who had very controlling parents may not have been allowed to make many decisions when they were young. As adults, they may have difficulties making decisions and choices due to lack of experience. They may find themselves unhappily married and in jobs they don't like. These people are especially susceptible to the tease of shopping addiction. It is overwhelming to go from no choices to infinite choices with a credit card in the wallet.

As the mother of a teenage girl who loves to shop with her friends, I can see the dangers inherent in shopping as a hobby for young people. My daughter tells me that several of her friends feel there is nothing else to do but shop. Are our children merely unimaginative and lacking in interests, or are they brainwashed by the media? We live in a city with an excellent school system where cultural opportunities abound. How then can we blame the child's lack of interests and creative hobbies on lack of exposure? Can we blame the media entirely? Can the parents be blamed? Should we forbid teenagers to shop?

# Teasing

Image is important to teens because of the peer pressure they experience. It is very easy to feel lonely in a crowd of children at school, and we know children can be cruel: "He had been the class scapegoat: obese, acne-ridden, easy to mock. . . . Instead of trying to make human contact, he planned where he would shop the next day. If he kept shopping, he thought, eventually he'd get just the right outfit. Then he'd have lots of friends, maybe even someone to love. . . . He'd finally feel attractive and popular, and he wouldn't be lonely anymore."[12]

Why weren't we compulsive shoppers when we were kids? Perhaps we felt we had some control over our lives.

One reason children are much more out of control of their lives than we were at their age is because parents are more afraid today. We don't allow young children the privacy of playing in their own backyards or around the neighborhood without adult supervision, because we are afraid they'll be kidnapped or molested. We want to know exactly where they are at all times. We are forced to make our children far more sexually knowledgeable than we were as children in order to keep them safe from AIDS and other diseases.

Like their adult role models, when young people feel out of control, they can go shopping. The tease of shopping makes everyone, young and old, feel powerful. For a person who feels out of control of his life, compulsive shopping is the quickest fix to feeling powerful. The sales people will praise your choices, give you the attention you crave, and try to make you feel beautiful, loved and special.

The tease of the promise of beauty, love, uniqueness, and power contributes to the shopper's euphoria. The compulsive shopper gets lost in the tease which becomes the trance. The high experienced by compulsive shoppers is not all that different from the high of other addictions. Like a cocaine addict, the compulsive shopper on a binge feels she can do anything, and acquire anything. This loss of logic can turn into occasional shoplifting, or even kleptomania, an obsession to steal things that one doesn't really need and could afford to buy anyway.

There are also those who love to shop so much that they become compulsive returnaholics as an excuse to shop some more. Jane, a young widow, reported, "Every day I go shopping and buy at least one item I don't need. That way I know I'll have something to do the next day: return it!" Some of these returnaholics have such a severe problem with intimacy that they can't even make a commitment to keep a purchase, never mind keep a relationship going with a person. Therefore, anything they buy must go!

Some people get so carried away by shopping that their binges may signal manic depressive illness (bipolar affective disorder). Manic people will purchase multiples of an item they don't need and more pounds of food than they could possibly eat. Fortunately, there are medications for manic depressive illness that help to prevent such manic behavior.

Like other addicts, compulsive shoppers suffer after they succumb to the tease of shopping and going on a spending binge. They feel worse about themselves after a binge than they did before.

Compulsive shoppers feel worthless and entitled at the same time. People who feel powerful by shopping soon find out they are not really powerful at all, but have been teased into shopping slavery by addiction. Compulsive shoppers must then deal with an obsession about money needed to pay expensive bills.

Lonely people sometimes succumb to the tease of shopping, because they feel a need to buy things to fill up the emptiness they feel inside. Emotionally deprived adults and children in grief after the loss of a parent (due to death or divorce) may begin shoplifting to act out the pain inside them. The relief of making a purchase or taking an item tease because it relieves the pain, but only momentarily. The person still feels empty.

There are support groups like Overspenders Anonymous and Shopaholics Anonymous, but they are not as widespread as the twelve step programs for alcoholism, drugs, gambling and overeating. Like other recovering addicts, addicted spenders have the problem of what to do with all the free time they have once they stop shopping. It is very important for recoverers to develop new hobbies and interests in order to resist the tease of shopping again out of boredom. Compulsive shoppers must learn techniques for delaying shopping to allow the urge to pass. It is helpful to avoid the tease, the pull of the stores, as much as possible in order to resist returning to self-destructive behavior patterns.

## COMPULSIVE EATING

A compulsive eater complains she never feels full. The extreme version of the compulsive eater is the person suffering from bulimia who eats enormous quantities of food until she feels uncomfortable and then the guilt and shame and fear of gaining weight cause her to purge by either vomiting, fasting, taking laxatives, taking diuretics, overexercising, or a combination of these. "If you are predisposed to bulimia or overeating, you should be extra watchful of your pace in winding down your compulsive shopping, so that withdrawal does not lead you into an eating disorder."[13]

Some professionals in our culture are more susceptible to eating disorders than others. Athletes, models, actresses and dancers fall into this category. Ballerina Gelsey Kirkland explains, "The bonds linking us were compulsory starvation, the dreams of food, and the drastic measures required to maintain our diets. We later induced vomiting by downing an emetic intended for babies. . . . I had an encounter with Mr. B [George Balanchine] in class which underscored his demand for starvation, a memory that is etched in my mind with all the pain of a fingernail being scraped across a blackboard. He halted class and approached me for a kind of physical inspection. With his knuckles, he thumped on my sternum and down my rib cage clucking his tongue and remarking, 'Must see the bones.'"[14]

# Teasing, Perfection, and Addiction

Compulsive eaters are constantly teased by clever food advertisements and tempting displays of food. Remember the potato chip commercial, "Can you eat just one?" When my friend told me, "I'm a seafood eater," I stupidly asked her what her favorite kind of fish was. Her reply: "I see food and eat it!" The free popcorn and peanuts in some bars and restaurants are to tease a person into eating them so his or her mouth will get salty and they will buy even more drinks to quench their thirst.

Restaurant chefs tease us with hefty servings. We have all seen enough roast beef heaped on a plate for the Lion King. The ultimate serving teases are the "All You Can Eat" specials and the one price buffets. Why are we so susceptible to the tease of overeating? Are we just like the little goldfish that will eat itself to death if there is too much food on top of its bowl? It is interesting that a gambling center like Las Vegas is famous for the inexpensive buffets offered by the hotels where there is gambling. Buffets have the advantage to a gambling establishment of being able to offer large amounts of food quickly so there is more time and money left over with which to gamble. Perhaps the owners also recognize that many compulsive gamblers are compulsive eaters as well.

It has been said that the addiction problem that affects one-third of Americans is eating and being overweight. If you add those people who only perceive themselves to be overweight, the total percentage of people who would consider themselves overweight would be staggering. "If we decide that being overweight is a disease and that obesity is biologically determined, then practically every American home is implicated in this disease. Moreover, since eating is legal, ubiquitous, and—for most people—pleasurable, overweight and overeating may be the hardest addiction to overcome. In addition, overweight/overeating—and not drug or alcohol abuse—is the fastest-growing substance abuse problem among the young."[15]

The big debate is whether the susceptibility to the tease of overeating or any other addiction stems from psychological or physiological problems. Some experts insist overeating is psychological. An individual may deny herself food because she feels unworthy of being loved. Another might overeat due to her upbringing. If a child is rewarded with a cookie for being good, we say it is the mother's fault if the child grows up to be a fat adult. Of course, mother happens to be fat because grandma gave her cookies, too. Was fatness inherited in this family, or merely the recipe for those good cookies? The recipe symbolizes the cultural influences of obesity. In my opinion, the chances are as great that it is the brain chemistry and the metabolism of this family which was inherited.

"According to research done at the Massachusetts Institute of Technology Laboratory of Neurendocrine Regulation, a clue may lie in the behavior of certain chemical messengers in the brain that normally regulate our hunger for sugars. . . . One such brain chemical, known as serotonin, is intimately involved with our appetite for sugars and other carbohydrates. Normally serotonin is released by cells deep in the brain, as a result of a long chemical chain reaction, as soon as we have eaten a meal rich in sugars. . . . Thus the act of eating carbohydrates ordinarily triggers a kind of natural, biochemical 'feedback mechanism' that shuts off the craving for more carbohydrates. . . . In some people, however, this carbohydrate-serotonin feedback mechanism may not work properly. Eating a little sugar doesn't end up suppressing their desire for more, as it normally should."[16]

Such people find themselves gorging on sugars or carbohydrates to the point of feeling sick from overeating. Prozac, a nonaddictive antidepressant, assists the body with serotonin. It is approved for use in the treatment of bulimia. Prozac has also been found helpful in alleviating the symptoms of premenstrual syndrome, according to recent research done at Beth Israel Hospital in Boston. Anyone who thinks she might benefit from medication should be evaluated by her internist, gynecologist, or psychiatrist.

Even if the cause of binge eating is physiological, the

result of an eating binge is a psychological problem. Since our society celebrates slimness, the person who binges will most likely suffer feelings of shame and guilt for overeating. It is the guilt that causes the bulimic person to purge, and the purging causes her to feel even more guilt. Consequently, the guilt causes depression. To reduce her feelings of depression she will often want to cheer herself up quickly with something that tastes good, and so the vicious circle continues. The fatter you are, the more depressed you get. The more depressed you get, the more you eat, the fatter you get. Food is seen as the solution as well as the cause of all her problems.

To get out of the vicious circle, a person must give up the guilt. Never aim for perfection, aim for improvement. You don't have to eat perfectly all the time. Just do your best one day or one hour at a time. If you binge in the morning, just say, "Well, I blew the morning but I am going to forgive myself for that and try to eat better the rest of the day." Remember, you are only human, and nobody is perfect. Everyone has problems. Some people are just more gifted at hiding their problems than others.

A person must also become aware of when, where and under what circumstances she is capable of being teased and seduced into overeating. A person must then adjust or avoid those situations as much as possible. Are you teased by your refrigerator? Stay out of the kitchen unless you have to be there. Are you lonely and bored? Try to make a friend by participating in a community activity or sharing a new hobby. Do you love to eat and read? Go to the library to read instead of the kitchen. When watching television, do something with your hands such as sewing or writing a letter.

Another way to avoid the tease of overeating or binging is to plan and prepare meals in advance. Otherwise, when you feel hungry, you will be teased into grabbing the most readily available foods which may be high in fat. You may wish to avoid high risk situations where you might feel uncomfortable due to a desire to overeat. You may leave a party or gathering early if you wish.

# Teasing

Another aspect of compulsive eating is that some people eat to distract themselves from their feelings. Psychologists talk about "eating" or "stuffing" your anger which means keeping the anger inside and then eating food out of frustration. This is often done unconsciously. The antidote for this is to make it conscious, become aware of how you are trying to distract yourself. Try very hard to "feel your feelings." By joining an Overeaters Anonymous program, which is free, you will learn about your behavior and get much needed support. You will then gain the strength to stay away from problem foods.

## COMPULSIVE GAMBLING

A compulsive gambler is a person who is governed by his own irresistible urge to gamble. Gamblers Anonymous was founded in 1957, but it took until 1980 for the American Psychiatric Association to recognize pathological gambling as a disorder of impulse control. The APA says that "most individuals with Pathological Gambling say that they are seeking 'action' (an aroused, euphoric state) even more than money."[17] I think this is ridiculous. Many addicted gamblers have borrowed and/or stolen large sums of money in order to participate in gambling. If you ask someone who has done this whether or not money is important to them, they will often deny its importance. This way they don't have to feel so guilty for never being able to pay it back.

If you want to prove that the money is more important to a gambler than the action, just ask a bookie not to accept more than a ten-dollar bet from a gambler. The gambler will be furious because he wants to bet more than a hundred dollars. As Don, a recovering gambler explained, "Excitement? What's exciting about gambling unless you're gambling a lot of money?" Don advised me to notice all the fancy cars in the parking lot of a Gamblers Anonymous meeting. "If all the people inside are complaining they are bankrupt, then why are they all driving fancy cars?"

# Teasing, Perfection, and Addiction

A gambler has a different view of money from the average person. Like all addicts, gamblers believe that what is the cause of all their problems is also the solution—namely, money. "A compulsive gambler with money in his pocket will always find a way to spend it. To him, money has absolutely no meaning. He believes he can always get more."[18]

Gamblers are teased by the casinos with offers of inexpensive hotel rooms and meals. Big gamblers are courted by the casinos with free stays at the hotels and preferential treatment at restaurants. Gamblers receive free drinks at casinos. Obviously the idea is that an inebriated gambler will lose his inhibitions and bet even more money while his judgment is impaired.

The credit card is a huge tease to a gambler. In the past, cash was required to place a bet. Now respectable establishments allow unlimited use of credit cards which helps put the gambler in a state of denial. However, this policy in the casinos may change. Deborah Kimbrow, the widow of a compulsive gambler, is suing a casino for fifty million dollars. According to the *Eye on America* television program, her husband committed suicide after losing $100,000 at the casino. Casino personnel kept giving him credit despite the fact that he had written bad checks to the casino the previous month. Should a compulsive gambler be responsible for his own behavior, or should the casinos play a role? The courts will soon decide.

Society contributes to the tease of gambling by encouraging people to participate in state-run lotteries and other forms of gambling. States with legalized gambling employ public relations people to tease customers into gambling by advertising the biggest jackpots and publicizing the winners. Casino owners don't even want to call it gambling any more. They want to call it "gaming" in order to deny the reality of it. Even Las Vegas is now promoting itself as a second Disneyworld.

The slang of gambling is also an enormous tease. A "nickel" bet really means a bet of five hundred dollars. A "dime" is one thousand dollars. A gambler will call his bookie and say he wants to put a nickel on the Patriots and a dime on the Celtics. The slang minimizes the amounts involved and puts the gambler in denial.

The convenience of gambling is also a tease. Lottery tickets are sold everywhere. "It was only after a betting office or gaming club opened up in their neighborhood that many of the gamblers lost control. In other words, with increased accessibility, a number of social gamblers rapidly became pathological."[19]

The tease of camaraderie is also offered while gambling. Like other addicts, gamblers have trouble with intimacy and feeling isolated. Thus, they are susceptible to the tease of false intimacy in the bingo halls and casinos. "When I think back, it's funny, but we never got together with each other anywhere but the bingo hall. . . . I felt I knew each one of them well, yet I was never invited to any of their family functions. I realize now that I was a bingo friend and nothing more."[20]

The actual physical environment of some gambling establishments also contributes to the tease of gambling. Like kiddie rides in amusement parks, casinos are gaudy, flashy, and contrived to look like playgrounds for grownups. The blinking colored lights, the fancy slot machines, the sounds of falling coins, and the sexy cocktail waitresses all contribute to an aura of excitement that draws people in.

All gamblers start out as recreational gamblers. "People gamble because it is fun, because they never have to gamble more than they are willing to, because they are often admired by others when their bets are sizable, and because it is a form of risk-taking that cannot harm them unless their gambling becomes an addiction."[21]

How can a game turn into an addiction? Linda Berman explains that "like alcohol or drugs, gambling can temporarily change a person's mood. It can heighten excitement to the point of euphoria. It has the potential to alleviate anxiety and depression, permitting people to remain out of touch with feelings they consciously or unconsciously perceive as dangerous. Gambling can raise some people's self-esteem and give them a sense of identity. Those who begin as social or recreational gamblers are at risk of becoming problem or compulsive gamblers if they experience the gambling as a mood-changing 'drug' and have an extraordinary need to change their mood. Anyone who is already abusing alcohol or drugs or is in recovery is also at risk."[22]

For a gambler, very often it is the tease of a big win or a long winning streak that turns him from a recreational to a problem gambler. As Richard, a new member of Gamblers Anonymous, put it, "I gambled because I thought I was special. Now I realize I am just like everybody else."

The chance of winning is the great tease of gambling. The gambler's logic is that if you won big once, you can do it again. The lure of easy money and coming "this close" to your goal are major teases for some people. When a gambler wins, it is his way of achieving perfection. A gambler's state of perfection is very fleeting, since he will soon lose again. There is also much suspense in gambling: the waiting and the anticipation are other forms of teasing. (See Chapter 13: Suspense Is a Tease.)

While the big win pattern is common to male gamblers, many female gamblers never have a big win. "More than half of compulsive gambling women state they initially looked upon gambling as a means of escaping from overwhelming problems, including childhood disturbances, troubled relations, . . . loneliness and boredom."[23]

"Although the ratio of male to female compulsive gamblers is five to one, the gap is closing. Women turn to gambling for the same reasons as men: to alter their moods, especially if they have suffered a loss or major blow to self-esteem."[24]

For those who succumb to the tease of compulsive gambling, gambling will become their entire lives. "The gambling fever got me and I no longer existed. I became 'gambling.' I thought of nothing else, wanted nothing else, lived for nothing else. My mind was racing every day."[25] Gamblers get a high, a burst of adrenaline, whether they win or lose.

# Teasing

Some experts believe there may be a physiological cause for gambling and that it may be found in the adrenal glands. This explains why some risk takers seem to need extraordinary excitement to give themselves shots of adrenaline, just to feel the way other people feel normally.

Unfortunately, more and more young people are succumbing to the tease of gambling. Researchers stress that unstable home environments, lack of self-confidence and society's obsession with money all contribute to the rise of teen gambling.

It's easy to look down upon gamblers. It's easy to say that gamblers are just lazy, greedy, immature, and don't like to work —that they lie, cheat, steal, and want something for nothing. What might be more fair and accurate to say about gamblers is that they suffer from pathological optimism. They really do believe that a big score is just around the corner. "Compulsive gamblers often are highly intelligent individuals who are accustomed to being the best, beating the odds and winning at every challenge. To them, gambling represents a new game to master."[26]

"Perhaps the best answer to the question of why compulsive gamblers continue to gamble is offered . . . in *Sharing Recovery Through Gamblers Anonymous*. The Blue Book says: 'We don't know and we cannot afford to care. Those who come to us need help immediately. There is not time for the intellectual luxury to explore each compulsive gambler's history and to interpret the results. There is no place in our Fellowship Program for debate on the merits of different theories of recovery, on the conflicts between varying schools of psychological thought. The benefits of introspection and speculation are paltry when compared to the rewards of helping others regain their lives."[27]

Like all addicts, gamblers have problems with intimacy. Rudy, a long-term member of Gamblers Anonymous, informed the group, "My wife and I had a problem with intimacy. I didn't have a problem. I didn't know anything about intimacy. I couldn't be intimate. So I didn't have a problem." Many people fear recovery because they fear having to tell the truth to themselves and others because they fear intimacy.

Marriage to a gambler is a complex undertaking. The partner recognizes the potential for intimacy inside the gambler, and this teases her to keep the marriage going. She is addicted to the emotional crumbs she gets from the gambler. As all compulsive eaters know, crumbs are an enormous tease. A gambler may be afraid of his marital relationship without the escape of his gambling. Peter explains, "I never used to tell the truth about anything. Truth was responsibility. So I made up stories. It was my way of avoiding being intimate with anyone."

Gamblers lie about where the money goes and where they themselves go. Tony confesses, "My wife would say, 'You must not love me if you gambled all our money away!' It was not personal to her. It was just the disease." When wives catch their gambler husbands lying, they often become suspicious of their every move. They become obsessed with wanting to catch them again.

The wife of the compulsive gambler may also be addicted to the tease of easy money when he's winning. She just doesn't like it when he's losing. The gambler's wife often resembles the wife of the heavy drinker. Sandra, a woman in her fifties who was married to an alcoholic for over thirty years, confessed that she didn't like her husband when he was sober because then he was dull and boring. Sandra also hated her husband when he was drunk. "I love him the best when he's had three drinks. Then he's amusing and fun, but not when he's drunk." The problem was that the poor guy couldn't stop after three drinks.

If the gambler stops gambling or the drinker stops drinking, all of a sudden life becomes predictable, and the wife doesn't know what to do. Predictability is just not a part of her reference frame. It is more than likely that she grew up with a gambler or an alcoholic parent or in some other kind of dysfunctional family. She is therefore used to the ups and downs of living with addiction, expects them, and may even be addicted to the tease of the roller coaster lifestyle of lying and stealing and the suspense of waiting for the next crisis. A roller coaster

# Teasing

is probably the greatest physical tease of all. You keep inching up, never knowing exactly when you will go flying down or turn upside down, and so the suspense, for some, is unbelievably exciting.

Because of her own insecurities, the wife of a gambler usually has a terrific fear of abandonment and is terrified of making her husband angry because she fears he might leave her. Therefore, even if she is against the gambling, she will continue to act as an "enabler." An enabler is the person who helps the addict keep his habit going. The wife will help the gambler by borrowing money for a "bailout." She will then feel she is indispensable to the gambler.

Sometimes borrowing alone cannot cover gambling debts. Since the gambler is addicted to the tease of easy money, he is also susceptible to the tease of even easier money via crime. It might even be easier to steal than to gamble but the penalty for stealing is greater, unless your bookie threatens you for nonpayment of all the nickels and dimes you owe him.

Is a gambler crazy to engage in illegal activity in order to cover his gambling debts? As Rocky, a recovering gambler, boasted, "Yeah, a gambler is crazy all right. Crazy like a fox! Most addicted gamblers never get caught when they embezzle or steal. How do you suppose they support their habit for so many years? When they do get caught, it's usually just by accident."

The vicious circle in gambling begins with the tease of "just one more bet." Some gamblers dig such deep holes for themselves that they can't see a way out. Many gamblers commit suicide. When gamblers finally attend a Gamblers Anonymous meeting, it is not because they *want* to stop gambling, but because they *have* to stop gambling. Gamblers show up at Gamblers Anonymous because they are having trouble with their marriages, their children, their jobs, the law, or because they are bankrupt or close to it. This is why trying to force a gambler or any addict to go to meetings is pointless. Unless an addict feels he has to stop, he doesn't.

# Teasing, Perfection, and Addiction

## SEX AND LOVE ADDICTION

*The addiction is truly an altered state of consciousness in which "normal" sexual behavior pales by comparison in terms of excitement and relief from troubles.*[28]

Patrick Carnes, *Out of the Shadows*

The sex addict not only has to battle the tease of his own sexual obsession but the tease of society's sexual obsessions as well. Personal relationships suffer greatly and, consequently, these addicts are extremely isolated and lonely. They don't know what true intimacy is. Like other addicts, a sex and love addict feels immeasurable guilt, shame, and self-hate. The major difference is that these people—many of whom engage in one or more of the following: exhibitionism, voyeurism, obsessions with pornography, child pornography, obsessions with masturbation, incest, rape, prostitution (as a customer or as the service provider), sexual harassment, bestiality, serious promiscuity—are regarded as criminal, immoral, or perverted by our society. Gay sex addicts suffer the additional stigma of homosexuality.

The sex addict may even agree with society's assessment of his or her behavior. This is why a sex addict will avoid seeking professional help. He or she is convinced of being judged. Where a sex addict will disagree with society is in terms of the motivation of his behavior. "Unlike normal persons, who seek love and sex to fill normal needs, addicts use them to lessen the pain that comes from problems in other areas of life."[29]

As a result of a failure to seek help, the sickness will be left unattended, and the sex addict may be punished instead. Some sex addicts are treated the way alcoholics were treated in the past when they were jailed for public drunkenness. Society can't seem to separate a person from his or her sick behavior. Some sex addicts will be viewed by society as embodiments of one behavior, i.e., he is a rapist, she is a child molester. These people are often jailed without being offered any rehabilitation.

# Teasing

Of all the addicts, love and sex addicts have the greatest access to their favorite tease. The sexual stimulation around us all is overwhelming. In films and on the beaches, people are scantily clad. Love stories and soap operas on television are increasingly more sexually explicit each year. Pornography magazines are sold in every corner store. Magazine ads are increasingly sexualized, and romance novels with sexy covers abound in the bookstores. Cable television and home video equipment bring X-rated movies into the home. Telephone sex services are also available at home. Escort services deliver. Like a gambler who thinks money is the cause and the solution, a sex and love addict feels that love and sex is the cause as well as the solution to all her problems.

Other teases for love and sex addicts are not so apparent. "For the exhibitionist whose pattern involves driving, simply entering a car becomes a cue to start the ritual. Scanning the street for potential 'scores' becomes almost part of driving."[30] Marsha confesses, "I started going out at night without my husband to rehearse for a play and had an affair with a fellow actor. Now, whenever I step into a theater, I get horny. Sometimes it is out of control. When they say, 'Take five,' I will go into the parking lot with someone. It doesn't matter who." Women who travel away from home on the job are now subject to the same temptations that were originally considered male. For some women, travel is thought of as sexual and the cue to want to act out.

As a social worker, I have been to many different twelve step program meetings, but I have never seen as many people at one meeting as I did at a chapter of Sex and Love Addicts Anonymous. There were more than sixty people there on a week night in a relatively small suburb. If attendance is any measure of the pain people are suffering, the distress must be immense. Unlike the Gamblers Anonymous and Alcoholics Anonymous meetings I have attended, there were many women at the SLAA meeting, and more women than men spoke about their problems.

Another difficulty for members of Sex and Love Addicts

# Teasing, Perfection, and Addiction

Anonymous is that they may find themselves teased at their own self-help meetings by the presence of attractive people there. As one of the female group speakers recommended to the men of the group, "If you like women of a certain size and hair color, I wouldn't recommend picking one of those for your sponsor."

Members of Sex and Love Addicts Anonymous try to offer encouragement to each other by sharing their doubts as well as their progress. Joe spoke first. "When I first came," he said, "I had faith that God will run everything fine for you, but when it comes to me . . . well, He has so many other things to think of."

Nate was worried, "I'm not good enough. I'm never going to recover. Everyone is going to recover except me."

Lana confessed, "I cried when I spent a day free from my addiction. A whole day. And I didn't think about acting out, and I didn't act out."

Stephanie added, "I spent so much energy looking good that people didn't know I needed to be hospitalized because my sexual behavior was so inappropriate. I used to feel that you kissed on the first date, had sex on the second, and got the U-Haul on the third."

Tim joked, "I'm such a control freak that the hardest part of the program for me is turning it over to God."

Lois shared, "I couldn't talk to a man when I was in withdrawal because if I wasn't going to go to bed with him, I didn't know what to say to him. I can see how much this disease has stolen from me. I want a real relationship, not just the junk you get from going to bed with someone."

Laura, a recovering love and sex addict, announced, "Pain is just a means to an end. You think withdrawal is really bad, but you go through it and the pain passes. In reality, your previous behavior was much more painful, but you just were not awake enough to know you were in pain."

Our cultural views on sexual role playing also contribute to sex addiction. Men are rewarded with admiration by other men for their sexual conquests and activity. They are seen as macho.

# Teasing

Men will often provide alibis for one another. In our culture, many men feel that women control when sex happens, and the new woman is seen as constantly teasing men. Such men complain of having to chase "it" and having to give up more, in terms of dollars, to get "it." Certain men feel the more money they have, the more powerful they will be in terms of having access to sex. These men often feel unworthy in their relationships and believe they could easily be replaced by another man with greater resources. Men of this ilk rationalize their view of women as sex toys because they think women view them as money trees.

Sex addicts will discuss feeling emotionally deprived when they were children. According to many, they felt lonely, unloved and unsafe. Their parents and extended families were emotionally unavailable to them. As a result, they used sex since childhood as a way to comfort themselves. Soon the sexual comfort replaced the need for people. Eventually, sex became their most important need and the focus of their lives.

Sex addicts are so insecure that they constantly worry that their sexual needs won't be met. One girlfriend or wife just isn't enough. Ralph confessed, "You have to have some people to fall back on."

The addict whose tease is merely visual rationalizes that just watching couldn't be so bad. Yet spying can be time and money consuming. Arlene, a pretty woman in her forties, told me that her husband always drove the longest way to get anywhere which would afford him the maximum opportunities to look at other women. She complained that it took him forever to get home from work. Sophie, an obese woman in her fifties, couldn't drag her husband out of porno shops where he chose to spend most of his free time. Sophie complained that money needed to pay the bills was being wasted on pornography and telephone sex services.

Why do married partners stay with sex addicts? They are often raised in unstable homes themselves, are afraid of the unknown and afraid to be alone. Co-addicts "often seek relationships in which they dominate, or nurture because they can be intimate with minimum risk."[31] "Instead of seeing sex as the most important need, co-addicts often believe: *Sex is the most important sign of love.*"[32]

Successfully recovering from addictions to alcohol, love, and sex, a young lesbian proudly proclaimed, "I finally realized that the sunset is enough, and I am enough. I don't need a drink in my hand and a beautiful person with me to be happy."

## NICOTINE

Cigarette smoking is a tease just like any other addiction because after awhile most people do not continue to smoke for pleasure, but in order to avoid uncomfortable withdrawal symptoms. Young people may start smoking due to the tease of peer pressure. They smoke to show off, feel more grown up, seem more sophisticated, be accepted by a certain crowd, alter their mood, relax, or keep from overeating.

As with other addictions, the nicotine addiction is a tease because smoking will not solve anybody's problems but will soon cause more problems for the smoker than he had in the beginning. In addition to the health problems with which we are all familiar, such as cancer, emphysema, heart disease, stroke, and babies born with low birth weight, there is also the problem of impotence. *The Boston Globe* reported on the front page on December 2, 1994 that "Smokers are 50 percent more likely to suffer from impotence than nonsmokers."

Smokers are now terribly unpopular because of second-hand smoke. Bad breath, yellow teeth, smelly clothes, smelly houses, and the risk of causing fires are additional problems. Cigarette smoking is also expensive. The price of cigarettes keeps rising as government keeps adding higher taxes to the purchase price.

Nicotine, the main addictive ingredient in cigarettes, may

not alter perception or drastically change an individual's personality as do other addictions, but it does cause significant changes in the body and the brain. In 1987 the Surgeon General's report "Nicotine Addiction" announced that cigarette smoking is as addictive as heroin, cocaine, and alcohol.

Despite all of the drawbacks, the tease of smoking is enormous. As with other addictions, smoking is part physiological and part psychological. While there are many medical aids such as patches and chewing gum to help smokers quit, it is still an extremely difficult addiction to break because "Commercial cigarettes are an unparalleled delivery system for getting the drug into the blood and to the nervous system in the most efficacious way possible."[33] The aroma and the actual smoke in the air are enormous teases for people trying to quit. When smokers hang out with other smokers because nonsmokers don't welcome them, they are constantly tempted to light up.

Part of the tease is the physical ritual of the smoker. "Buying cigarettes, taking off the cellophane wrapping, taking off the gold paper and extracting a new, aromatic cigarette from the pack are almost as important as the pharmacological aspects of smoking. They are, for the smoker, what preparing the fix is for the heroin addict."[34]

Psychologically, smoking is an enormous tease, because smokers associate an incredibly high number of other activities and situations with smoking. Smokers think of coffee breaks as smoking breaks. Caffeine powerfully reinforces and encourages the use of nicotine. A smoker might wish to light up while he is on the telephone or watching television. Some people always smoke after sex or after a meal. Some like to smoke while driving.

Smokers are constantly teased because reminders of their cigarette habit are everywhere. Cigarettes are sold at every corner store. Their houses and cars still contain ashtrays. Cigarette manufacturers sponsor sports events. A smoker is also teased by the many respectable people, who have made enormous contributions to society, who continue to smoke in public. "If they can do it, why can't I?"

For ideas on how to resist the tease of lighting up, call the local branch of the American Cancer Society and ask to be sent free information on how to quit.

All recovering smokers must be prepared for the tease of sudden cravings which might occur at any time after they quit. A recovering smoker can be teased by the smell of cigarette smoke, the company of other smokers, feelings of nostalgia for a place or situation where he used to smoke, a long ride in the car. All the recovering smoker can do is understand these cravings are to be expected and that the craving will pass. "It has been estimated that it takes about eleven years to remove a long-established tobacco addiction from every cell in the body, and at any time up to then the habit could take hold again."[35] Many recovering smokers would disagree and say that the habit could return at any time during the course of their lives.

## CAFFEINE

In 1994 researchers from Johns Hopkins University reported that "the caffeine in coffee, tea and cola can produce addiction similar to that engendered by alcohol, tobacco, heroin and cocaine."[36]

Due to the strong connection between eating and drinking coffee, caffeine and sugar addiction can become a cross-addiction. Those who take lots of cream and sugar with their coffee will often gain weight and be in a total state of denial as to the cause. Like smokers, the "java junkies" associate drinking coffee with many other activities which tease them into drinking another cupful.

Some people kick the coffee habit only to be teased back into another type of caffeine drink such as cola drinks or tea or chocolate. Addiction to caffeine in any form can cause problems.

# *Teasing*

Paul, a forty-year-old engineer, was rushed to the hospital from work after going into convulsions. He had no previous history of seizures. Paul said the first question the neurologist asked him in the emergency room was whether he drank a lot of diet soda. Paul confessed that he was a caffeine addict and that he drank at least one liter bottle of a diet cola every day. The doctor told him there is a recent theory that large quantities of diet drinks cause convulsions, but it has not yet been proven.

Our culture contributes to the tease of caffeine addiction. "Let's go for coffee" doesn't necessarily mean "for coffee." It is our idiomatic expression for going to a restaurant for a chat and a drink of some sort. You can't go into a restaurant for breakfast without a waitress asking if you want a cup of coffee. Even people who don't enjoy coffee often love the smell of it: another enormous tease for the caffeine addict who is trying to cut down or quit.

Phyllis, a young widow in her early thirties, told me in therapy that she had begun her first sexual affair since the death of her husband and that she had been having trouble sleeping. It was tempting to assume that guilt was interfering with her sleep. However, when I asked about her personal habits, she told me that she had recently begun to drink twenty cups of coffee per day. Apparently, around the time she began her affair, a new free coffee machine was installed at her workplace. She was teased into trying coffee for the first time in her life because it was free. She quickly became addicted. Now, when she couldn't sleep at night, she would get up and make herself a cup. She was unaware that caffeine is a stimulant that would keep her awake.

Free coffee at work is an enormous tease for a recovering caffeine addict. I'm always curious as to why some companies offer this. Do they want their caffeine addicts to stay awake and alert, or are they just trying to keep them happy? Can you just imagine what would happen if businesses left free alcohol next to the free coffee?

Another enormous tease for coffee addicts is the variation

in the different types of coffee available today that could help the coffee addict remain in denial. "Last week I went into a coffee house to get, you know, a cup of coffee, only to be told that actual coffee was unavailable. Would I like a tasty cappuccino, cafe au lait, or espresso? . . . No way. This mutant coffee thing is getting out of hand. It's even hard to get a cuppa mud at the local convenience store. . . . Today, convenience stores all have an Isle Du Cawfay or some damn thing. . . . I'm not against this stuff, but it's not what I look for in liquefied coffee: I want a blister on my lips and a knot in my stomach. I want my coffee black, bitter and scalding. Give me that little pleasure, America. I promise I won't sue you."[37]

*The Boston Globe* reported that java junkies have been meeting every Friday night in Portland, Oregon since April 1994, the first twelve step coffee-addiction support group in the nation.[38] Perhaps we shall soon see Caffeine Anonymous groups springing up around the country.

### ALCOHOL

*Growing up in an alcoholic home, I was emotionally damaged as a kid, and alcohol solved all that. It made me feel good. I was happier and funnier. My shyness disappeared, and alcohol helped me to fit in.*[39]

Dennis Wholey, *The Courage to Change*

As a mother, I worry about my young teenager who will soon be faced with the same teasing by her peers to drink that I faced when I was young and continue to face as an adult. I worry that my daughter may not yet have enough self-confidence to resist those who tease about alcohol. I advise her to say, "I don't want any. Period." I tell her that she doesn't have to justify her choice to anyone. I suggest that if anybody continues to pressure her that she should be willing to repeat herself firmly a couple more times. I then remind her that she has the power to end the conversation by saying, "I'm not willing to discuss it any further." She should then leave if she has to. She must always remember to bring carfare or call home for a ride. Some young people have even called the police for a ride home to avoid riding with a driver who has been drinking.

Just as certain professions seem to be prone to eating disorders, certain professions seem to carry a higher risk of alcoholism. Medical people are one such high risk group. Men in uniform, whether they are letter carriers, police officers, or members of the armed forces, are another.

The teases of alcohol are many. "What harm could there be with just one drink?" is the standard line. Drinking to excess can seem to be normal behavior and not excessive to those people who only know others who drink. This is one of the reasons alcoholism is so easy to deny. "Everybody does it," or so it seems. Some people who lose their inhibitions when drinking are teased into thinking that alcohol must be a stimulant. In actuality, alcohol is such a depressant that it can cause impotency.

Denial is the biggest tease of all to an alcoholic. People who still manage to function and make money will be excused by their employers and their families for their drinking. Others, who are slipping, will blame their drinking and resulting problems on others rather than take responsibility for their actions. Alcoholics will get very angry at anyone who tries to discuss their drinking with them or who tries to encourage them to take responsibility for their drinking. Alcoholics will try to hide their drinking habit as well as their liquor. They'll start drinking before they show up at social events, so no one will be able to figure out how much they have consumed. Some people will succumb to the tease of buying their liquor by the case, saying they do so because it is cost effective, when they really just want a large quantity on hand.

Social events are an enormous tease to an alcoholic. Some recovering alcoholics are so threatened by the teases which present themselves at social gatherings, such as toasts and drinks on the house, that they refuse to attend family weddings, holidays, and other celebrations in order to avoid liquor. One twenty-six-year-old woman didn't want to accompany her mother to her cousin's baby shower because she was afraid alcohol would be served and that she wouldn't be able to resist the tease. "My mother stopped speaking to me when I said I couldn't go to the baby shower, but she just doesn't understand!"

There are both physiological and psychological reasons for alcoholism. Without trying to minimize the cultural patterns which influence drinking among certain ethnic groups, I truly believe that the susceptibility to alcoholism is primarily genetic. This belief was reinforced for me during my work with a twenty-one-year-old woman. Laura came into therapy complaining of having been raped once and molested twice during her first semester living away at college. It soon became clear that all her horrible sexual experiences occurred while she was drinking heavily. Laura told me that liquor was everywhere at her college and there was no way she could resist the tease of it up to that time. It appeared that if she could stop drinking, she would no longer get into trouble by putting herself into situations where everyone was drunk and anything goes. Since I knew Laura's parents and knew they didn't drink, I was surprised that this young woman displayed alcoholic behavior. When I told her about my surprise, given the lack of family history, Laura explained, "Well, you see, my father is really my uncle." Apparently, her mother divorced her biological father because of his alcoholism and married his sober brother who then raised Laura as his own daughter.

There are certain myths about alcohol that contribute to the tease factor. One is that drinking alcohol warms you up on a cold day. "What happens is that when the blood vessels on the skin's surface become enlarged, you lose warmth from the body and so become even colder. The more alcohol you drink, the more body heat is lost."[40] Then there is the myth that the most

# *Teasing*

mature and sophisticated people in the world are all experts on alcohol. That is one of the worst teases into alcoholism and the message that liquor advertisers attempt to achieve. A recent newspaper ad for a liquor boasted, "For some reason, you stop getting carded and start drinking us at just about the same time."

## DRUGS

Although there are too many different kinds of drugs to consider them all, a few of the tease factors of the more popular addictive drugs such as tranquilizers, heroin, and cocaine will be discussed.

### Tranquilizers

Tranquilizers are a tease because people can become dependent on them without realizing it. The reason most people don't think of tranquilizers as addicting is that people don't take Valium (diazepam) to get high. They take it to temporarily relieve anxiety, to calm down or to fall asleep. Since most people are able to obtain prescriptions for tranquilizers from their physicians without too much coaxing, there is the implication that tranquilizers could not have any ill effects. Besides, the pills are so small: how could they possibly do any harm? The reality is that tranquilizers are very physically addictive and can cause withdrawal symptoms.

Another tease of tranquilizers is they promise to act quickly. Anxiety will be lessened within an hour of taking them. As is typical with other addictive drugs, the positive benefits of the drug will only last a few hours and another pill will then be needed to continue to relieve the anxiety.

Tranquilizers tease an individual into postponing his or her emotional pain, ideally to a point in time when the person can better handle it. Unfortunately, many of us believe in the saying, "Don't ever do today what you can put off until tomorrow." As a result, once someone starts a course of tranquilizer treatment, he may not wish to stop or even be able to stop.

### Heroin

Heroin provides a number of teases. Initially, heroin feels terrific. It is the quick fix, and it does seem to solve one's problems. But the momentary problem solving is just a tease. Later, heroin users must continue to take their drug in increased dosages, no longer to feel terrific, but to feel just like the rest of us feel normally.

"Physical addiction means that, in time, the body actually cannot function without the once-alien chemical and comes to rely on it. The human body is almost infinitely adaptable and can learn to accommodate many poisonous and deadly substances. This is what happens with heroin: it affects both brain and body cells in a very intimate way, and alters the workings of every cell in the body. That is why people become dependent on it."[41] Severe withdrawal symptoms are experienced from heroin after six to twelve hours of the previous dose.

"But there is another danger . . . namely that when people start taking powerful drugs to alleviate any real or imagined pain, this can make them intolerant of any bodily or emotional discomfort at all. One reason why it is particularly hard to wean addicts off their fix is that, as soon as the slightest crisis looms, they will be tempted to return to their former panacea. . . . Users can find it hard to tolerate anything like bad news in the post, a crick in the neck, stiff joints, a late train, red traffic lights, or any minor inconvenience in life. The merest setback to plans or hopes can send them in search of the drug again. This is the most seductive and the most dangerous effect of heroin dependence."[42]

Even if the physical addiction is overcome, heroin may still remove the individual's ability to cope with everyday life. This inability to cope can drive the recovering addict back to his drug.

Another tease of heroin use is that it gives people a purpose and a way of belonging even if it strikes the rest of us as a bizarre way of accomplishing those goals. A person who feels lost and who feels he doesn't belong anywhere will soon find his life completely structured around the drug and his new addict friends. To avoid withdrawal, the lives of heroin addicts become so dominated by the need to buy more heroin that they are unable to think of anything else. Not only do the addicts become slaves to the drug physically and emotionally, but they become enslaved economically also. Because the drug has traditionally been so expensive (although cheaper versions are coming onto the market), it has consumed all the addict's time and energy to keep his supply up. Obtaining and using the substance can become a full-time job and the only job the addict is capable of holding on to. Eventually, most addicts are forced into criminal behavior to support themselves. Heroin users will eventually become addicted to their own roller coaster lifestyles.

## Cocaine

> *Did I love Patrick or cocaine? Or, did I love Patrick for giv-*
> *ing me the cocaine? Or, did I love the cocaine for giving me*
> *Patrick? I was never quite sure. I was sure that I wanted more*
> *of whatever it was.*[43]
>
> Gelsey Kirkland, *Dancing on My Grave*

A hit of coke is the cocaine addict's way of achieving perfection. The tease of cocaine is that it promises to make people feel powerful, optimistic, intelligent, and in control.

Cocaine is just a tease, because the high cannot last. A person can remain high on coke from ten minutes to an hour, depending on the dosage. After the high, the person may feel depressed and irritable. Other disadvantages include possible death by overdose due to heart failure, as well as strokes and brain seizures. Sniffing coke causes irritation of the membranes in the nose and throat and a resulting susceptibility to colds, flu, nosebleeds, and blocked sinuses.

Despite the horrible side effects, another tease of cocaine is that it has a glamorous reputation. Some very ambitious and successful people use cocaine. "The substance tends to be taken by people who want to feel good all the time and who have not realized that life does not admit of this feeling on a permanent basis. Cocaine takers are those who become impatient when life does not conform to their often unreal expectations."[44]

It is hard to resist the tease of peer pressure when it comes to taking drugs, especially cocaine, which promises to make the initial user feel good. One psychiatrist who focuses on cocaine addicts, David Musto, described the situation in this way: "The question we must be asking now is not why people take drugs, but why do people stop. In the inner city, the factors that counterbalance drug use . . . often are not there. It is harder for people with nothing to say no to drugs."[45]

# 12

# Money is a Tease

*Rarely did I have any money. . . . Kramer upbraided me*
*each time. . . . I was stealing from him, making him miserable!*
*Never in my life had I felt so distressed, never had I felt more*
*hopeless, more enslaved.[1]*

Herman Hesse, *Demian*

**M**oney is the classic tease. For many people, the more they
get, the more they want, the more they spend. They are
never satisfied. Money has universal appeal, not for its own sake,
but for the tease and the unspoken promise of what people think
money can buy. If you ask someone, "What is money?" you will
probably hear not what money is but rather what the person
thinks money would do for him. Inevitably the responses are:
"Freedom. Retirement. Security. Travel. Servants. Cars. Yachts.
Planes. Respect. Sex. Clothes. Jewelry. Club memberships."
Money is worshiped in our society because it is seen to have god-
like properties, bestowing the seemingly perfect life on those fortunate enough to possess it. This is how money and perfection
become linked. It is ironic that the very same people who say
money buys freedom are often those people who are workaholics

and enslaved to the pursuit of earning money. Greedy people, like the legendary King Midas, have totally succumbed to the tease of amassing money.

Now if you ask a thoughtful person, "What are the two most important things in life?" you might hear, "Health and love," or "Family and health," where family and love are meant to be the same. It is, of course, obvious that money cannot buy health or love. Yes, money can buy beautiful clothes and the skills of makeup artists, hairdressers, and manicurists in order to help an individual attract a potential partner, but money cannot control the emotions of another person. A person who loves money and has none might agree to marry you if you have money, but you will never be as sure of that love as you would be if you were without money. Yes, money can buy better nutrition and access to quality medical care, but money cannot take away AIDS, cancer, or so many other terrible diseases.

Despite the numerous things that money cannot buy, most people believe that money can buy happiness. When a wealthy person gets cancer, a divorce, has a mental breakdown, commits suicide, or his son dies, people tend to put aside the fact that he had a lot of money. I feel that people truly need to believe that money can buy happiness because it gives them the hope of one day gaining the magic ingredient which will enable them to control their own happiness, to control their very lives. The tease of money, then, is the unspoken promise that vast sums of money will make one better, happier, and more powerful.

The other side to this logic is that we can blame money, or the lack of it, for not being better, happier or more powerful. For instance, Carol, one of my patients, has a fantasy that it would be much easier for her to lose ten pounds if she were to spend three weeks at an exclusive spa which specializes in weight reduction than if she were to attempt to lose weight in her own home. The fact that she cannot afford the two thousand dollars per week it costs to attend such a spa, or the fact that she chooses not to spend her limited resources in this manner, means that in her thoughts the reason she is overweight is because she is not rich. Does this sound logical? Of course not.

Money and the pursuit of it is such a great tease that it becomes one of the greatest motivating factors in the world. This is especially true in the United States because we never had a monarchy or a strict class or caste system. People are continually teased and inspired by stories of self-made American men and women. Thus, they feel if someone else can make a fortune, why can't they? When a sex study indicated that Americans were not quite so sexually active as we had imagined, sex fantasy author Erica Jong deadpanned, "Totally predictable. Americans are more interested in money than sex."[2]

To accomplish the goal of obtaining vast sums of wealth, some people will try to get it in almost any way possible. People will pursue professions they are not suited for in an attempt to earn a high salary. People will invent the most ridiculous devices and manufacture the most seemingly useless articles thinking they may strike it rich. Thousands of people write novels, songs, and screenplays each year that will never be published hoping to become overnight millionaires.

The commodities market is also a terrific tease. The price of gold or silver keeps increasing, and we think we will hold onto our gold for just one more day before we sell it to see if it goes any higher. Then our plan may backfire as the price goes down.

For some people, blue collar and white collar, legitimate ways to earn money do not satisfy or accomplish the goal quickly enough. Those people may decide to pursue the tease of money with such a desperation that they will commit terrible crimes and risk lengthy jail sentences—even capital punishment—in its pursuit.

Money is also a terrible tease because it puts a price tag on things that perhaps should never have a price. Prostitution strikes many as abhorrent because it makes an exchange of intimacy and love, or the illusion of intimacy and love, for money. People will murder and kidnap for a price. Are these people born psychopaths or sociopaths or does the tease of money drive some people to outrageous ends or out of their minds?

A widow sometimes will feel offended when she opens an envelope containing a life insurance check because she feels her husband's life has been swapped for money. In a similar way, the determinations of medical malpractice lawsuits where a death is involved are difficult for many people to understand (such as earning income potential of the deceased) especially when nonsensical sounding lawsuits brought against film stars are frequently settled for much more money than the loss of life. We ask how much a Michelangelo or a Rubens painting is worth and the word that immediately comes to mind is "priceless." How much is the life of one's child worth? Again, the word "priceless" comes to mind. Unfortunately, what is priceless to one person has a price to someone else, and the courts would come up with a bottom line figure that might be greatly offensive to the person suffering such a loss in the settlement of a lawsuit.

In this discussion about the tease of money in our lives, it is interesting to stop for a moment and reflect back to a period of time in our history when there was no paper money or system of credit or electronic banking. Marc Shell's book, *Money, Language, and Thought* tells us that "America was the historical birthplace of the widespread use of paper money in the Western world, and a debate about coined and paper money dominated American political discourse from 1825 to 1875. The 'paper money men' (as the advocates of paper money were called) were set against the 'gold bugs' (as the advocates of gold, in opposition to paper money, were called). . . . Congress, it was said, could turn paper into gold by an 'act of Congress' that made it money."[3] Sounds like the tease of the alchemist who promised to turn tin into gold!

Part of the problem was that "paper money differs from coined money in an intellectually significant way. While a coin may be both symbol (as inscription or type) and commodity (as metallic ingot), paper is virtually all symbolic."[4] Karl Marx wrote: "Gold circulates because it has value, whereas paper has value because it circulates."[5]

Of course, credit cards are an extreme version of paper money, and to many people the credit card symbolizes the ultimate tease in life. We know this because so many people go bankrupt every year due to their unrestricted use of credit cards. Credit cards are especially threatening to young people who don't have the maturity to defer gratification. The absolute purpose and tease of the credit card is to assist the user in his denial that he is not actually spending money at the particular moment in time that he is using his credit card. We can all relate to that monthly shock we experience when we open our credit card bills and realize, "Oh, my God! I guess I really was spending money after all, wasn't I?"

There are many situations where the tease of money does a person no good. If you were stranded on a desert island, you would gladly exchange any money in your possession for water and food. In wartime, the homes of the rich are bombed just the same as the homes of the poor. Money, of course, is of no use to us when we are dead. Any special privileges we secure for those who follow us to remember us by are just that: a plaque on a hospital wall is very nice, but you can't see it when you are dead. Those who believe in an afterlife realize that they can't buy entry into heaven.

Despite all this, millions of people continue to buy lottery tickets and make trips to Las Vegas, Atlantic City, or, if they are wealthier, London or Monaco, and fantasize about winnings—a big tease.

# 13

## *Suspense is a Tease*

*Every night she comes to me. I wake and she is there,*
*smiling, whispering to me. Make him pay, Danny, only you*
*can. Make the truth come out. Don't let me down. But she*
*is teasing me. Let her down? Does she need to ask me?*

Susan Hill, *Mrs. De Winter*

Suspense can be delicious. Suspense is any "anxiety or appre-
hension resulting from an uncertain, undecided, or mysterious situation."[2] We love to feel the tease of suspense because
we feel so wonderfully relieved when the tension is resolved.
Suspense is to literature and film what foreplay is to sex. The
best suspense, like the best foreplay, makes us literally hold our
breath. Like foreplay, "if the writer reaches the climax too early,
readers will feel let down by the time they get to the final page."[3]
"The major ingredient is suspense, so tease and titillate, but
never give away the conclusion."[4]

Elements of teasing suspense are involved in every work
of fiction, not just in mysteries and suspense novels. Suspense is
what makes the reader turn the page to answer the question,
"What happens next?" If the reader already knows what

happens, then how it happens is the cause of the suspense. Suspense is what makes you willing to stay up late to finish a good novel or watch the end of the film on television. At that point, the tease of the ending compels you to stay with it, and you are no longer in control. In *How to Put Suspense in Your Story*, Heidi Vanderbilt writes, "Every story, whether suspense or not, asks the same question: Will the protagonist get what he or she needs? In mainstream fiction, the need may be to understand, to love, to grow. In suspense fiction, the need is to survive (though survival may be interpreted broadly)."[5]

Suspense thrillers, in film or literature, are far from being passive entertainment. The audience is just as involved in what is on the screen or page as the characters are. This way the viewer is put to work to solve the puzzle and guess the climax. The viewer is teased into a state of total arousal as the anxiety and anticipation build. Since the viewer is living vicariously through the characters' emotions and situations, the viewer wants to know how he, himself, is going to end up. The viewer or reader is taken beyond the realm of curiosity and becomes desperate for the situation to resolve itself.

Another attraction for the viewer of a work of criminal suspense is that he or she is allowed the tease of a false intimacy with a murderer, the kind of person one would never get to know in the course of the viewer's everyday life. For this murderer to be believable, he has to be real. This is what made Dean Koontz's *Mr. Murder* a best seller. The author writes, "Being present at a death is to share one of the most intimate experiences anyone will ever know in this world. After all, no one except treasured family members and beloved friends are welcome at a deathbed, to witness a dying person's final breath. Therefore, the killer is able to rise above his gray and miserable existence only in the act of execution, for then he has the honor of sharing that most profound of all experiences, more solemn and significant than birth."[6] What Koontz does is create an intelligent character who is vicious and yet possesses some understandable human qualities. Although the reader may learn to understand the murderer, he knows he doesn't have to forgive him.

The criminal mind can be fascinating to a law-abiding person because the criminal dares to do what others only fantasize and tease each other about. Patricia Highsmith writes: "Perhaps I have some severe and severely repressed criminal drive in myself, or I would not take such an interest in criminals or write about them so often."[7]

Although we are fascinated by the criminal mind, we do not approve of stories where the bad guy wins at the end. We want the criminal to be discovered, sent to jail, made to feel terrible and guilty, or even suffer greatly. We do not want to be teased into becoming criminals. We just want a few vicarious thrills and then we want to go to work in the morning.

Viewers enjoy the feeling of mastery after they have conquered the tease of fear in the protected setting of a film or a novel. As Marilyn Stasio writes in *Under the Spell of Scary Stuff,* "With the detective-hero as our ego stand-in, we enjoy both the vicarious thrill of looking our secret terrors in the eye and the intense pleasure of punching them in the nose."[8]

The force behind suspense is fear—there is something to fear. We are teased in a work of suspense to worry that something that has not yet happened is going to happen; and we don't want to see it happen. We don't want this something to happen because we have come to like and appreciate our hero, and we don't want our hero to get into trouble.

Fear can only be achieved if the viewer or reader is sympathetic to the hero and can empathize with him in his dangerous escapades, and if the villain is credible. For a threat to be real, the anti-hero must be at least equal in strength to the hero. What the successful suspense work does is to create an appearance of verisimilitude, of truth. The more fantastic the story, the more supernatural the characters, the more convincing must be the personalities, the settings, and the background.

Charlotte Armstrong writes that it is not enough to tie

someone to the railroad tracks to cause suspense, but that it has to be someone we like, and we have to at least hear the approaching train. "Suspense is fear lest something bad happens to us or to someone whose side we are on. . . . The ordeal is converted to suspense with the addition of a time limit."[9] Then there must be hope that our hero can save the person tied to the tracks.

This is precisely why suspense is a tease. We think the victim on the tracks will be saved but we can never be sure, at least until the television commercial has ended and our program reappears. One moment we think yes, the next moment we think no, and then finally and hopefully there is a yes at the end.

Alfred Hitchcock was the ultimate tease. After deliciously torturing us with suspense, he often did not supply an ending to his dramas but forced his viewers to imagine their own endings. This was an added tease and nowhere near as satisfying as being told for sure what actually happened at the end of the story. What is almost as bad as an Alfred Hitchcock's teasing ending is watching a two-part suspense drama on television that says, "Tune in tomorrow evening for Part Two of this drama."

The pace of a suspense story is rapid and energetic. Often, the suspense story contains several subplots. These subplots which also tease the viewer add to the suspense.

What makes for good suspense, real suspense? According to Cecilia Bartholomew, "A good story always has a man in the closet. In the entertainment story, it is enough to see the intruder hide in the closet and to wait with mounting suspense for the moment when he jumps out. In stories of more lasting value, the writer must make it clear why the man is in the closet, and the better the reason, the better the story."[10] The author must therefore know his characters intimately and know what they would or would not do in any given situation. The function of this technique is twofold; it makes the characters believable and causes the viewer or reader to care about them so much that he or she sits on the edge of his seat.

Going to a suspense movie today is hard work. Popcorn

# Suspense is a Tease

gives you the energy you need to get through a thriller, and the repetitive activity of eating it helps to bind your anxiety. You may bite your fingernails or munch on your cuticles. You have to cover your eyes or bury your face in your partner's shoulder. You must restrain your impulse to run out of the theater. You know you are risking nightmares, but it is worth it.

Perhaps our attraction to suspense stories which involve life-and-death struggles is due to our fascination with our own ultimate suspense story. Usually, the personal "suspense story" involves the moment and the way each of us will die. It used to be that a baby's birth was suspenseful, not so much because of the exact moment of birth, but because the sex of the baby was suspenseful. Scientific tests can now end this question and predict the sex of a child. However, scientists continue to work to prolong the suspense about our own deaths. Maybe some day the geneticists will be able to predict the years of our deaths. Maybe some day the cryogenicists will be able to predict our moments of rebirth. For now, we shall all have to be content with the tease of this ultimate thriller.

# 14

## Coping With Adult Teasing

*Grown people were always on the edge of telling you*
*something valuable and then withdrawing from it, a form*
*of bully-teasing.*[1]

Lillian Hellman, *Pentimento*

Although being teased can sometimes be fun, especially when the teasing is part of a good adult relationship, there are times when it is not fun, when, in fact, teasing is painful for the recipient. Here are some suggestions for stopping teasers in the act—when you want to.

First, try to figure out what the teaser is trying to do before you buy into the tease. Try not to react or overreact until you understand the teaser's motivation. Is the teaser just trying to get your attention, or is there a more ambiguous message? Check out the teaser's body language and facial expression. If the teaser is being playful, there may be a clue in the teaser's face or voice or in his remarks that tells you the teasing is harmless. If you cannot figure out the teaser's message and the tease is not upsetting, give the teaser the benefit of the doubt and assume he is being playful.

The most important thing to remember when reading this chapter is that no person can control the behavior of another. Therefore, in trying to stop or prevent unwanted teasing, all that a person can do is change his or her reaction to that behavior and hope that these changes will affect the behavior of the perpetrator. By changing reactions, you will also change the consequences for the perpetrator.

Do your best to joke or invent a teasing comeback of your own or laugh at the tease—even if it requires effort. If you don't make light of the tease, an unfriendly teaser will feel that he accomplished his mission of getting under your skin.

If there is an audience surrounding the teaser, watch and see how its members are reacting. Is the teaser teasing you only because he is playing to his audience? Your response will influence the audience, no matter whose side they are on. You can defuse the tease by choosing to treat even an obviously negative remark as a joke. If you can genuinely laugh at your own vulnerabilities, so much the better.

Know your own emotional vulnerabilities. What kind of comments are guaranteed to irritate you—comments about your hair, punctuality, accent? Try to understand why you are so vulnerable on these points. Maybe, if you think about them enough, you will desensitize yourself to them and be able to laugh at yourself. There isn't a person who doesn't have some emotional vulnerabilities. Some people just hide them better than others.

If you are being teased at the workplace, try to separate those remarks which are personal from those which say something about your professional capacities. Try not to get upset about general teasing remarks. If your professional capabilities are being teased into question, you may wish to speak up and be assertive to nip the behavior in the bud.

Review your history of teasing, taunting and bullying. When were you the victim? When were you the bully? What kind of teasing was practiced in your family—friendly or sadistic teasing? Try not to let the past cloud your judgment about your present teasing situation. Please read the next two chapters on childhood teasing in order to remind you of your childhood experiences and how they may affect your view of the present. There are also numerous strategies for helping children deal with unwanted teasing that are perfectly applicable for helping adults also.

Remember to try and take each new tease one tease at a time.

In order to keep teasing playful, one must follow the rules. A good idea would be to post these rules at the workplace, your clubhouse or anywhere else you wish to modify the teasing environment. Hopefully, the teasers will read these Rules of Teasing and consider them in advance of dishing it out.

## THE RULES OF TEASING

1.    Teasing plays off the truth. It is not the truth. If teasing is truth, it's not teasing. It's insulting.

2.    Save your teasing for people you know well so there is some way to predict their response. Avoid teasing strangers and casual acquaintances. Also avoid teasing people from other cultures who may not understand your own teasing culture.

3.    Try not to poke fun at any serious problems that the person may have.

4.    Don't tease about things that a person cannot or would not want to change. Don't tease someone about their name or their height. Those are very old jokes.

5. Never tease people about their weight or any speech impediments they may have. This is cruel.

6. The safest thing to tease about is behavior. You can poke fun at a person's hobbies or traits.

7. Remember that the teasee sets the rules. If he or she doesn't like the teasing, stop. Good intentions mean nothing in the world of teasing.

8. Unwanted sexual remarks are not teasing. These remarks are sexual harassment and illegal.

9. People who are obsessive about being in control usually don't like to be teased.

10. Never tease anyone at work about his professional capacities. This is very demeaning and threatening to the livelihood of the individual.

11. Try to think about your objective, what you are trying to do with your teasing. Perhaps what you need is a serious discussion with the teasee.

12. If teasing is the only way you know to express yourself, try to develop a new style. To figure out a new style of relating to others, do a lot of listening to others while trying to understand them and their needs.

13. If you must tease, give nonverbal hints that your verbal sting is meant in a playful fashion. A wink, a smile, or a shoulder poke can soften the blow. Notice how Jay Leno laughs and shakes his shoulders right after making fun of someone.

14. Remember, it's fun to kick someone off his high horse, but not if the person is going to break his neck.

15. If you dish it out, people will expect you to take it when your turn comes.

16. If you can't take it, don't dish it out.

# 15

# Solutions for Parents and Teachers

*To a child that is picked on, having a good friend, being accepted for what you are or just simply being left alone, would be like a dream.[1]*

Summerhill Presentations,
*The Broken Toy*

Children's teasing is different from adult teasing. Children's teasing is often playful, but it is rarely ambiguous. When children's teasing is meant to be mean, it is indeed very cruel. For this reason, there is a fine line, when discussing children's "teasing," between putdowns, teasing, taunting, ridiculing, tormenting, provoking, harassing and victimization. For the purpose of this chapter, the word "teasing" will mean "unwanted teasing."

"When children handle teasing effectively, they learn important lessons: self-confidence, empathy, resiliency, the power of the individual to defuse teasing, the power of the group to combat offensive or hurtful behavior. Dealing with teasing effectively can in fact nurture children's beliefs in the power of legitimate authority to protect the individual—and ultimately in their own ability to make a difference."[2]

# Solutions for Parents and Teachers

The old saying, "Sticks and stones may break my bones, but names will never hurt me" is obviously untrue. At its best, teasing allows children to release their aggressions and to abuse each other without bodily harm. At its worst, teasing can cause more harm to the victim's developing self-esteem than violence. Without healthy self-esteem, a child cannot grow up to be self-confident and strong. Teasing causes children to feel mad, embarrassed, out of control, and scared. We have learned that "No matter how well the subject is taught, no matter how good the teacher is, children cannot learn if they are afraid to go to school."[3] "Studies suggest such anguish and isolation can affect students long after they leave school."[4]

Teasing also harms the perpetrator by giving "the teaser a sense that abusing or exploiting others is the way to feel powerful, good about oneself . . . while reinforcing an attitude in the teaser that in its extreme can lead to serious bullying—even criminal—behavior. In an atmosphere in which teasing is unrestrained and can cross the line to become harassment, both victim and perpetrator may ultimately grow cynical about the power of legitimate authority to protect the individual."[5] "Bullies whose behavior is allowed to continue are five times more likely than their classmates to wind up in juvenile court, to be convicted of crimes, and, when they become adults, to have children with aggression problems."[6]

Teasing also harms its witnesses. "Even students and adults who are witnesses are affected. They must deal with the lowered self-esteem and loss of control that accompanies feeling unsafe and unable to take action. The result is children and adults who do all they can to avoid recognizing when someone else is being hurt."[7]

Every child, parent and teacher has witnessed teasing, bullying or rejection. Often, one has either done it, or had it done to them. The adults have experienced teasing from both ends, as adults and as children themselves. Yet parents and teachers rarely recognize childhood teasing for the dangerous game that it is, and when they do, it may be too late. Children may also not understand that they don't have to allow other kids to mistreat them.

This chapter is divided into two sections: 1) Help for Parents, and 2) Help for Teachers. Since there is much overlap between the sections, I suggest the chapter be read in its entirety. The ability to stop unwanted teasing is not a science, but rather an art, and therefore acquiring it will require a period of trial and error. What works between two children or two adults may not work between another pair of children or adults. To combat taunting and victimization in the schools requires a partnership of parents, teachers and school administrators.

## HELP FOR PARENTS

There is nothing more painful than watching your child suffer. There is also no pain like emotional pain. Children who are taunted and bullied suffer such intense distress that they may feel suicidal or violent as a result. I have treated several teenaged clients who wanted to end their lives after being unmercifully teased. The problem is that not all children will share their experiences of being taunted or bullied with their parents. They may be too ashamed or embarrassed about their fears or their rejections.

### Symptoms of Teasing

The most significant distress indicator that something is wrong is a sudden drop in school performance or school achievement. Taunting and bullying will distract a child's attention away from learning. A child may develop school phobia, a disabling fear of school, which causes him to no longer want to attend.

A child may pretend to be physically ill to avoid going to school, or may become actually ill with headaches, stomachaches and fatigue and may have trouble eating or sleeping or have frequent nightmares.

# Solutions for Parents and Teachers

A child may come home in different clothes than he had on in the morning because someone stole his clothes or because he got into a fight and dirtied or tore his clothes. A child may come home with unexplained bruises from fighting.

A child may come home hungry after school because someone stole his lunch or his lunch money. A child may say he's lost his lunch money or school supplies when these items may have been stolen from him.

A child may not want to go outside to play at recess or in the neighborhood after school because he fears being bullied.

A child may say he hates school when what he actually hates is his bullying experience on the school bus.

A child may have lowered self-esteem and a generally fearful attitude that he may not be able to explain.

Parents must not dismiss these distress signals, but pay close attention to them. When it comes to teasing, parents who help their children to work out today's problems will avoid worse problems tomorrow.

## What Parents Can Do

In order to help your children who are being teased, please consider the following suggestions:

1.  Be a model of appropriate social behavior toward your child and others: teasing and putdowns are often learned at home. Praise a child frequently for appropriate behavior and for getting along well with other children.

If your child does something wrong, try to separate the child from his behavior and avoid name-calling. Say instead: "That was not a nice thing to do, Tommy. How else could you have done that?" rather than, "You are a real brat!" or "What a baby you are!" Negative criticism of children reinforces the behavior. If you tell a child he is a "real brat" often enough, the child will actually begin to believe you and act in a bratty manner accordingly. Also, if you call your own child bad names, why shouldn't he call other children bad names?

If your child does something terrific, give positive praise. Say: "That was very nice of you to do. Thank you," instead of "You're such a good girl!" because the role of always being the "good girl" or the "good boy" puts pressure on a child.

If your child hears you gossip frequently and criticize mercilessly at the dinner table, for the smallest transgressions, your child will do the same. Children learn intolerance at home. Racial epithets and criticisms of the cultural heritage of others will definitely be repeated outside the home. Children need to learn to embrace diversity.

2.    If you find that you are overly critical of your child, do not hesitate to say, "I'm sorry" right away and tell him you still love him, that you didn't mean what you said, but that you were momentarily angry. Children need to know that grownups make mistakes and that they can acknowledge and take responsibility for their words as well as their actions. This will enable your child to do the same.

3.    If a child asks you a question and you do not know the answer, be honest and say you don't know. Advise him that if the question is so important to him, you will try to find out the answer. Children should know that grownups don't have all the answers. They need to learn not to be "know-it-alls," but to develop open minds.

4.    Try to model good sportsmanship with your friends and teach it to your child. A couple of years ago, a home run was disallowed in a Little League baseball game because the child who

hit it did not step on home plate when he came around the bases. There was a huge fuss over this. This is not exactly good sportsmanship. The child who hit the home run will carry the pain and embarrassment of that incident with him for the rest of his life.

5.      Make sure you give your children of both sexes permission to be equally assertive about their needs. Some female children have a tendency not to be as assertive as male children. Children need to be assertive if they are going to withstand the pressures of being tormented and bullied. "Here's a scenario I encounter all the time: A little boy is bothering a little girl. When she retaliates, for example, by messing up his drawing, the teacher pulls the girl aside and says she needs to understand the boy's problems. The message the girl gets is that the boy's problems are more important than her feelings. And so, many girls learn to avoid conflict—even with other girls."[8]

If you have a tendency to be controlling with your children, teach them about control and also teach them to stick up for themselves with you!

6.      Try to remember how you felt as a child when you were taunted, tormented, or rejected by other children. This will help you to understand the pain of your children. On the other hand, try not to overreact to the slightest offense against your child because of your past sufferings. Attempt to separate your past from your child's present as much as you possibly can.

7.      Educate yourself as much as possible about childhood conflicts. There are some good books on these subjects to read, such as *Siblings Without Rivalry* by Adele Faber and Elaine Mazlish, published by Avon Books in 1987, and *Raising a Thinking Child* by Myrna B. Shure, published by Henry Holt & Co. in 1994.

8.      Work with your Parent Teachers Association and your

school councils to request that your school adopt clear guidelines about verbal taunting and physical bullying on school grounds at recess, on the busses, in after-school clubs, and in the classroom.

Insist that appropriate punishments be handed out to offenders. Robert Evans of The Human Relations Service of Wellesley, Massachusetts, advises: "Adults in the community must work hard to agree on some basics that they would all get behind and support at school and at home, so schools wouldn't be alone in the task of trying to shape responsible, social behavior."

9.    Ask your Parent Teachers Association to suggest that the schools fund social skills training programs for students and teachers. If the school cannot afford such programs, help the PTA to raise individual donations or grant monies for them.

### For Parents Whose Child May Be a Victim of Teasing

If your child shares with you that he or she is being teased at school, please consider the following suggestions:

1.    Really listen to your child. Acknowledge and validate his feelings of anger, fear, embarrassment and being out of control. Tell him that you would also be scared if this were happening to you now.

Let him talk to you at his own pace. Don't force the conversation. If your child gets upset while talking about being teased, don't pressure him. Let him know you will be there for him when he's ready to share.

2.    Be supportive. Let your child know that you will stick by him and help him through this hard time. Try not to criticize the way your child has handled the situation up to now. Your child may not be able to take any more criticism at this sensitive time. You don't want him to think that you, too, are rejecting him, or that he'll never be able to measure up to your expectations. You

may wish to share a story from your childhood when you were bullied and how the situation was successfully resolved, but do not tell such a story if it will make your child's fear worse. The point here is to help your child realize that he is not alone, that others have had this experience and that you understand.

3.    Try to adopt a positive attitude to lessen your child's fears. Let your child know that you are confident that he will be able to work the problem out successfully.

4.    Do not be fooled if the child acts really brave on the outside. He may be struggling inside. Confidence in dealing with bullies comes only from experience.

5.    Try to get as accurate information as possible from the child as to what happened. Document the who, what, where, when and why in case the harassment of your child continues. You need to be careful about this. One child took a special notebook to school to write down the taunting remarks, at the request of his parent. He then flaunted the notebook in front of the other children as they were taunting him. This incensed the other children and made things worse for the child.

6.    Try to determine the problem. Is the child worried about the bully himself and what the bully will do to him, or is the child upset about what the bully said? Your child may just need some reassurance that what the bully said was untrue. If a very young child is upset about the content of the remarks, make sure to ask your child if he knows exactly what the remarks mean. Your child may think he was insulted when he was not. For instance, if one child calls another child a "slowpoke," an extremely sensitive child may get upset and hurt by this. If you reassure your child that the other child calls everybody a slowpoke and it is not a big deal, then your child may not take that sort of remark so personally in the future.

Similarly, one first grader called another first grader "gay." It was determined, as you might suspect, that the child doing the name-calling had not the slightest idea as to the meaning of the word "gay" to signify a homosexual, but was imitating statements he had heard elsewhere.

Try to decide how serious the threat of the behavior is toward your child. "There's a difference between your child being teased about lunch and someone stealing your child's lunch money."[9] Don't treat any threat to a young child less than seriously.

7.    If your child was truly insulted by a deliberately mean remark, try to demonstrate the technique of positive reinforcement. Teach your child to "self-talk," to say to himself, "I'm a good person. What this other child is saying just isn't true. The other child is the one with the problem. Not me."

8.    Try to determine how vulnerable your child may be to certain types of teasing. "Or if an older child is teased because he can't throw a baseball, he could practice with you until he improves. . . . With some questioning you may find that a child who's dubbed Big Mouth may be alienating her peers with constant interruptions. In that case, you might explain to her why interrupting is irritating and suggest that she try counting to twenty-five each time she feels the impulse to cut someone off."[10]

9.    Allow your child to do as much of the thinking about the problem and the possible solutions to it as possible. Your child is feeling he has lost control due to the taunting. Help him by giving him some control now. Educate him about his options and ask him which options he prefers and why. It helps self-confidence for the child to come up with the solution rather than the adult. School psychologists often have children come to their office who say things like, "My mother said to do this, but it doesn't work," or, "My mother said to do this, but I don't really want to."

You want to avoid this type of behavior as much as possible.

10.     Many parents will simply tell a child to ignore the taunter. Since this does not always work, the child may get frustrated. Teach your child that ignoring might work and then it might not. You should be aware that some professionals are against ignoring the bully. "Not responding will often cause the teaser to raise the ante by calling out a more pointed jab. Few children can ignore this type of continued verbal abuse. When the victim finally reacts, he has lost the battle and is an easier target the next time."[11]

11.     Advise your child to avoid the perpetrators of the teasing as much as possible. Suggest your child tell the taunter, "I don't want to play with you right now." Billy may gravitate toward Joey because he's the person in power, even though Joey has taunted Billy in the past. Children don't have the same level of experience as adults. They may not assume that just because a child taunts them one day, that the child will continue to do it later that day or the next day.

Suggest that the teacher change your child's seat, either in the classroom or on the school bus. In some cases, you might even suggest a child take an alternate route home from school to avoid trouble. This is not the same as giving in. This is an attempt at defusing a volatile situation.

Discuss with your child the option of walking away from a future confrontation. Walking away is not the same as ignoring the behavior. The child may wish to say, "I don't want to get in a fight with you because I don't want to get into trouble." If your child is much smaller than the bully, reassure him that he is not being a sissy by walking or running away, but that it may be the smartest and safest thing to do.

12.     Discuss the option of talking the matter over with the guidance counselor at school for some suggestions on how to handle the problem.

13.    Gayle Macklem, President of the Massachusetts School Psychologists Association, suggests, "Consider a neighborhood strategy to deal with a bully for a younger child. For instance, if your child is bullied while he waits for the school bus, ask an older child in the neighborhood to stand next to your child to give him backup and emotional support."

14.    Emphasize the power of laughter. Can your child laugh at himself? This will also rob the bully of the pleasure of making someone feel bad. Perhaps, if the child has a sense of humor, he can try a comeback line of his own, provided this will not lead to escalation of the taunter's aggression. The child might also apply nonverbal strategies which are discussed in the next chapter.

15.    Teach your child to acquire an air of authority. If your child says to the bully, "I don't like that. Why did you do that?" in a firm, assertive voice, the bully will not have succeeded in his mission.

Tell your child to warn the perpetrator that if he keeps up his bad behavior, your child will tell the teacher and then the perpetrator will get into trouble. Usually such a warning will suffice or at least allow the child to tell on the perpetrator later without feeling guilty that he is squealing. After all, the perpetrator was warned!

16.    Explain to your child why it is so important to tell the school about behaviors which are dangerous and destructive so your child will not be afraid to "squeal" or "rat" on the perpetrator.

If dangerous and destructive behaviors occur, notify your child's school immediately. If the behavior occurred outside of school or on the weekend, notify the local authorities. Instruct your child to report any future threatening incidents to the nearest adult at school.

17.    Help your child understand the motivations of the bully. The bully wants to humiliate someone, make them feel bad. The bully thinks that if he acts tough, he will gain power and control. "To understand why another child is turning to bullying can sometimes help your child cope. He or she can then see the bully as less omnipotent and threatening—just another youngster with problems."[12] Hopefully, when your child sees the bully as less threatening, he will be able to be more assertive in challenging him.

18.    Remind your young child that other young children are fickle and quickly change their minds. Whoever is the bully on Monday morning may be the victim on Tuesday. The child who supports the bully on Monday may join forces with you against the bully on Tuesday.

19.    Encourage your child to make friends at school. Bullies usually direct their barbs at loners. Ask your child if he would like you to phone a friend's parent to invite a new child over to play at your home, or offer to take your child and a new friend some place special. Some kids need help in learning how to make friends, sharing toys as well as feelings, and taking turns.

Lois Lang, a counselor at the Maimonides School suggests, "It is important to remember that if a child has a good relationship with his peers and if he knows how to play and conducts himself well, he will be forgiven for a lot of inappropriate stuff for which other kids will be teased. The point is, if you can help your child to learn the social skills necessary to make friends, the teasing your child experiences will lessen."

20.    If your child continues to be a victim of bullying or if he is a victim in other settings as well as at school, perhaps some individual therapy or group counseling sessions would be helpful in changing your child's behavior. Your child needs to be helped to feel competent in certain areas, and his new feelings of competency will boost his self-esteem.

# Teasing

### What Parents Should Not Do

Parents should never assume that tormenting and bullying is a natural rite of passage. It isn't. That's like saying sexual harassment is a natural occurrence at the workplace. While bullying and sexual harassment may be common, they are not "natural" or necessary.

Parents should not unwittingly set their child up for being teased. For example, at birth, avoid giving the child a name or nickname for the other children to poke fun at.

Parents should not criticize their child or call him a bad name in front of his friends in case the criticism should become ammunition in the hands of the child's peers. It's always better to talk to your child privately to correct behavior.

Parents should respect their child's own taste in clothes. There are very few things in life that a young person can control, and how he presents himself to the world is one of those. If clothes don't match, you might suggest options without enforcing your own style on your children.

Parents should never assume that childhood taunting is no big deal and their child ought to handle this problem by himself. Help the child to come up with a plan to combat the taunting.

Parents should never assume that physical threats by bullies are empty threats. Physical threats should always be reported to school authorities or law enforcement officials.

Parents should never encourage their child to fight, even though this may be a tempting choice. Physical violence can escalate to very dangerous levels. Fistfights can lead to knife fights, which can lead to gunfights. School administrators will suspend both children who are fighting without asking who started it.

# Solutions for Parents and Teachers

(Some experts disagree with this. Grace Hechinger writes, "Your own attitudes about fighting will govern what you tell your children. We told our boys that they probably should not fight for something or about something unless it was really important to them. If it means a lot, fight for it: but don't fight for minor reasons. In the last analysis, whether or not a child fights is up to what he or she considers to be at stake. Children usually have a good idea of what they can do in a given situation without acting like a daredevil or a coward."[13] (Of course, a parent must never give weapons to their children under any circumstances.)

Parents should never confront the child who is bullying their child, but should solicit help from school officials. If you confront the bully, you send a message to your child and to the bully that your child is helpless. Lois Lang advises parents: "Never get too angry and critical at the child doing the taunting because the child's enemy on one day often becomes his friend the next day. If you get too angry at the offender, it makes it that much harder for the kids to be friends the next day."

Nor should parents try to confront the parents of the bully. Parents who do will often find themselves bullied by those parents. Once again, try to get the support of the school or a third party to resolve the issue.

Parents should not expect perfect behavior from their children or their friends, especially young children. A mother of a kindergarten child went to see a psychologist to discuss that her daughter was not being respected by the boys at school. "I taught her to say 'no' firmly when her personal space was being invaded, but it doesn't work. What should we do? The boys don't listen. What's going to happen when she's sixteen and in the back seat of a car?" This woman could not understand how hard it is for a five-year-old to grasp certain ideas. Small children have less ability to reflect and control their behavior. This mother was "catastrophizing"—projecting current behavior forward—the idea that if it is this bad now, it can only deteriorate later. Remember that children are children developmentally, biologically and psychologically. The balancing act is, don't expect too much too fast, but don't expect too little too late either.

### For Parents Whose Child May Be Bullying Other Children

If your child is the bully, do not be his enabler. An enabler is a person who helps someone else continue his inappropriate behavior. A couple of years ago, in a nearby town, there were two kids who published a list of scurrilous attacks on other kids. They made copies of the list and passed it around to all the kids at school. When the school found out who did it, the two teenagers were suspended. When the parents of the suspended teens found out, they went to court and said their children's rights had been violated because they were suspended. The school was forced to go to court and defend its position.

Do not enable your children to act inappropriately, but teach them to bear responsibility for their actions and accept the consequences of inappropriate behavior. If you enable your child, your child will think he can keep up his inappropriate behavior because you will always be there to bale him out as well as bail him out later!

Don't enable your children to be bullies by teaching them to feel superior to others. Clearly, we are raising some children who lack empathy and compassion for their victims. These children actually feel justified in what they are doing. We must figure out how to balance giving children a healthy dose of self-confidence without causing them to feel falsely superior to others.

We must never teach our children that we are superior to others because of the color of our skin or our faith or our sex. Instead, we should teach children reasons to be proud of who they are and to feel fortunate if they possess genes for beauty, strength, speed and intelligence, but never to feel superior. Just as luck gives us these genes (after all, we didn't choose our parents), luck can take these attributes away. In a matter of moments, a serious car accident can take away someone's beauty, and a head injury can take away someone's intelligence. Teach a child with money to be grateful for being so fortunate. Also, teach the child to never feel superior for having money. Teach him or her generosity toward those less fortunate without calling attention to his own status. Explain that just as a poor family can suddenly win the lottery and become rich, wealth can also be lost. A highly paid parent can lose his or her position, the stock market can fall, and real estate can become worthless.

If your child is modeling your own bullying behavior, you need to put an end to your own bullying. Family therapy may be needed to change long existing patterns.

Parents should not use physical discipline to punish children of any age. Physical discipline will backfire and could cause the bully to use more physical force and humiliation on his own targets. Instead, parents should discipline their children by removing privileges such as the television and the telephone and by adding extra household chores.

Parents should avoid leaving their children unsupervised if they have a problem bullying others. Parents should try to be encouraging and optimistic and use positive reinforcement toward their child despite their anger at him. If not, the child will sense their hopelessness and their fear that nothing will ever change. Once that happens, nothing ever will.

HELP FOR TEACHERS

Ellen Cunniff, Principal of the Hunnewell Elementary School in Wellesley, Massachusetts analyzes teasing in school this way: "Every child should have the right to have a good day. Teasing is the most common violation of that right. It is a very serious problem and it is perplexing to adults. We'd like to have a better handle on it, but we have to spend most of our time making sure kids don't fail to learn."

Teachers witness more childhood taunting and bullying behaviors than any other group of adults. Because it occurs so frequently in the schools, some teachers may have the dangerous attitude that these behaviors are "normal." These teachers should remember that bra-snapping used to be considered "normal," too, but that it is no longer tolerated. If you begin to see taunting and bullying behaviors in the same light, you will quickly realize that, while the behaviors may be common, they can have serious negative and hurtful consequences. Such behaviors are truly unnecessary.

Just how pervasive is the problem? "Approximately 15 percent to 20 percent of all United States students experience some form of bullying, national surveys show. And the problem is getting worse, school experts report."[14] A survey of 204 middle and high school students in several apparently safe midwestern communities showed that 75 percent (most of them middle-schoolers) of those surveyed had been bullied, and 90 percent of those bullied said they suffered side effects. "More disturbing," say the authors of the survey, "the students by and large indicted adults for failing to recognize the severity of the problem."[15]

Sometimes teachers and school staff members don't do anything about teasing because they don't know it is going on. Teachers must boost their awareness of what is occurring in their classrooms and in the cafeteria, the playground, and the hallways as much as possible. If you are a teacher, try to keep your eyes open. Remember that the worst taunting goes on outside the classroom and on the busses. Teacher aides and school bus drivers should be trained not only to be on the watch for bullying, but in how to deal with it.

# Solutions for Parents and Teachers

If you are a member of a school staff, you must learn to handle situations and complaints of taunting, tormenting, and bullying very sensitively in order to keep the channels of communication open between you and your students. If you do not, you may cut off communication and may unknowingly send a troubled student away whom you might have helped.

By the time a complaint of taunting reaches you, usually it is not the first time the taunting has occurred. Most children hate to squeal on taunters, and they view telling a teacher as a last resort. Nancy Papagno, a school psychologist, has noticed about so-called squealing: "A third grader can tell a teacher. A fifth grader is leery of telling a teacher. A sixth grader will never tell a teacher. Telling a teacher is a risk because the teacher may tell the child, 'Just ignore it!' or 'You're a big boy!' or the teacher might bring the offending child over and then it becomes an even bigger deal. Teachers need to be sensitive about how they work on teasing complaints."

If, after an initial complaint of taunting, the teacher doesn't hear any more about it, do not assume the behavior has stopped. The child is probably not coming back with more complaints because he thinks no one is going to do anything. It is important for adults to remember that the behavior will persist if they don't get involved. The victim may think the person to whom he reported the bullying either condones the behavior or doesn't care about him. The worst case scenario is that a teenager may think that a high school teacher is also intimidated and afraid of the offending students. The victim may feel he is forced to accept the bullying behavior and may act out his built up resentment either days or years later.

Sometimes children will get tired of telling adults about bullying if the adults don't do anything about it or if the adult tells a kid to ignore it. What teachers need to figure out is, which behaviors need to be addressed and which behaviors can you overlook? Certainly, you were hired as a teacher first and as a taunting consultant second, and you can't spend every moment getting involved in childhood conflicts. But you may be able to set aside a few moments a day with the children or a longer time once or twice a week to deal with these issues.

Anthony La Verde, a school psychologist in the Newton, Massachusetts public schools, advises: "Teachers have all heard of ignoring as a good intervention. I tell them not to ignore behavior that they're worried about becoming contagious, or they can expect an epidemic of bad behavior if one kid gets away with it. I tell them not to be afraid to confront a behavior. Teachers may not do anything much because they've been involved before and they know what it's like. Parents of the victims get adversarial. It isn't easy to prove the behavior. The perpetrator will deny it. Teachers are also cautious and concerned about litigation and their own personal liability." One of the real issues of our society recently has been the number of lawsuits brought against professionals who, in earlier times, were seen as more or less immune to litigation. Teachers are no exception.

In order to prevent taunting and bullying, teachers must be aware that they sometimes set up the children as well as themselves for being teased. Children will make comments and wisecracks and will often mimic their teachers. This is often an attention getting and ego preserving behavior. This is also a way to save face when a teacher has reprimanded a student. Teachers must talk to students with respect if they want the respect returned. When my oldest daughter was in third grade in a different school system than we are in now, she came home from school upset because the teacher called a little boy in her class a baby. She said all the children called him "Baby" outside at recess and for the rest of the day. If she knew at the age of eight how unjust this was, what was going on in the mind of the teacher? My daughter said she hoped the teacher never did it to her!

Sunburst Communications suggests that when teachers hold discussions about behavior, they "guard against inappropriate self-disclosure in class. . . . One rule of thumb is to keep the depth of self-disclosure roughly the same across the group, so that no one student gets in over his or her head."[16]

Teach your students about the how and why of teasing, taunting and bullying. Children need to understand the motivations of the taunters and how they pick their victims. They also need to know how teasing hurts the victims. A sixth grade teacher conducted a very successful class discussion on the motivations of kids who taunt and bully others. One of the points raised by a student was that students who taunt and bully others are often insecure people who take their frustrations out on others. The teacher reported to her colleagues that, after this discussion, incidents of taunting and bullying were greatly reduced because nobody wanted to be labeled "insecure" as mentioned in the class discussion. In other words, the bullies did not want to be taunted by being told about their insecurities.

One of the most significant issues is that students should feel free to answer and ask questions without having to feel fear or embarrassment if they should give the wrong answer, or ask a common knowledge question. Why would anybody want to raise his hand if he is going to be laughed at for a wrong answer or not knowing what everyone else knows?

One of the ways you as a teacher can create a safe, open, and healthful climate in the classroom is to model it yourself by trying to have an encouraging attitude with students, and by showing respect for their thoughts, feelings and opinions. To do this, you must also have or develop what seems like infinite patience. Patience is just as difficult for experienced teachers to maintain as it is for parents and others who deal with children on a regular basis. The rewards for being patient will generally make the effort worthwhile. If you are losing or have lost your patience, please seek advice from your administrative staff or a psychotherapist.

Another way to create a safe environment for class discussions is to utilize topics which have no one right answer. Open-ended questions which begin with "What if . . ." or questions that involve critical thinking will give permission for students to think and be appreciated.

If, despite your best efforts, your classroom is interrupted by a child who yells out in the middle of class, "This sucks!" in response to a homework assignment the child does not like, you have three choices:

1.     Take the issue to the group. Gayle Macklem recommends, "The teacher should ask the class, 'Is this okay with the rest of you? Is it okay to interrupt the class and yell out using this sort of language?' Together they must decide it is not. Together the class must figure out that everybody will be entitled to make a mistake in the classroom. Everyone needs to feel comfortable and safe in the class. The class will not tolerate such outbursts."

2.     A second choice would be to ask the child to stay a moment after class and then say, "I don't know what things were like before, but I can't accept this type of behavior in my class. If you're upset about the homework, come up and see me privately, but don't call out 'This sucks!' in the middle of the class." The teacher is modeling the behavior and should then remind the child, "I didn't react to your line in front of the whole class because I didn't want to put the spotlight on you. I'd expect to be given the same courtesy."

3.     The least helpful response by the teacher would be to say, "Sorry! You have to do the assignment anyway!"

If a child is not behaving appropriately in class, you need to know something about the child's environment and background in order to develop a successful intervention. Some children have reputations. Some are impulsive. Your personal relationships with these children will give you some insight. If you have a highly reactive, impulsive and out of control child, turning his behavior over to the group for corrections may not be a safe thing to do. A child who has more self-esteem and who is not out of control will make turning it over to the group more powerful.

In a classroom where the teacher is in control and has set standards, rules and expectations, such outbursts and putdowns are unlikely to happen. If they do, use the group to establish norms and behaviors that will be acceptable in the classroom. This approach may be a bit frightening to an inexperienced teacher, who may wish to be mentored at first by a successful experienced colleague.

Occasionally, the teacher will also have to support the person whose behavior is inappropriate. For instance, in one class there was a boy who was easily angered and couldn't control himself. The other children were trying to correct him all the time. When the boy got upset, his classmates would say, "Oh no! Here he goes again!" This would further upset the boy. The teacher was involved in a classic dilemma. The child's behavior was inappropriate. The other children were impatient and understood that he was interfering in their learning process. The teacher decided that the best way to handle the situation was to take a strong stand with the other kids and to say, "I'm the teacher here. I'll take care of this." Although the child's behavior was incorrect, the teacher would not allow the class to take it out on him.

Schools, as well as individual teachers, need to set up codes of conduct for what sort of verbal and physical behaviors are tolerated. These rules should be explained at the beginning of the year and reviewed throughout the year. Too many teachers make the mistake of going over the rules at the beginning of the year and then forgetting about them. New teachers, especially, are often shocked by how frequently rules must be repeated. For some children, rules must be reviewed every day. For a child who is out of control, the rules may need to be printed out and kept on his desk.

# Teasing

Some excellent guidelines for classroom rules are:

- We will respect others in this class.
- We will cooperate with others in this class.
- We will respect what others have to say in this class.
- We will listen to others until they finish speaking and we will do so without interrupting.
- We will respect the property of others in this class.
- We will allow everyone to physically pass.

In addition, the schools need to be clear and consistent about enforcing codes of conduct. When a problem occurs, it should be dealt with immediately. This will help the victim's self-esteem and send a message that such behaviors are not tolerated. Immediate response will also discourage future incidents.

Students should become familiar with the codes of conduct about bullying and know what their own roles are in enforcing them. "The possibilities include speaking up, supporting those who are being hurt, attempting to defuse problem situations, and seeking an adult's help."[17]

A school may decide to conduct a student survey to determine how serious is the problem of taunting and bullying. To encourage honest responses, do not require students to write their names on the surveys. Let students as well as parents know the results and solicit parental help in working on the issues. At the end of Chapter 17 is a sample Teasing/Bullying Survey you may wish to use for your school.

In Massachusetts, the Education Reform Act mandates the formation of school councils composed of school staff and parents to set goals and objectives. These councils must form an annual school improvement plan which includes: enhancement of parental involvement in the life of the school, school safety and discipline, and establishment of a school environment characterized by tolerance and respect for all groups.[18]

Teachers and parents will often miss what is happening at

school. Adults tend to overprotect the victims rather than teach them how to handle taunting and bullying. We need to teach children who are victims the skills we have been discussing. Then we need to coach them to use these skills because they will need practice. Children who are victims give the aura that they are helpless and won't do anything about bullying. Most of the time they are really scared. In trying to help the victim, you must decide what a child is capable of doing to protect himself and stop the bullying. Victims need to figure out the motivations of the bullies so they can better handle such situations in the future. Victims also need to boost their self-esteem to feel more competent.

Schools should provide counseling services for the bullies as well as the victims. Bullies need to learn to understand themselves and why they behave as they do as well as how they affect their victims. Bullies also need to learn other ways to feel powerful and in control.

Students should have the chance to work in cooperative groups as well as independently in order to understand the importance of community and receiving help from others. There is no better way of getting to know and understand people than by working with them. This helps to eliminate teasing.

Social Skills Programs

Teachers should be activists for including social skills programs in the curriculum of their schools, starting with the youngest children. Many such curricula are available. In Massachusetts, the services of *The Reach Out to Schools: Social Competency Program* at the Stone Center at Wellesley College have been much in demand. This program "builds self-esteem, problem-solving skills, and a classroom environment of collaboration and cooperation. In the process, it enables students to establish growth-enhancing relationships in their lives."[19] Pamela Seigle is Program Director and coauthor of the program along with Gayle Macklem.

# Teasing

Another curriculum is a video called "No More Teasing," offered by Sunburst Communications of Pleasantville, New York. The video is not a story film, but a sequence of acted out vignettes to help children figure out different techniques for handling teasing.

Another is "The Broken Toy," a 1993 film by Thomas Brown for Summerhill Presentations. It is a dramatically acted out story about a quiet and shy twelve-year-old boy named Raymond who is being bullied. The bullies feel very guilty when Raymond gets hit by a car, are joyful when he recovers, and are taught an invaluable lesson.

*U.S.A. Today* reported recently on two other programs to help children deal with teasing and bullying. One is a teacher-training program called *Bully-Proofing Your School* from Denver, Colorado, which has been taught at approximately 200 schools over the last two and a half years. The other is "Project Achieve," developed at the University of South Florida in Tampa, which can be used to train school employees, particularly bus drivers and cafeteria workers.

Not all educators are convinced of the value of social skills programs used in the schools. One principal confessed to me, "I feel the social skills programs give children the verbal comment ability to combat teasing, but the programs don't stop teasing." A school psychologist shares, "I don't really think that groups that teach social skills are productive. The kids will put on a good face and say the right things, but that doesn't change their behavior. In order to do that, there have to be more consequences and more discipline. Kids need to be suspended from school. If the school doesn't permit the behavior, it will stop."

Gayle Macklem offers this rebuttal. "A one shot assembly or a one shot program to teach children how to compliment others will not solve the problems of taunting and bullying in the schools. You must use the classroom group to solve the classroom's problems. For instance, we were dealing with a third grade class in a school that made use of our School Competency Program. This particular class went to the gym one day and behaved in such a way as to make the gym teacher feel very frustrated. She let them know she was frustrated. The class asked her if they could have a few minutes themselves at the end of the class to solve the problem. They took five minutes. When the teacher returned, the children said they realized they needed to change their behavior and they figured out how they would do it. They had changed the norm for the class! Instead of it being fun to play Get-the-Gym-Teacher, these children used their problem solving techniques to figure out that it was okay to say you made a mistake, okay to take some responsibility when you cause someone else a problem. They had the capacity, the empowerment to do something about it all by themselves. This was very impressive."

Robert Evans values the use of social competency programs in our schools, but he sees the issue in larger terms. He feels that the schools alone cannot make up for the powerful influences of the family and the community which may be lacking. "You can't measure the success of the social skills program by having schools which display no evidence of teasing. If some basic building blocks that turn kids into responsible citizens are left out of their families and their communities, we should do something in the schools, but we shouldn't feel guilty if we can't stop all the teasing. We certainly can't overcome ethnic prejudices that kids learn at home. I'm still in favor of social skills training in schools, but I'd hate to rely on it solely for change.

"Frankly," Dr. Evans continues, "I can't imagine a world without teasing. There are always kids who will be bigger and better and stronger at sports. Ten-year-old girls will always have their cliques. I think everybody teases and always has. The question is how much. I don't think kids' teasing is always so cruel. Sometimes it is playfully competitive. With teasing, kids are learning, practicing, testing their social skills. . . . The question is, where do you draw the line? I don't think there is a place on

earth without putdowns, but we want them within some manage-
able limits, where it's not the dominant tone."

I believe that the social skills programs have a much
greater chance of preventing taunting and bullying if they are
used universally within a school system or county wide. If only
one elementary school uses social skills training and then feeds
into a middle school where four elementary schools combine, it
will be difficult to measure the success of a program. But if all
four elementary schools participate, results should be more
apparent.

Children need to be taught social thinking as well as
critical thinking. Children should not blame others for their
behavior, but learn to take responsibility. They need to learn
empathy, that others have feelings too. They must become aware
that their actions can seriously hurt others and that they have
choices about this. Rules protect everybody, not just them or the
other kids. Everyone makes mistakes and that is okay because
mistakes help you learn. While feelings may not be rational,
everyone has choices about how to express feelings. Children also
need to learn to take their time in making decisions to ensure
they are making healthy, positive choices. Finally, they need to
learn who to trust and how to trust, and that trust develops over
time and is earned. These are lessons that can be taught at home
or at school, at places of worship or in therapy. It would help if
these important lessons were taught and reinforced in more than
one place in order to help them penetrate the minds of our children. There is much research and study still to be done.

# 16

## Helping Children Cope With Teasing

*Beezus was always saying she was a pest. The big boys and girls on Ramona's street called her a pest, but Ramona did not consider herself a pest. People who called her a pest did not understand that a littler person sometimes had to be a little noisier and a little bit more stubborn in order to be noticed at all.[1]*

Beverly Cleary, *Ramona the Pest*

Just who are the victims of childhood bullies? "To find out the answer, David Schwartz, Ph.D., and Kenneth A. Dodge, Ph.D., of Vanderbilt University, and John D. Cole, Ph.D., of Duke University, organized play groups of unacquainted first or third grade boys and videotaped the boys' interaction for an hour a day for five days. The videos revealed that both personality traits and group dynamics contribute to the problem. Chronic victims of bullying displayed more passive, submissive behavior than other group members. They were less likely to start a conversation, to attempt to persuade another boy to follow their suggestions, to engage in cooperative play, or to participate in rough-and-tumble games. Submissiveness acts as a reward for the bully's aggressiveness, reinforcing his belligerence. The play group's admiration for such aggression further rewards the bully and intensifies the problem."[2]

"Chronic victimization is a three-step process, Schwartz and Co. report in *Child Development*. First, the eventual victim submits to persuasion. Capitulation reinforces the victimizing behavior of peers, who then up the severity of coercive acts. The victim changes in response to victimization. Unless victims learn social skills, they are at risk for behavior problems."[3] Another problem is the rest of the kids will stop liking the victim if the child is repeatedly victimized because victim behavior is not admired in the peer culture.

Sunburst Communications advises that "Victims tend to be shy, self-effacing, retreating, frightened."[4] According to a fifteen-year-old girl who was interviewed, "The bullied person is always sad and depressed and doesn't have any popular friends."[5] We must consider the reasons why a child would tend to be shy, self-effacing, retreating, frightened, sad, and depressed:

1.    Some children are temperamentally shy which may be inherent in their personalities.

2.    A victim may have been the target of past physical, emotional or sexual abuse at home. It may be that the victim expects abuse, has given up trying to fight it, and has withdrawn into himself.

3.    A child may have experienced significant trauma or loss, resulting in fear and anxiety in relationships with peers. Some of these children have been hurt so severely in the past that even low levels of teasing can reactivate earlier trauma and cause the children to withdraw more. This behavior causes even more taunting and bullying, thus, the vicious circle continues. Children who suffer special problems such as learning disabilities, physical disabilities, depression, or problems in social relations are part of this group. These children may not be shy, but may be fearful and

anxious due to their histories. (See Chapter 19: Children with Disabilities and Teasing.)

Andrew O'Hagan described the victims of his childhood. "The kids who were targeted were thought deviant in some way—maybe they were serious, bright, quiet, keeping to themselves."[6] Obviously, the quiet, shy child may appear to be weak and vulnerable to the bully, but the victim may provide an additional element of interest to the bully which is less obvious. Perhaps the quiet, shy child who keeps to himself seems mysterious to the bully. The bully must draw the child out by forcing a reaction in order for the bully to feel he can control the child. The quiet child may strike the bully as a challenge, first to get to know and understand, and, later, to dominate.

Unfortunately, some children put the blame on the victims. Hazler, Hoover and Oliver reported: "One seventeen-year-old boy agreed: 'Sometimes when people get bullied, they deserve it because of the way they acted.' Another student was cited for 'her mentalness and lack of common sense,' both of which, the writer said, she could have controlled. Victims commonly reported feeling isolated and lonely during the time they were bullied. Some of this might have been due to other causes, but as one seventeen-year-old boy said about being bullied, 'All it did was make me more of a loner and more generally antisocial than before.'"[7]

Psychologist George Batsche of the University of South Florida has described a typical victim profile. "Chronic bully targets," he says, "are often anxious, quiet youngsters seen as physically weaker or less assertive than classmates. A minority, perhaps one in five, are 'aggressive' victims: they provoke others and then smash back when bullies bite at their bait."[8]

What kind of teasing is actually going on and when does it start? I asked my daughter Jenny when she was five years old and in kindergarten if she knew what teasing was. She got very emotional and replied in an angry voice, "Yes I do! Teasing is rude!" Getting so upset demonstrates that by age five, some kids have already had a lot of experience with teasing.

Experts say that children tease before they talk. Infants like to play peekaboo with their hands covering their eyes. A toddler will "hold a toy out to another, for instance, only to pull it away when his playmate reaches for the prize. . . . At the toddler stage, teasing is usually playful and conspiratorial; it enables very young children to 'recognize and explore their ability to affect other people,' explains Marilyn Segal of Nova University in Fort Lauderdale, Florida. 'For instance, you say no when your toddler starts to climb onto the coffee table . . . but she proceeds anyway and gives you a big mischievous grin. Her expression tells you that she's inviting you to join in her fun.' As preschoolers progress toward the elementary years, their reasons for teasing become more varied and complex."[9]

By the time a child is in kindergarten, he may become verbal and obsessed with bathroom humor and says things like, "You're a poopie." The child is not being mean, just silly. When children are in kindergarten or first grade, up until about third grade, they tease about concrete things. Children who are overweight or speak differently or children who act babyish will be teased.

Teasing starts to get mean and becomes problematic in elementary school usually by third grade. Now the children start to insult one another. These kids will tease each other about the way they dress, the style of their hair or their sneakers. One third grade girl was getting teased because she wore frilly dresses to school instead of following the grunge dress code like everyone else. The middle of grade school is usually when children start wanting to dress like their classmates. The wish to conform and dress alike may simply be a wish not to get teased for being different.

Exclusion starts in preschool. When children go out to play, the interactions are so short that, to keep the play going, kids have to exclude a child who tries to join in. If the new child feels rejected and stops trying to be included, he ends up feeling isolated. Third and fourth grade is when children become adept at inclusion and exclusion. They begin to form little groups as a way of belonging. But in order to belong, you have to exclude others. This makes life very painful for those excluded.

From first grade up, children will start to be teased about their achievements in school and their athletic prowess. Children who don't know how to read well or kids who raise their hands and give the wrong answer will be teased. Children who are clumsy may be teased. There is a universal roar in every school cafeteria whenever a student drops his lunch tray.

Sexually oriented teasing begins in third grade where kids may begin to be teased for wanting to play with the same children of the opposite sex who they played with up until second grade. When they reach fifth grade, children may be teased for having a crush on somebody of the opposite sex.

There is enormous pressure to conform, especially regarding dress. Teasing is also about "being cool." Nancy Papagno advises, "Teasing is more powerful as the kids get bigger, especially when the big kids pick on the little kids. In elementary school, there is more bickering instead of big kids picking on little ones. We showed a film about teasing to the third graders. They were more concerned with being teased by older sisters and brothers than they were about being teased by kids in school."

Papagno continues, "It is interesting what happens when the fifth graders move up to the middle school in the sixth grade. They go from being at the top of the heap to being at the lower rung. The eighth graders will then pick on the sixth graders. The sixth graders will be afraid to squeal. It's like hazing in college. Our fifth graders know this in advance and so they will suffer some anticipatory anxiety about going to junior high."

Kids may be teased in middle school if they don't behave socially the way they are expected to. Kids who are over involved in fantasy may also be teased. If they are over involved or have a preoccupation with Star Trek or the Power Rangers or if they have imaginary friends, they may be teased. Kids who don't behave in class by screaming out or acting out in other inappropriate ways can also be teased.

During the peak popularity of teasing, children may be teased because they are different due to their appearance or behavior. Children who are overweight, wear eyeglasses or hearing aids may be teased. Those who stutter, have a lisp or have acne, scars or deformities, may be teased, as well as children who have learning disabilities or physical handicaps.

Children who are physically challenged may be teased at school and may tease younger siblings at home. Nine-year-old Tasia, who is blind, confessed that she "had her share of groundings and other various punishments for teasing her younger sister—who is sighted—and tripping her with her cane."[10]

Kids may be teased for sticking out because they are too smart, dumb, tall, short, loud, quiet, strong, weak. They may be teased for doing their schoolwork and for not doing their schoolwork. They may be teased for hanging out with the out crowd. They may even be teased for wearing bike helmets in some neighborhoods. It might not be considered "cool" to bring a bag lunch from home in some schools. And if the child does bring a bag lunch, what is inside it might not be "cool," especially if the child brings healthy food instead of junk food.

Children may also be teased for any loss of control of bodily functions. A child who is still crying in fourth grade may be teased and called a crybaby. Children hate throwing up in school, for which they may be teased. If a child has a bathroom accident, burps or passes gas, he may also be teased.

It is interesting that grounds for being teased or bullied in one school may not necessarily be grounds for being teased in another school. A child who doesn't fit into a small homogeneous community may fit into a larger, heterogeneous community where looking a bit different is not so unusual. "A fifteen-year-old boy who recently changed schools reported he was bullied in his former school because he was 'not so good in sports.' He wasn't being bothered in his new school, where students apparently didn't hold sports in such high regard."[11]

A parent of a high school student at Phillips Academy, a well-known prep school in Andover, Massachusetts, shared, "The standards at this private school are different. Things that make a kid popular at the public Andover High School, being good in sports or being attractive, don't work here. Here all the kids have respect for is brains. The most popular kids here at Phillips are the smartest."

Gayle Macklem suggests, "Boys and girls have different experiences with taunting and bullying. A boy who can't take taunting has an extremely difficult time in his peer group. Some kids are highly sensitive by temperament and cry easily. These kids are easily stressed, highly anxious and will over interpret statements made to them. These boys will misinterpret playful teasing remarks as hostile remarks. The mothers will bring in the sensitive little boys who cry a lot. The parents seem to be acutely aware that little boys who cry won't be accepted."

About girls, Macklem says, "The girls we are the most concerned about are those without language skills. Girls do more talking than boys. Language skills have to be developed for a child to be popular. Sensitive girls have many of the same problems as sensitive boys, but interestingly enough, we often see more boys because they make the most noise about it. Girls with poor language skills may not report the problem. You have to look for the girls with problems so you don't miss them."

While writing this chapter, I had a flashback of the female bully in my junior high named Ginny who tried to push me down a steep flight of stairs when I was in the seventh grade. I remembered going to see the assistant principal with my mother and how painful that was. The assistant principal threatened to expel Ginny if she didn't leave me alone. It worked. Ginny was too scared to even look at me after that.

# Teasing

If you are taunted or bullied, stop and think. Consider the following options. (Try not to get frustrated and upset when one of the options doesn't work.) The way to be successful is often to use a series of these strategies. The strategies are listed from easiest to hardest to use. It may be that more than one strategy and more than one use of any particular strategy will be necessary. While you are using these strategies, think to yourself, "I'm a nice person. I try my best. I don't deserve this. The person taunting or bullying me has the problem, and it's not my fault."

Since the bully is the one with the problem, try and figure out just what his problem is. This will explain his motivation for trying to give you a hard time. In essence, the bully has a problem and he is trying to give that problem to you. You should also consider whether or not there is any basis at all for the teasing. For example, a hospital intern described a child who was getting teased about his mother being overweight and unattractive when she was really beautiful. The child didn't stop to figure out the reality of the situation which was that there was no basis for this teasing. Apparently, the teaser had some real questions about his own mother—some kind of fear of lack of self-confidence, or feelings of embarrassment, about his own family. Children often don't stop long enough to think that there is no basis in reality for their being teased. When there is a basis, teasing can be the most hurtful.

The simplest strategy is to try and ignore the teaser and hope she will go away. What you are doing is not giving her the chance to taunt or bully. Don't get frustrated if ignoring her doesn't work. It may and it may not. There is a chance that the bully might misunderstand your strategy and think you are just too scared to say anything.

If you are ignoring the bully and that doesn't work, try to express yourself to her without words. These are called nonverbal strategies because they don't involve words.

# Helping Children Cope With Teasing

## General Nonverbal Strategies

In each of the following nonverbal strategies, try not to cry, look down, seem upset, or act embarrassed. Instead, look and act confident, even if you are feeling scared inside. Stand up straight, shoulders back, hold your head high, face the person, and act assertive. Your goal should be to look sure of yourself and calm. This shows the bully that she has no power over you.

Give a nonverbal message that is neutral and will defuse the teasing. Just as bomb squads will try to defuse ticking bombs, you are trying to make light of the teasing situation so that it won't blow up in your face. Give the bully a strong look with your eyes and walk away.

Give a nonverbal message that says, "You can't get to me" without words. Then smile at the bully as though to say, "Thanks for paying attention to me," and walk away.

Try to give a nonverbal message that says, "Get lost." To do this, just glare at the person and then walk away.

Another way to handle nonverbal strategies is to act not only calm and confident, but aggressive. "No matter how intimidated, uncomfortable, or unhappy the victim is, he must stand his ground. He must laugh, look interested, and seem to be completely untroubled. His whole demeanor should convey aggressivity (rather than passivity) so he should stand firmly on both feet, with arms folded, and gaze steadily at the teaser. If it is feasible to do so, the target child should move closer to the teaser and follow him, should he move away."[12]

## General Verbal Strategies

If ignoring and nonverbal strategies don't work, and you need additional help, try different verbal strategies. These are strategies using words.

# *Teasing*

You might begin by making a defusing statement to play the situation down. You might say something mild like, "I don't have a problem with you." Then walk away.

You can try to "own" the putdown. You do this by humoring the bully and agreeing with him. "Yeah, I'm short. I'm trying to grow but I can't." You can also say:
"That's right, but . . ."
"It's my problem but I'm trying to work on it."
"I can't help that."
"I wish it weren't so."
"My mother makes me."
Then walk away.

If that doesn't work, tell the bully how you feel in a message that is short and clear. Tell the person in words that you don't like what he's doing. A child will tell a counselor, "Why do I have to say anything? He knows I don't like it."
The counselor asks, "How do you know that he knows?"
"Because I cry."
That's not good enough. You have to say it in words. Speak assertively to the bully in a firm voice. Remarks to stop the teasing might be:
"Cut it out."
"Quit bugging me."
"Leave me alone."
"Don't do that."
"Don't say that."
"I don't have time for this."
"I don't want to play this game any more. Do you understand me? This game is not appreciated."
"Hey! I don't like that! It bothers me!"
"Can you please stop teasing me? I don't like it."
"Why are you teasing me? I didn't do anything to you."
"That's not funny."

# Helping Children Cope With Teasing

"Stop it."

"I don't like you teasing me. Please stop."

"That's not really nice. Could you please stop?"

"Thank you for telling me."

Then walk away.

You can also try to give a verbal message that will affect the person by changing his or her mood. You can try to:

Try kindness. Give the person a compliment.

Try to make friends with him. This approach will be the least expected and may throw him off guard.

Ask the person to come over after school.

Offer to help the person do something.

Ask the person a question about himself or herself as if nothing had been said.

If that doesn't seem to be working, fight back with words. Give it right back to him. If he says you dress funny, try to reverse the tease: tease him about the same thing he was teasing you about. Tell him, "It takes one to know one." Some other comebacks might be:

"You're not really mad at me. You're just having a bad day."

"Twinkle, twinkle little star. What you say is what you are."

"I'm rubber. You're glue. What you say to me sticks back on you."

"I'm rubber. You're glue. It bounces off me and sticks to you."

"Do you always blame someone else for your problems? Why blame me?"

Strategies To Use When Teasing Becomes Physical

Teasing can escalate to fighting. If the bully tries to pick a physical fight, just say, "I don't want to fight with you because I don't want to get in trouble." Then walk away. Never strike the bully first.

# Teasing

About fighting, Dr. LaVerde advises, "I tell high school kids that it's not going to help them if they get in a fight because they will get suspended. The rule is that if two people are in a fight, they both get suspended. Nobody tries to figure out who started the fight."

If another child strikes you when there are no adults around and you cannot get away from the bully, you may have to strike back. Of course, this can be dangerous. Staying out of the bully's way as much as possible is the wisest course.

If the bully has any sort of weapon, try to run away from the bully as soon as possible and get help from a trusted adult.

Try to keep away from this person in the future. This is not the same as ignoring him. This is just trying to stay away from trouble and harm.

If the person does not keep away from you and continues to invade your space, he is stalking you. In the world of adult behavior outside of school, stalking is illegal. Tell a teacher or other responsible adult. If you tell the person in charge and get no results, tell your parent, the vice principal or the principal.

Consider an "intervention" approach where you band together with other kids who don't like the bully's behavior either and confront him as a team. You might choose to ask someone bigger than the bully to help you by teasing the bully back.

Make an appointment to see the school guidance counselor or school psychologist for help in handling these types of situations. The guidance counselor may try to work though the problem at both ends, with you and the bully.

If the teasing involves physical abuse or if you are terrified, always tell an authority such as a school administrator or even the police. This situation could be dangerous. Terror is a very real emotional response that your body is giving you to warn that you are in a dangerous situation. Get help immediately!

Try practicing your reactions to a bully with your parents. One of you pretend to be the bully while the other pretends to be the victim. Then switch roles. Practice different strategies. This will increase your self-confidence and help you deal with the problem.

# 17

## *Help for Bullies*

*We made Linda say,* I am Blubber, the smelly whale of class
206. *We made her say it before she could use the toilet in the
Girls' Room, before she could get a drink at the fountain,
before she ate her lunch and before she got on the bus to go
home. It was easy to get her to do it. I think she would have
done anything we said. There are some people who just make
you want to see how far you can go.*[1]

Judy Blume, *Blubber*

A good definition of bullying comes from Hazler, Hoover, and
Oliver in *The Executive Educator:* "We defined bullying as
aggression in which one student or a group of students physically
or psychologically harasses a victim over a long period of time. It
is unprovoked and repeated. Often, the bully is perceived as
stronger than the victim, which means the victims don't feel they
can retaliate."[2]

"Bullies," according to Maher in a recent article, "are
basically unhappy children, suffering through a hard time in
school or at home. Generally, they feel inferior, and they pick on
someone to gain what looks like a superior position." He goes on

# Help for Bullies

to tell us that bullying is most acute "between the ages of twelve and sixteen, 'when many students aren't feeling great about themselves."[3]

There are three types of bullies: the Popular Bully, the Bully-Victim and the Bully's Buddy.

## THE POPULAR BULLY

The popular bully is the child with good self-esteem who may be a popular child. This is a more aggressive child. Dr. LaVerde feels that teasing by a popular bully is "a way of relating for kids who are well put together."

Why do popular kids feel the need to tease? As Ellen Cunniff explains, "Teasing is what kids do, and they don't think about it. It's certainly nicer to think it's done unconsciously than to think the kids are being offensively mean. There is enormous peer pressure for acceptance. Status is fleeting. Popularity is insecure. Teasing reinforces the popular status of some kids by putting other kids down. If they think putting down other kids will make them cool, they'll do it for peer recognition. Putdowns become the norm of behavior. The entrance criteria for the most popular group may be how much you put down the other kids. Teasing is seductive. You get teased into teasing!"

Lois Lang suggests, "It is important to remember that the most popular child may not be the most terrific kid. It's also important to remember that chances are the most popular and powerful girl in the sixth grade will be forgotten in the ninth grade where she is not powerful any more."

Hazler, Hoover and Oliver interviewed students about why kids become bullies. "'I feel that most of the time, the people who are doing the bullying aren't doing it to hurt the person's feelings, but to seem more popular and cooler to their friends and/or the in-crowd,' reported one fourteen-year-old. 'I think

they also think it makes them seem stronger than other people.'
Many other students said basically the same thing: what bullies
crave is social influence. They want to compensate for their own
inadequacies. . . . Students often reported that bullies did not
want to hurt others so much as help themselves. 'It wasn't to hurt
them but to try to be in the main crowd and not be in lower
groups,' reported a fifteen-year-old boy. To an extent, this appears
to work despite its twisted logic: many students we spoke with
apparently believed bullies had more social status than victims."[4]

Bragging is tied to teasing. "You guys aren't cool. I am."
For some kids, unfortunately, bullying is just a way to have fun at
school. Some kids really think that teasing others is both fun and
funny. ·

### THE BULLY-VICTIM

The bully-victim is the child who is a bully and a victim.
He gets taunted also. He is provocative and always looks for something to happen in a group. This child has poor self-esteem. He
may be hostile because he expects the group to be hostile to him.
This is the child who displays what I call "Offensive-Defensive
Behavior" or behavior that says, "I'm going to get you before you
get me." He will project onto someone else what he is afraid of in
himself. His motivation is, "If I call you fat and ugly first, then
you won't call me fat and ugly. I get to be the bully and then I
don't get teased."

This child may be acting out problems he is facing at
home. He may be picking on kids at school because his parents
or older brothers and sisters pick on him. Some bully-victims
might have been raised without empathy or compassion in abusive or neglectful homes. As a result, these children have never
been able to process feelings of guilt. They may be conditioned
to lack trust and always assume the worst in others. They might
feel that other people are out to get them.

# Help for Bullies

This child may be taunting others as an unconscious cry for help. It may be a way of attracting negative attention so a grownup will figure out that the child is suffering problems beyond his control. For this reason, parents and teachers should give the bullies as well as victims special attention.

Some of these children are temperamentally aggressive, and taunting serves as their outlet because no other outlet may be available to them. Taunting and bullying helps them to feel better, more powerful, bigger, stronger, in charge and in control. Taunting, in such a case, will actually help the child to boost his low self-esteem.

## THE BULLY'S BUDDY

The bully's buddy is the child who would never generate the bullying but he does nothing to stop it. He supports the bully whom he admires and/or fears. The bully's buddy, consciously or subconsciously, views himself as a potential victim who supports the bully for fear that if he does not, he will be the next target. The logic is that it is better to be on the giving end of teasing than on the receiving end. The buddy fears becoming a scapegoat for some individual or for some group. He also has a need to be accepted by the dominant group of children. This child is much more than a witness. He is viewed as being the bully's teammate.

## MOTIVATIONS FOR BULLIES

Motivations for bullies include the following:
1.    To get attention.
2.    To prove they are not vulnerable. Bullies are motivated to distance themselves from something or someone they perceive to be bad or stupid. Kids who get held back in school often get

teased, as does a child "who looks different . . . such as a child with a hearing aid or glasses. . . . By hurling verbal taunts or making rude comments, children distance themselves from the source of their fears. . . . 'I'm not like you' is the message their teasing conveys," explains child development specialist Diane Lynch-Fraser.[4]

3.     To exclude another child in order to solidify their own circle of friends. Kids will put down others for being friends with "nerds," for instance.

4.     To overcome feelings of jealousy. The victim may have something that the teaser does not; the victim might also be better at doing something than the teaser. Furthermore, a child may be teased for being the teacher's pet or for being perceived as rich. Latency age children, those of ten or eleven, are aware of their own weaknesses. Teasing is a way to minimize just how good the other child is and make the teaser feel more important. Sometimes a child will excel in one area but be weak in another. As a result, the child will be teased about the weaker area.

5.     Some kids tease for revenge. A teacher shared, "We had one child who was scapegoated in the third grade. When he finally became a fifth grader, he said, 'I'm going to do to them what they did to me!'"

6.     Some children get sadistic pleasure from teasing. They truly enjoy upsetting, bullying and embarrassing other people. Kids might say very mean things to each other in order to hurt and to poke fun. One elementary school teacher told me he heard an overweight boy being called such names as "Fat Kid," Blubber," and "You Fat Fuck!" while the other kids laughed. Kids make fun of the way other kids dress. And kids who go to special reading class will be teased.

Some children use body language to put other kids down. For instance, they roll their eyes. A popular boy may establish eye contact with a friend across the classroom. Then the two will jointly laugh at a child whom the popular boy doesn't like. Kids pick up on this stuff immediately. Some children will get physical,

refusing to allow another child to pass. Some children will tortu-
ously tickle other kids.

7.     Teasing is also a way for children to test different aspects
of their personalities. "Many of the battles they wage among
themselves are, in fact, a direct result of their sometimes clumsy
attempts to form relationships."[6]

A recent article in *U.S.A. Today* quoted school psychologist Susan Safranski as saying that, "bullies tend to develop in
less supervised environments. With a rising number of single
parents, dual-career families and latchkey kids, close adult mon-
itoring may be at a premium. . . . Television often fills the void,
and it's loaded with (unpunished) violence. . . . Most healthy kids
will roughhouse or mildly tease each other, so every little tiff
doesn't equal a bully's rampage."[7]

Has the problem of mean kids always been with us?
Certainly Andrew O'Hagan's article, "Growing Up Nasty," confirms this belief. When O'Hagan, now an editor with the *London
Review of Books*, was ten years old in Scotland, he confesses,
"We had been walking the mile to school in the company of a
boy, smaller and younger than ourselves, a fragile boy with gin-
ger hair named David. . . . Occasionally, when he didn't walk
straight or carry our bags or speak when we wanted him to, we'd
slap him or hit his hands with a ruler. Over time, we started to hit
the boy hard. Though we'd set out on time that morning, by now
we were late, having spent half an hour on top of an out-of-the-
way railway bridge practically skinning the screaming boy's legs.
. . . If all of this sounds uncommonly horrific, then I can only
say that it did not seem so then; it was just the way most of the
boys I knew used up their spare time. . . . We didn't stop to
think, or did our parents, that something dire might result from
the darker side of our extracurricular activities."[8]

If the problem has increased and kids are worse today
than when we were young, then what is influencing the changes
in their behavior? Dr. LaVerde believes, "Kids are just as nice

today as kids used to be, but they have a harder edge to them due
to the influence of our modern media. The interior of the child
is soft, but the exterior is harder. There is a lot of peer pressure
to be very strong, tough and cool. Kids who are alone are okay.
Kids in groups are not as nice."

Some kids who tease lack empathy and so they may not
perceive their behavior as terrorizing to other kids. We do know
that if we call a highly sensitive child a name, it may hurt. The
same name applied to a second child may not hurt the second
child at all. This makes teasing a risk. We need to establish
norms that say if the child doesn't like the teasing, the teasing
must stop. If you can't predict the response to your tease, lay off.
The perpetrator of the tease needs to take responsibility for his
actions.

LaVerde continues, "Television programs such as *Married
With Children* show that teasing is a way to achieve verbal supe-
riority and power. When kids watch that, they find that the
barbs, the clever one-liners, are attention getting. Some of these
same programs teach children to disrespect their parents. For
example, fathers are often portrayed as ridiculous beings. Kids
on the sitcoms often act angry and mean with their families as
well as in their schools."

As for language, LaVerde says, "Television has lowered the
standards for language we use. A generation ago a kid would say,
'This stinks!' Today a kid will say, 'This sucks!' This has a harder
edge and makes the kids sound harder. Television actually models
poor behavior for our children."

He also claims that "The news media, also, has toughened
up our kids. People fear crime more as the news media portrays
the world as falling apart. If this is an angrier, meaner world,
then adolescents perceive they have to be tough to stand up to it.
Being tough, violent and nasty sometimes gets kids what they
want. It is a means to an end. Kids also see the good guys being
tough, violent and nasty in movies. In the old days, John Wayne
would fight according to the rules and he would win and he

wouldn't say nasty things. Last night I saw a Steven Seagal movie where the good guy was doing nasty things!

"Sports heroes, too, are modeling poor behavior for our kids. Taunting in sports is a strategy used by some professionals to win. If I can taunt you or upset you, even though I have nothing against you personally and I might even like you, and if I win, then I have accomplished my purpose. This kind of winning by intimidation is universally done in male sports down to the junior high level. This represents a change in attitude about playing sports. The National Basketball Association recently put rules in place to decrease taunting and directed referees to enforce them. The NBA calls it 'trash-talking.' If the kids' heroes are doing trash-talking, why shouldn't they?"

While physical bullying can be immediately dangerous and destructive, verbal bullying can also lead to violence either directly and immediately or indirectly and many days, months or years later if a defenseless child commits suicide or lashes out at others. One study of aggression in children done in Finland in 1987 made "use of a peer nomination and teacher rating variable for offensive aggression: 'attacks without reason, teases others, says naughty things'; and another for defensive aggression: 'defends him/herself if teased, but does not tease or attack others without reason.'. . . . Offensive aggression at age fourteen was significantly predicted by aggressive behavior at age eight, while defensive aggression was not. Intercorrelations of rating variables at age fourteen showed that offensive aggression was related to weak self-control and defensive aggression to strong self-control. Only offensive aggression at age fourteen predicted criminality at age twenty."[9]

## CONSEQUENCES OF TEASING AND BULLYING

The 1990s have dramatically demonstrated the disastrous consequences of childhood teasing and bullying. Susan Smith, the young mother from Union, South Carolina who confessed to drowning her two young sons in her car in November 1994, was a victim of "cruel teasing from other children after her father shot himself through the head when she was eight years old."[10] She attempted suicide twice in her youth.

Eric Smith of Savona, New York was only thirteen years old when he murdered four-year-old Derrick Robe by bashing him with a large rock in 1994. Eric had been teased all of his life at school and on school buses. Eric scratched his own picture out of his school yearbook. He felt his sister and the kids "treat me like trash," spitting and screaming at him. When he was nine, a child taunted him by saying that his father was not his real father and that only his sister was wanted by his real father. A sad, depressed child, Eric stayed back in school, wet the bed until age eleven, killed small animals and once tried to strangle his pet cat. He intermittently became deadly angry. He once asked his father for help with his anger, which he never received. Supposedly, a child once said to him, "I bet I can beat your head in."[11] It is simple, in retrospect, to see the profound rage which built inside this youngster and eventually erupted in the form of violence against Derrick Robe.

In March 1993, two-year-old James Bulger of Liverpool, England was abducted and murdered by two ten-year-old boys.

In December 1994, American newspapers reported: "A thirteen-year-old schoolboy's suicide in a central Japanese town was the second in the last few weeks, sparking fresh concern about bullying and suicides, police said. The boy's body was found on the same day that Prime Minister Tomiichi Murayama held a special cabinet meeting to discuss the first death and Japan's Education Minister urged teachers to crack down on schoolyard bullying. . . . Shoji Sota, vice principal of the school, said the boy was a victim of bullying in October, when schoolmates scribbled on his bag and injured his head by throwing a chair."[12]

In October 1993, a magazine article discussed the case of an intelligent fifteen-year-old student in Westchester County,

New York who was "contemplating suicide. Almost from the first day of school, seven to eight classmates mocked his successes. It started as locker room teasing, when they would want to stay after practice to work out, and he wanted to study. Maher [the school principal] says: 'They tormented him every time he did well on a test, called him a nerd,' and picked fights. Later in the year, the desperate sophomore finally confided in a school counselor, and the problem landed in the principal's office."[13]

In January 1995 in a small northeastern town, a "fourteen-year-old . . . boy was suspended for five days following an incident last week in which he allegedly slashed a fellow student with an X-Axto knife, allegedly in response to persistent teasing. . . . 'He went to punch the kid and he had the knife in his hand,' Officer Milne said. 'He said he didn't realize he'd had the knife in his hand at the time. Apparently there's been some friction between the kids.' Assistant Principal Tony Corvino described the cut as not much more than a scratch."[14]

Knives and scratches may be what some small towns are made of, but life is tougher in the big cities where some bullies are armed with guns. "A survey from the Centers for Disease Control found that one in twenty-four students in 1990 had carried guns within the previous thirty days. A year later, the number of armed students had increased to one in eighteen. Survey respondents said they had armed themselves for self-defense, but the guns aren't protecting anyone. In 1990, more than four thousand teens died in shooting incidents, though not all were school-related."[15] Do all schools need metal detectors, guards and law enforcement personnel on the premises?

### TECHNIQUES TO CHANGE BULLYING BEHAVIOR

Since bullying behavior and victim behavior usually start as early as preschool, it is very important to try to influence children early on. This takes total intervention; cooperation among the child, the parents and the school is essential. Unfortunately, such a unified approach doesn't often happen. In order to achieve it, we need to change the climate in the schools.

Bullying is learned behavior which needs to be unlearned. Furthermore, bullying may be reinforced by systems in the family or in school where the behavior is often supported. Those systems need to be addressed and changed.

With younger children, bullying is more physical. As children get older, bullying is more verbal. It takes some cognitive development to be effective in verbal taunting. A child has to be perceptive and to be able to look at another child and ask himself, Can I get away with taunting him? Is he shy, handicapped, very sensitive?

If you want to help a bully change his behavior, you need to work with the child. Certainly, if the behavior gets the child what he wants, his bullying is reinforced. The bully also needs to know there are less hurtful ways to be powerful, be in control and get reinforcement. To do this, you have to get to know the child on an individual basis to find out his developmental level, his intelligence and his skill level, and whether the child has developed any empathic skills.

It is very effective with the smallest bullies to give them roles where they can be helpful, such as making the child the coach or referee of the team. This will give the child another way to feel powerful and in control without taunting others. The child must also be reminded continuously that schools can't tolerate hostile teasing and that this is not acceptable behavior.

A bully can change his role if he can learn some positive behaviors and skills. In order for a young bully to participate in skills training, such as learning to give compliments, he must be amenable to a reasoning approach. If the child does not yet have the ability to comprehend and reason things through, you may have to give the child "Time-Outs." This means the child must spend a certain period of time away from the other children. Hopefully, during his "time out" he will reflect on what has occurred and his role in it while he regroups for more productive play.

The period between first and third grade is the most critical time for making an intervention with any child, whether the child is a bully or a victim. By the end of third grade the child has probably earned a reputation and acquired a label in his peer group. This label does not seem to change easily. If a child is rejected, ignored, or isolated in his peer group, he tends to keep this same role through school. Unfortunately, the negative roles don't seem to change as the child grows, even though positive roles might. What is valued early on may not have the same power later.

When you are dealing with slightly older children, such as a bully in the second grade, you may have fewer opportunities to give the child a leadership role. Instead, you might help the child to be a planner and help her to make friends.

In interactions, children with attention deficit disorders will often try to be the best and win. These kids are generally less mature and don't always make wise decisions. They are often impulsive in their decision-making. This goal of winning might not be the best approach for them, because it may not get them the friends they crave.

By third or fourth grade, a child must be helped to realize that winning all the time is not a guarantee of happiness. Sometimes athletic parents foster the goal of winning above everything. Adults often seem to forget there are other goals of sports in addition to learning about competition, such as the goals to keep children safe and teach them skills.

Working with a fourth grade bully is not a simple intervention. If the goal of the child is to be powerful, you must teach him other ways to do this without running roughshod over the other kids. The child must be taught empathy and a concept of fairness. It may be fair to playfully tease an equal the child's own age and grade, but it is unfair to pick on a much smaller or younger child.

# Teasing

In order to change the behavior of a bully who has good self-esteem, the bully has to get something positive back. Punishment is not enough of a motivator for this type of bully to effect a change. One way to help the child feel more powerful is by signing him up for an athletic team with a coach who is good at teaching kids sportsmanship.

Other effective interventions for elementary school bullies are those which teach a child to form prosocial behavior by helping others. Instead of simply sitting out recess outdoors or in the gym, the child could help the teacher in the classroom, in the office or help clean up the cafeteria. A child could also be asked to stay after school to help. An older child may be asked to tutor a younger child or help plan a school activity. The child could also be asked to do something nice for the victim. A teacher could try to teach a child to be empathic by doing some role playing where a bully is the victim. Finally, a child could be asked to keep a private journal where he must record daily good deeds and good thoughts toward others.

Behaviors are often well established in sixth grade. It makes a big difference whether a school system places sixth graders in the middle school or the elementary school. A sixth grader is the big kid in the elementary school and may be perceived as powerful, but he will be a little kid in the middle school and will be perceived as having relatively much less power.

Children may be very afraid of a sixth grade bully, so there needs to be intervention at this level. Also needed is a school culture that does not approve of the behavior. There are not many places that use a whole school intervention. However, all teachers, staff and kids need to be trained about the rules and how to enforce them with appropriate consequences. More than just punishment and more than just suspension of offenders is needed. Kids need to be placed in small group training where they can learn alternative behaviors and learn to pay attention to the consequences of their own behavior. Kids who are isolated and rejected should be placed in a small group and norms established for that group. One suggestion is that when that group goes out onto the playground, each child will have a responsibility to go and stand next to any other child in the group who is being bullied. When two or three children are standing together, it is easier to be assertive. There is safety in numbers.

For a sixth grade bully with good self-esteem, a mixed counseling group in school with the school psychologist is a good recommendation. If this bully picks on specific kids, put the bully and victim together in the group and assign them to work on academic tasks together. This will enable the bully to see his victim as a real person with feelings and competencies.

For a sixth grade bully with poor self-esteem, self-control training in a small mixed group where the victim can be taught to give the bully some feedback is a good idea. When a kid bullies, she may not realize she has gone too far or she may not perceive she is doing something hurtful. These kids should be paired, one bully and one victim together, in an academic learn-ing situation. In any of these groups, don't put too many aggres-sive kids together who will outnumber the victims.

Eighth and ninth grade bullies, kids in upper middle and high school, need some very firm limits because intervention at this age is more difficult. Make sure that the school culture does not support the bullying behavior. It doesn't work to merely pull the child out of the classroom for a private talk with the school psychologist. This doesn't change the peer culture. Teachers need to change the rules of their classrooms.

By tenth grade, the hallways become a major environment for bullying behavior. Fortunately, older kids have more cognitive capacity and can be talked to and reasoned with. Individual counseling may be effective momentarily, but intervention where teenagers are talked to in small groups is more helpful. Staff must be placed in the hallways to make sure taunting and bully-ing doesn't occur. Telling kids they can't do it and to cut it out just isn't enough.

A tenth grade bully with low self-esteem, who is himself getting harassed and bullied, may have some other issues at work, too. For instance, he may have a nonverbal learning disability. These kinds of kids don't easily perceive other kids' feelings. They just don't know how to read them. Some may also suffer attention deficit disorders.

If a tenth grade bully has very little self-control and is very hard to work with, she may have to be kept out of the hallways. You can do this by changing her schedule so that she must leave her last class two minutes early and get to her next class two minutes early. That's a preventive intervention, better than punishing her. With a less competent child, it is a good idea to find some place where the child can be helpful so she can feel good about herself if only momentarily.

In dealing with consequences for bullying behavior, you need effective school structure. Some schools will suspend children. The only negative thing about suspensions is that children sometimes like to be out of school and school personnel lose access to the child. For this reason, some professionals prefer in-school suspensions. An in-school suspension is like a time-out. It gives a teacher or administrator the time to work with a child and help him to understand the ramifications of his behavior, the problems he causes for himself and other kids. Another way to modify behavior is to give an in-school suspended child books to read on problem-solving techniques and request the child write about these techniques and then practice them.

Bullies must be reminded that their behavior has legal ramifications for the future. If a twelve-year-old boy pushes another child into a locker, the attitude may be "boys will be boys," and if a twelve-year-old girl trips another her action may be thought of as "children's play." But if the same child does it again when he or she becomes eighteen, there will be legal consequences. Kids need to be helped to understand the seriousness of their actions and the possibilities of physical injury.

For a more impulsive bully, you must figure out what's going on with the student. Does he have a nonverbal learning disability? Is he developing internal standards and controls? Can he understand consequences? Is he depressed? Is he being victimized at school, at home or in his neighborhood?

The parents of a bully need to be brought to school after those who've witnessed a bullying incident are less angry, perhaps one month after any punishment has taken place. Bullying of this type is a long-term problem. Sometimes the parents of a particular child are brought in repeatedly during the time when everyone is emotional. However, this doesn't usually work. Parents who feel angry may also harbor feelings of incompetence, defensiveness and failure. When parents come in after a cooling down period, they can sometimes be very helpful by sharing invaluable information about the child, such as the stressors in her environment which will be unknown to the school. Time with the parent allows the teacher to be empathic with the parent and improve communication between the child's home and school.

Nancy Rhodes explains, "The kids are using teasing and taunting as a form of intimidation. There was an angry fourth grader beating up a small first grader in our school, swelling his eye. I reported it to the principal and to the nurse, that the child had a swelling over his eye. I know the bully had been in to see the assistant principal before. The bully's punishment was that he lost his recess privileges for a period of time. That was not enough! Bullies are just not being punished severely enough in any of the schools. When a bully trespasses on someone's personal space, that's assault. Let's call it that!"

Dr. Evans disagrees with the use of the word "assault" to describe this situation. "There is a danger in over interpreting behavior," he says. "If you use the word 'assault' for every little fight, you cheapen the word and then you need stronger words. I think of 'assault' as occurring when the bullying is sustained, systematic, extremely violent and deliberate. I prefer giving the parent a blow-by-blow description. 'He banged the other child's head three times into the cement.' This is better than labeling it assault."

# Teasing

Our language, how we define the behavior, is part of the problem we face. "When we bring a parent in for a school conference about his kid's behavior, the parent will say their kid was 'just teasing,' when clearly the child was taunting, trying to provoke another child," Dr. LaVerde says.

He goes on to talk about the "lesser language" used in schools. "In talking to a parent we want to convey a serious problem in less extreme terms. We don't want to frighten the parents. In a sense, the parents are our customers and we are afraid to alienate them. We say the word 'teasing' to the parent instead of 'tormenting' because teasing sounds more innocent. Neither do we use the words 'stalk' or 'assault.' Instead of saying, 'Your child assaulted another child,' we say, 'Your child got in a fight,' when clearly one child assaulted another.

There are risks involved in the vocabulary schools use. If you tell a parent his child assaulted another, he may get a lawyer. The child who is assaulted could get a lawyer and sue not only the bully, but the school for failing to provide a safe environment. Perhaps we need a few of these lawsuits to change the system.

Perhaps we should force teachers and principals to use "straight talk." Let's forget about using the phrase "childhood teasing." There may have been a time when childhood teasing was mostly playful, but nowadays it's mostly negative and meant to cause a reaction.

Sometimes the outcomes of certain types of childhood teasing are useful to adults and, as a result, the adults may wish them to continue. Sometimes peer pressure will enforce the completion of homework even when the child doesn't want to do it. Sometimes a three-year-old will be teased out of diapers or his thumb-sucking by his preschool cohorts who make fun of him. These positives, while they may be helpful to adults, are painful to children.

# Help for Bullies

## RULES TO HELP DEAL WITH AND LABEL CHILDHOOD TEASING

Here are some new rules to help deal with and label childhood teasing:

1.      Childhood "teasing" not meant in the spirit of fun for both parties should henceforth be labeled childhood taunting. Let's clarify our terms. Let's see taunting for what it is: hurtful, serious.

2.      Childhood taunting should be called childhood tormenting when the taunting is repetitive and causes severe distress to the child, and the child's protestations have no effect on the child who does the tormenting. Tormenting should not be defined by how often the taunting takes place, but by how it affects the child. If the taunting causes great distress, it is tormenting.

3.      If a child follows another child around for the express purpose of tormenting him, the behavior is stalking. Bullying is another word for childhood tormenting and should be used to describe minor physical incidents such as bumping into, refusing to allow another to pass, and tripping, when there is no serious injury resulting.

4.      The word assault should be used if one child physically invades the space of another and causes bodily harm. Let's use the real words. If we now recognize sexual harassment in the schools and treat it as such, why not treat assaults and stalking the same way as they are treated in the real world—outside of the classroom? Children should be entitled to at least the same protection as adults. Children should feel safe in school.

5.      We need to empower the victims of torment and bullying and supply consequences for the perpetrators. If kids don't hear about any repercussions to bullies, they don't feel empowered. Consequently, they also feel that no one cares about them.

Teasing in childhood, as well as teasing in adults, is about power and control. One of the few things children can control in life is what goes into and out of their mouths—that includes words as well as food. Children will tease when they realize they have personal power. Thus, teasing becomes a driving force in their personalities.

Dr. Evans responds to the question, Are kids worse today? "They are worse behaved—absolutely," he says. "Anybody who works with kids can see a marked deterioration in social and school readiness. Kids are not dumber, but they do come to school less able to stand in line, less able to stay with a problem, less able to be quiet and listen while another kid talks. Kids are less controlled, less restrained, less prepared to be good citizens, less prepared to self-regulate, to be able to say, 'Am I going too far? Am I hurting the other kids?' The truth is that kids' behavior is worse today, but so is the behavior of adults. The overall level of civility is worse."

As a society, we are clearly not as civil as we once were. Language that was once considered obscene is now commonplace. Sexual scenes that were once censored from television are now flaunted in the daytime when children can tune in. Parents have not yet figured out how to balance full-time jobs with quality time with their children in order that they may better supervise them, set an example for them, and have the time to teach them the social skills they need. To help with the problem of dealing with childhood taunting, tormenting and bullying, clearly we adults must first look in the mirror.

# 18

## Sibling Teasing

*You are a dependent, Mama says; you have no money; your
father left you none. You ought to beg, and not to live here
with gentlemen's children like us, and eat the same meals we
do, and wear clothes at our mama's expense.[1]*

Charlotte Bronte, *Jane Eyre*

Teasing begins at home. Children learn to tease from their
parents, grandparents, siblings and other relatives long
before they go to school. There are indeed several major differences between general childhood teasing and sibling teasing.

The first and most significant difference is that with sibling teasing, the victim and the teaser live together. This means
the victim will often be unable to get away from the teaser. In
cases of severe and malicious tormenting and bullying, it means
that the person torturing your child could be another one of your
own children.

In today's world of step, blended, foster, and adoptive
families, it is also possible that the child in your home who
tortures your child may not be biologically related to you.
Some children may feel they have more rights, power, and

position than other children in the house, and they may wish to exert their power by taunting, bullying and assaulting the others. Some children may be jealous of the others and act out their resentments by taunting.

A second difference between general childhood teasing and sibling teasing is that if one of your children is taunted or bullied on a routine basis by another one of your children, you may feel forced to take sides against another member of your family or another person in your household. It is much easier to be supportive to your child and to be upset with a bully when the bully is unrelated to both of you and lives somewhere else.

A third factor is that boys and girls who live together know each other extremely well. They know each other's flaws, weaknesses and vulnerabilities. Brothers and sisters also know each other's secrets as well as their life histories. This means that they know exactly what buttons to push to get strong reactions.

Siblings love to tease each other about very sensitive subjects that they might not dare tease other kids about, for example, their love lives, wetting the bed, or what they look like naked. Older siblings always seem to know when a younger one has a crush on one of their friends and will use that information against them. A parent suggests, "This may sound far out, but I think sometimes siblings of the opposite sex will start a fight as a way of dealing with sexual feelings they might have for each other. It's one way to maintain a safe distance."[2] Author Janet Bode agrees: "Sexual interest often takes the form of teasing or anger. In a way, it's safer to argue than to face the fact that you have these warm feelings. So you control your affection by fighting."[3]

Familiarity in addition to opportunity equals increased levels of all types of childhood teasing, taunting and bullying behaviors. When the factor of sibling rivalry is thrown in as well as general childhood insecurities, that is a combustible mixture.

Parents cannot do anything to change the familiarity or opportunity to taunt among their children, but they can help to ease tension between them by trying to ease sibling rivalry as much as possible. Sibling rivalry can't be entirely eliminated because it is built into the equation of a family, but parents can do their best not to exacerbate the situation. This boils down to two words. No comparing! This is asking a lot of a parent who is tempted to call out, "Why can't you be neat like your big brother?" or "Your big sister never forgets to brush her teeth!" Comparing children, however, only illustrates a deficiency in one and damages the relationship between them.

Never compare report cards or appearance. Children will translate such comparisons into "You must love him more than me because he's better than me." Comparing behavior of two siblings is not even relevant because one child's behavior has absolutely nothing to do with that of his sibling.

In trying to resist the impulse to compare children, remember to put into words the behavior you hope the child will be able to modify. "I wish you wouldn't whine so much!" is far better than "Your big sister never whines!"

"Experts say it's better to keep the focus on the child's potential for achievement, without bringing up a sibling. Ask: How can we help you: improve your grades; practice harder; keep your room cleaner?"[4]

It is best not to make favorable comparisons either. If you tell a young child, "Doesn't your big sister look pretty today?" this translates for the child to, "You mean I don't?" Best to give compliments directly to the child you are describing.

Instead of comparing, let each child understand he is special in his own way. In our home, we tell Marissa that she is special because she is the oldest, and we tell Jenny that she is special because she is the youngest. When you stop comparing children, it shows you are accepting each child for her strengths as well as her weaknesses. Ultimately, we all wish to be loved for our uniqueness. As the authors of *Siblings Without Rivalry* write, "I told them all the story of the young wife who suddenly turned to her husband and asked, 'Who do you love more? Your mother or me?' Had he answered, 'I love you both the same,' he would have been in big trouble. But instead he said, 'My mother is my mother. You're the fascinating, sexy woman I want to spend the rest of my life with.'"[5]

If your children share their bedroom space, their close proximity may intensify the conflict situation. Lack of privacy gives anyone—child or adult—the feeling of being out of control of his environment. Some children will taunt or bully a sibling as a way to punish the sibling just for being in the way. Siblings will commonly argue over territory and possessions in the house. "He's touching my stuff!" "That's my toy!" "She crossed over into my side of the room."

A strategy for dealing with territorial issues is to give each child a private space in the house. This is most important when children share bedrooms. It is ideal to give a child who shares a bedroom a corner somewhere in the bedroom or elsewhere in the house that is completely private and may not be touched by any sibling without permission. Children who share bedrooms may also wish to take turns having the room to themselves for several hours at a stretch in the daytime, especially when they have friends over.

Children commonly take their frustrations out on their younger siblings because they are there and available. Kids who have had a bad day at school, because a teacher or a friend yelled at them, may come home and take their hurt feelings out on their little brothers and sisters—to do so makes them feel powerful and back in control. Since there is an element of unconditional love between siblings, siblings feel safe getting angry at each other because they won't leave. Consequently, home becomes a place where a child can test behavior without being penalized too severely. I was the middle child of three sisters growing up. My little sister used to say, "I wish Mommy and Daddy would have another baby so I could have someone to pick on, too."

Sometimes kids will tease and pick on each other just to get their parents' attention and to figure out where they stand with their parents, especially as compared to their siblings.

# Sibling Teasing

Children may say they don't want the parent to compare them to each other and yet they will still try to provoke the parent into doing it—e.g., by trying to make the parents take sides in their teasing arguments. When I was a child, my little sister bragged about how she could manipulate our father. "If we fight and Daddy comes upstairs to see about it, I'll make tears in my eyes and then he will believe me!" I got back at her later in a not very nice way by telling her that she was adopted when she wasn't.

Sometimes kids tease and taunt each other as a way of getting negative attention. Sooner or later children figure out that when they get along well, their parents ignore them. So if they want their parents' attention, they better start misbehaving. It also makes some kids feel powerful if they can deliberately provoke and upset a parent. Therefore, if parents allow their taunting each other to rile them, the children will have accomplished their goal, and the parents will be responsible for helping to perpetuate their behavior. "My kids fight because they love to see the show I put on. . . . They finally admitted to me that they were banging on the wall between them and pretending they were fighting. It was all made up to get me up there six times a night. They thought that was terrific."[6] My six-year-old will admit that she thinks it's fun to provoke her older sister so she can get her into trouble!

Another reason siblings tease is to alleviate boredom. One of my patients, a twenty-six-year-old woman named Donna, grew up with four older brothers. They terrorized their adorable little sister whenever their parents left them alone and made even worse threats so she'd never tell. They turned the lights off when Donna played in the cellar and locked her in closets. She reported the worst thing they did happened when she was eight years old. At that time, one of her brothers routinely jumped on top of her while she was sleeping and put a pillow over her face. I suspect that her preference for dating younger men was due to her need to control any man in her life and her fear of older males.

# Teasing

The way to avoid this kind of victimization between siblings in a family is supervision. Before trusting children to babysit each other, interview the smallest children in the house about what goes on when you are away, giving them permission for honesty. Vow to protect them if they confess to being abused by their older siblings. When leaving younger children with their older sibling, it is a good idea to occasionally come home earlier than they expect, to see how they are managing.

To overcome teasing and taunting and bullying at home, help your children with conflict resolution. Teach them how to put their feelings into words so they can discuss what is the matter instead of wanting to hit or name-call. In order to do this, parents must model the desired behavior themselves. Parents who have been guilty of name-calling or any kind of hitting must stop it. If a parent can do it, why can't a child? If a child calls another a bad name, remind the child that there will be no name-calling allowed in their home any longer. Instead, say "Tell your brother what's bothering you!" If children don't have a chance to air their grievances, frustration and anger builds up inside them and then they may act out by teasing, taunting and bullying. Allowing them to vent their anger and frustrations is an important step in making everyone feel better.

Giving children the confidence that they can find other ways besides teasing and taunting to resolve their differences is important. They need to understand that they each have hidden strengths they haven't yet developed. A child may tell a parent, "'He's making ugly faces. I'm scared!' Instead of viewing the child as a victim, a parent can help her see her potential strength. 'I'll bet you could make a really ugly face back at him if you wanted to.'"[7] Remind a child who has a self-image of being mean, that he has a gentle side, too.

Sometimes translating behaviors for your children helps. If a little child is teasing a big sister while she is doing her homework, the reason may be that the little one just wants some attention. Explaining this motive to the big sister might encourage her to promise to play with her younger brother if he will leave her alone long enough to finish her homework.

The important thing is to keep the communication open between the children and between parents and children. Parents must always intervene if one child abuses another physically or mentally. Intervening does not solve the problem, settle the dispute or take sides, but keeps the lines of communication open. If a parent gets involved in solving their problems, children will always want the parent to get involved. When children take responsibility for settling their own arguments, arguments lessen.

Parents must take their children's safety seriously. Some parents ignore or under react to taunting and bullying in the home because they feel these are "normal" behaviors between siblings. While such behaviors may be common in families, they are not to be condoned in any way.

The authors of *Siblings Without Rivalry* suggest five steps in helping children resolve disputes:

1. Start by acknowledging the children's anger toward each other. That alone should help calm them.
2. Listen to each child's side with respect.
3. Show appreciation for the difficulty of the problem.
4. Express faith in their ability to work out a mutually agreeable solution.
5. Leave the room.[8]

Most important, members of a family need to establish new norms about which behaviors will be tolerated and which behaviors will not. Physical roughhousing as well as tickling should only be allowed if both parties are enjoying it.

What are the results of sibling teasing and bullying later in life? Dr. Sandy Graham-Berman, a clinical psychologist at the University of Michigan, after conducting two studies, warns parents: "Sibling conflict that is out of control harms social and emotional development."[9]

On the other hand, there are some who will insist that surviving sibling teasing can have positive effects. Forty-year-old Abby, just getting married for the first time, confides, "I was the youngest child and the only girl in a family of five older brothers. They teased me unmercifully. I spent my entire life trying to defend myself and stand up for myself. I am now a very successful business consultant with a master's degree in psychology from Harvard. I think my conflict with my brothers helped me become the very positive, assertive and ambitious person I am today."

Perhaps we can rationalize experiences like these and say that only children, who have not benefited by the experiences of sibling rivalry and sibling teasing, have problems of their own. If an only child has not ever been teased by his parents, he may feel confused when he enters school and experiences the school culture of teasing.

# 19

## Children with Disabilities and Teasing

*Mocking laughter from behind me. Then a voice. "Yeah, he's in the Dummies' class. Aren't you, Rice?" A fist punches my shoulder. "You got no brain between your ears. Just rice."* [1]

William Bell, *The Cripples' Club*

Unfortunately, being different provides a motivation for being the victim of teasing. There are many types of disabilities that would put a child at risk for being teased. These include: cancer; learning disabilities; blindness, deafness, or mental retardation; severe physical trauma such as scarring and deformities; arthritis or muscular diseases; being wheelchairbound; emotional or mental illness; and chronic diseases such as asthma, diabetes, and epilepsy/seizures; as well as others.

Most children who tease and taunt other children with disabilities do so because they:

1.    Lack understanding of the physical condition of the individual.

2.    Are unable to see the person as an individual with feelings.

3.  Fear that the disabled person's condition could happen to them and they would be unable to manage their lives in the disabled state.

An excellent way to help children deal with the disabilities of others is offered by the "Understanding Handicaps" program,[2] a disability awareness curriculum originally developed by Understand Handicaps of Newton, Inc. for students in the Newton, Massachusetts public schools. This program is currently serving approximately 870 Newton fourth graders in fifteen elementary schools.

The goals of the Understanding Handicaps program are:

1.  To recognize the commonalities in us all.

2.  To help children understand that a disabling condition is only one of many traits that help to make a person the individual that he or she is. We learn more from what we can do than from what we cannot do.

3.  To help children understand that every person is unique and that no one person is affected by his own disability exactly like anyone else.

4.  To help children avoid the use of pejorative labels that destroy an individual's self-esteem. When one person labels another it hurts because it reduces the labeled person to just one characteristic which is his disability. Instead of saying "that blind girl," it is better to say "that girl who is blind." People have disabilities. Disabilities are not people. It isn't a fair or accurate portrayal to pigeonhole a group of children when there is so much individuality in every group.

5.  To foster informed, helpful and respectful responses to people with disabilities by educating children about various disabilities through use of a wide variety of materials and activities.

6.  To introduce children to adult guest speakers who have the various disabilities discussed in the Understanding Handicaps program. The guest speakers tell the children about their disabilities and how their disabilities affect them, how they adapt and function according to their personal needs, and answer questions.

# Children with Disabilities and Teasing

7.    To simulate various disabilities with hands-on and adaptive activities for the children so they will gain respect and empathy for handicapped individuals.

This chapter will limit the discussion of teasing and taunting children with disabilities to children with cancer and leukemia, children with learning disabilities and children who are blind. A discussion of the teasing which may occur when children have these particular disabilities will hopefully help the reader to be sensitive to the kinds of teasing that children with other types of disabilities might experience.

## CHILDREN WITH CANCER, INCLUDING LEUKEMIA, AND TEASING

While treatments for cancer are greatly improving, enabling more and more children to go into remission and return to school, cancer is still a disease of mystery, fear, misconceptions and misinformation. When children are confronted by things they are afraid of and don't understand, unwelcome teasing and taunting can occur. Kids who return to school after cancer treatment are worried about a lot of different things. They worry about being teased for their appearance or disabilities—baldness, weight gain or weight loss, surgical scars. They may also worry about any nausea they may have at school. These children may fear that they will fall behind in their schoolwork and be unable to catch up. Their own continued good health is a major source of concern as well as any physical limitations, risk of injury or infection or illness they may incur at school.

According to psychologist Nancy Frumer Styron, "Kids who have cancer don't get teased as much as we think they would, but the kids will anticipate and worry a great deal about getting teased. Sometimes the teasing just doesn't happen."

The Dana Farber Cancer Institute in Boston where Styron practices conducts a school reentry program for children with cancer where a nurse and staff person go to the child's school, talk to the class, and give out information. The purpose is to ease the anxiety for the class as well as the child coming back. Classmates get a chance to ask questions such as, "Can I catch it?" "Is he going to die?" "What's a tumor?" "What does his pretend leg feel like?" and "Will he die in school?" The child with cancer may attend the session or choose not to. The program is not presented if the child does not want it.

An example of a child with cancer not being teased is found in the story of Ian O'Gorman's return to school after surgery to remove a malignancy from his small intestine. Ian's chemotherapy treatment resulted in baldness, and his classmates' reaction was described in *People* magazine. "The Bald Eagles were born when thirteen of his friends and one fifty-year-old teacher at Lake Elementary School in Vista, California, shaved their heads in solidarity. 'We didn't want him to feel left out,' said fellow fifth grader Erik Holzhauer.'"[3]

Some children return to school in a weakened condition. This happens when a child is in the hospital and can only come back to school periodically. The adjustment to schoolwork and school itself can take a toll on a child both physically and emotionally. Some take medicine and feel nauseous from it. Some kids are unable to do what other kids can do or are too tired to make it through the day. Some kids can only go half a day. They may have chemotherapy Monday, come back to school on Tuesday feeling nauseous, but then feel okay on Wednesday. They may have to be out for three weeks if they catch chicken pox or whooping cough because their immune systems are weakened. Much depends on how old the child is, what type of cancer he has and what kind of treatment he is getting.

Dorothy and Sheila Ross advised children with leukemia returning to school about how to handle bullying if it occurs:

1.    "The first principle concerns the characteristics of bullies. . . . Usually a bully only picks on children whom he thinks cannot, or will not strike back. The bully expects his victim to

show discomfort or cry, endure the teasing in silence, or with-draw. If the victim retaliates in kind, the bully usually will stop and seek out another, more satisfying victim. This change in the bully's behavior may not occur until the second retaliation because the bully may view the first counterattack as a fluke. It is essential to prepare the target child for this possibility and to emphasize that it is highly unlikely that he will continue to be harassed after the second attack."

2.     "The second principle concerns the fact that one's own behavior is often a major determinant of others' behavior, specif-ically, that how a child acts about his physical appearance will, to a great extent, determine how others react to him. The child who exhibits obvious discomfort or embarrassment . . . is tacitly invit-ing negative reactions, such as teasing, from his peers. It follows that one solution to being teased is to change one's outward behavior about the characteristic that has elicited the teasing response from others."[4]

The Rosses have developed several aggressive verbal strategies to help children with cancer who may be bullied when they return to school. One of their excellent tactics is to use words to show that the child is really the boss. The child should say to the teaser, "'Okay, X, I want to see you here tomorrow so we can talk some more about my [focus of teasing]. See you tomorrow.' [Point at teaser.] 'Now, don't forget.' Note that when the instructions say 'point' this means an aggressive, jabbing (but not touching) movement with the forefinger. If the teaser is a boy, the target child should use his last name when talking to him"[5] because last names sound tougher, as do actual first names such as Margaret for a girl, instead of Maggie.

The second of the Rosses' strategies is to use words to topple the teaser and gain a superior position. The child can say, "'X, you remind me of someone.' [Pause. Look thoughtful.] 'Now, who in the world is like X? I got it. Kindergarten kids sound like that. Say it [teasing statement] again, X. I want to hear you say all that baby stuff again.' Call to some of your friends, saying, 'Come and listen to X, he says this every day. Everyone, listen now. Okay, X, say it nicely.'"[6]

The Rosses also suggest that the child can use the teaser's own words to make the teaser look foolish. "Keep asking the teaser, 'What did you say? What did you say?' Then when he stops, say, 'That was good work, X, you said it four times for me. Come back tomorrow and I'll let you say it four more times.'"[7]

Another technique of the Rosses is to try to make the teaser look incompetent. For example, in helping leukemic youngsters who are returning to school bald, they suggest, "A *general* response here is, 'X, you said that [teasing focus] yesterday. Don't you know any other words? You need a lot of help. Ask your mom to teach you a new word about baldness tonight, then you can say it for me tomorrow.' *Specific* responses should also be used. For the taunt, 'You've got leukemia, you're going to die,' the child may want to say the following to underline the teaser's incompetence: 'X, you just don't know the right words. You don't talk about going to die, you say *terminal.* Now let's hear you say it again *properly.*'"[8]

Another strategy is to make an asset of the teasing topic. For example, "*Baldness*: 'If it just stays this way till Halloween I'm going trick and treating as E.T.' (Telly Savalas, Yul Brynner—pick the most appropriate.) 'It's the only time in my whole life that I could wash my hair in ten seconds.' *Paleness*: 'If it just stays like this till Halloween I can be an instant ghost.' 'If I could get on a television commercial for taking iron pills, I could get rich on this.'"[9]

If the person continues to taunt or bully, the child can advise him or her that the type of behavior they are showing is not allowed in school and if the person keeps it up, the child will have to tell on them.

If the person still doesn't listen or respond positively, the child should stay away from an argument and end the discussion. This means that the person is not being reasonable.

# Children with Disabilities and Teasing

## CHILDREN WITH LEARNING DISABILITIES AND TEASING

Psychologist Nancy Papagno advises that, "Some children with learning disabilities will be teased by other kids who, trying to be cool, will rank on them. 'Why are you in that retard class?' Often, learning disabled kids, who by definition have average intelligence, will hear this. The teasers are trying to make themselves feel better. 'I need ways to make me feel better. I'll feel better if you feel lousy.' Others will think, 'I'm cool.' This kind of teaser does not always work for an audience. This teaser can tease independently. He may tease and be cool among the kids, but he may stalk the kid away from the audience. This teaser is on a power trip. We had a child who suffered from facial grimaces, a kind of tic disorder, and a few of the other kids would make fun of him."

Special Needs teacher Nancy Rhodes states that sometimes teachers will set their special needs children up for being teased. "Teachers may shout out the weakness of a child in front of his peers so their peers would know there was something different about them. For example, some children are slow at processing information and need to think through the question before they answer. The teacher needs to say to that child, 'You think about it. I'll get back to you.' A teacher who lacks insight may stare at the child waiting for the answer. This is humiliating to the child. The teacher is unable to empathize, as he or she has never been in that situation. This teacher has set the child up for being teased.

"Another way teachers set kids up for being teased," Mrs. Rhodes continues, "is the way they group them. The strongest, most assertive child in the group will often pick the task he wants to do, leaving the other children to scramble for the less popular chores. The learning disabled child might then get stuck with the job which is his weakness, such as writing, and then he looks bad to the other kids. It's best to place a learning disabled child in a democratic group where the kids are taught to take turns with various chores.

# Teasing

"Still another way to help kids is to always change how the picking of the 'firsts' is done. There is often tremendous pressure on kids to be picked first, both by the teacher and by his teammates. Kids must somehow learn that firsts are not always so important, whether in the classroom or on the athletic field."

A related problem occurs when children are allowed to pick partners for various activities. A child who is isolated, rejected, unassertive or learning disabled may be left without a partner. This is most painful in middle school when teachers are less likely to choose partners for kids. Sometimes if a child is left out, the teacher will say, "Okay, you can join that pair over there." Now that pair has three kids and invites inappropriate comments. Sometimes if a child is left out, the teacher will say, "You can be my partner," which is even worse.

When my husband Alec was eight years old and away at camp, he was hit on the head by a horseshoe while he was attempting to take a shortcut across a field. He became unconscious and was taken to the hospital where his head received eleven stitches.

As a result of that accident, my husband appeared to be slow when he returned to school. His mother took him to Children's Hospital in Boston where a neurologist told her that the accident had caused Alec to be retarded and that he would probably never graduate from high school.

When his second grade teacher recommended that he repeat the grade, his mother enrolled him in private school. There, a gifted, interested teacher realized that Alec couldn't read because he had forgotten the alphabet which he had learned before his head injury. After she retaught him the alphabet, he eventually caught up to the other kids and rejoined his former classmates in public school.

The elementary school years were difficult for Alec emotionally as well as physically. "I had trouble following other people's thoughts. I said disjointed things. I appeared stupid and was teased about being stupid continually. Every kid who wanted to make himself feel better would call me 'Dummy.' I decided I'd better get to be good in sports if I wanted any respect. That was the only real advantage to what happened to me. I began to excel in sports. My big brother was the only kid who didn't make fun of me. I think it's because he felt sorry for me." My husband now has a Ph.D. in physics!

## BLIND CHILDREN AND TEASING

Since so much of childhood teasing is visual, making fun of children who are too short, too fat or have pimples, I was personally very curious to find out if blind children tease each other and, if so, what they tease each other about. To research this, I interviewed James Callanan, a counselor at the Carroll Center for the Blind. The center runs programs for teenagers, as well as adults, in life skills such as Braille, computer, mobility training, making choices, learning to take care of oneself, and socialization.

Mr. Callanan advised me that a child who is the only legally blind student in a public school may be teased by the other students. He may be called names such as, "Blinkie" and "Four Eyes," or labeled "That blind boy" or "That blind girl." The blind child may feel he doesn't have enough friends. He may be overprotected by his parents and not allowed to do things that his sighted siblings are allowed to do. The blind student in high school will miss such activities as getting his driver's license and having a part-time job in a fast food restaurant or a gas station like the other kids. Blind children encounter a lot of people talking about them in their presence as if they weren't there, for example, "What does he want?" instead of just asking the blind child himself.

Blind children, like children with any other physical challenge, want to appear "normal." Consequently, many blind children do not like to use canes or other available aids such as telescopes or monocular scopes which are used for reading print on street signs, or special glasses to enable them to see the blackboard in school. Mr. Callanan says some of the blind children he has worked with have "passed" for years as being sighted because they haven't used their aids. The blind children who "pass" often are those who constantly bump into things, or drop something and then can't find it.

Blind children will often form small groups which exclude others and will tease other blind children who don't fit into their own category. There are different degrees of blindness. There are those who are congenitally blind and those blind since birth who cannot see at all. There are also "adventitiously" blind people, mostly adults, who became blind due to a disease like diabetes or an accident. There are also legally blind people (those with vision less than 2/200) who have some usable low vision and can see shapes and colors. Often the adventitiously blind will integrate with the congenitally blind. Sometimes there may be a small group composed only of children who are totally blind. The less mature children may hang out together. Blind children who have more skills, leadership and athletic, are more active and may also band together. Then there may be groups for children who are more intellectual or groups for kids who have more vision.

Sometimes, at the Carroll Center, a child with low vision will meet a totally blind child for the first time and feel threatened. The low vision child may use name-calling against the totally blind child or complain about the totally blind child in order to distance himself from the child.

Some blind children do not yet have good social boundaries and they will be teased about them. Some of them are inexperienced in making friends and may try to get too close to a new person too soon, instead of building a relationship gradually. A particular blind child may not have good social boundaries because he is simply desperate to make new friends.

A blind child who participates in a residential program for a number of weeks may feel free from his parental restrictions. He may also feel he can act out by staying up late, hanging out with other kids and listening to loud music.

A blind child may have a romantic relationship with another blind child. Although they may not be able to see each other, one will ask sighted friends if the other is pretty and desirable. Sometimes it happens that after twenty-four or forty-eight hours as a pair they cannot stand one another. If this happens, they may be teased for their fickleness. This is interesting because, in the sighted world, many couples are bound together by nothing more than visual physical attraction.

Some blind children will bully each other. They say things like, "This is my seat. . . . This is my group. . . . This is the show I want to watch."

Some blind children will get teased for what they wear. A blind child may not be able to see what he's wearing, but he knows if it's good or bad, or in style, or if it matches. Blind children want to wear the same fashionable jeans and sneakers that sighted children prefer. They will use their senses of smell, touch, and hearing, and they will ask questions in order to know what's cool.

Some blind children will tease each other for being very immature or silly, for drooling, or for being too talkative. They may be teased if they cannot think in the abstract but only in the concrete. Some blind children will be teased for the rocking mannerisms and the "eye-poking" (thumb knuckle in the eye and rubbing) that are common to blind people. Some blind children will grimace or smile at inappropriate times, or "parrot talk" which means they will say a couple of your words right back to you. Some of the children talk too much and do not listen enough. Some will talk too loudly and be unaware that they are drawing attention to themselves. Then they will be teased for it.

There is always the possibility that any mental health problems of a blind person may be overlooked due to the emphasis placed on his blindness. A blind person who suffers depression or manic-depression or the ritualistic thinking of an obsessive-compulsive may not be diagnosed.

# Teasing

While some blind children may be desperate to make friends, there is a danger that other blind children or blind adults will isolate themselves in their world of electronic gadgets. Many blind children are heavily into stereos, compact disks, computers, telephones and the Internet. Mr. Callanan calls these kids "the wireheads." The computers have become their friends.

Blind children may tease each other because they have difficulty handling confrontations. There is the possibility that they have been overprotected by their families, thus, they may not be used to doing things on their own. Blind children might have trouble with their assertiveness, especially with those in authority such as employers. Some blind people have what Mr. Callanan calls the Pearl Harbor Syndrome. This is when anger causes the person to explode and then run out of the room. At the Carroll Center there are special programs for assertiveness training, to help with personal empowerment, the development of self-esteem and conveying feelings. These are difficult skills for anyone to master, sighted or blind, but especially so for the blind who may suffer other losses in addition to their vision. Reverend Thomas J. Carroll, founder of the center, documented the twenty losses of blindness, some of which include: the loss of physical integrity, confidence in the remaining senses, reality contact with environment, ease of written communication, social adequacy, and self-esteem.[10] Vision helps to ground a person. Vision affects balance. Vision is like the gyroscope of the human body. Without vision, a person may feel like he doesn't fit physically anywhere.

Some blind people make light of their lack of vision by saying that blindness is an "inconvenience." Mr. Callanan doesn't believe that. He thinks if a blind person believes such a rationalization they are into denial, even if they are congenitally and totally blind and do not mourn their loss of vision the same way an adventitiously blind person would mourn the loss of theirs. Mr. Callanan believes that when you face your challenge and adjust to it, you empower yourself. He thinks the experience of being blind must more resemble that of a blind teacher who said, "Some days I like being blind. Some days I hate being blind. Some days I forget I'm blind."

## CHILDREN WITH OTHER DISABILITIES AND TEASING

Children with other disabilities may get teased. Some kids have arm or leg amputations and other physical changes. Some may be coping with protheses of various types. Children who take steroids may appear bloated. A child may also appear skinny, heavy or pale. Other kids with handicaps who may be teased include those with diabetes, kids on dialysis, or those with food allergies. Children may be teased due to any unusual paraphernalia they must utilize such as cane, crutches and wheelchairs.

Dr. Styron, the psychologist, adds, "I knew a kid who got teased for wearing hearing aids. 'How come you have to wear those dumb things in your ears?' The teacher spent the whole day telling the class that we all have differences. Some kids wear glasses, some have different color hair. Some differences are what we look like, some are how we hear or how we see or how we learn. Everybody is different, but we just all have different ways of manifesting that."

An excellent resource for parents and teachers on being different is *It's O.K. to Be Different* by Dr. Mitch Golant with Bob Crane. It is a Tom Doherty Associates Book and was published in New York in 1988.

# 20

## Children Teasing Adults

*Speak roughly to your little boy,*
*And beat him when he sneezes:*
*He only does it to annoy,*
*Because he knows it teases.*[1]

Lewis Carroll

I looked in the refrigerator and announced to my family, "Well guys, I'd better go to the supermarket. We're down to the bare bones in the refrigerator."

"What?" my spoiled seven-year-old questioned. "You mean all there is to eat in this house is bones?"

Hey, are we the Addams family or what?

When children tease adults, they are primarily trying to gain attention, play, flirt, rebel, annoy or create mischief. Rarely are children trying to be mean to adults. Most young children don't yet have the intellect to be ambiguous or sarcastic. Children love to tease adults because they get to turn the tables on the people who are usually in command. Teasing makes kids feel in charge. The end result of all teasing behaviors is that

# Children Teasing Adults

children feel powerful because they caused a reaction.

It is healthy for children to playfully tease adults. Their teasing demonstrates they are assertive, competitive, and have a sense of humor. It also shows they feel safe and accepted by the adults they choose to tease.

One day I announced a treasure hunt in our house for my green eyeglasses which I had lost. Jenny, then five years old, came running to me and screamed, "I found them! I found them!" What she had in fact found and presented to me were her pair of little girl's green sunglasses. Jenny thought this tease was a scream.

A favorite way children like to tease adults is by mimicking them. This occurs when you ask a child a question and he asks it right back to you, or you scratch your head and he scratches his. Children will keep it up until the adult turns blue! Children also mimic each other. They can be very persistent at it and continue for long periods of time. Children also like to make funny faces at grownups, especially faces that resemble the grownup's.

Kids have more patience than adults and seem to thrive on repetition. They love to play "Knock, knock. Who's there?" over and over until it becomes a tease and they decline to stop. They love to sing songs which annoy the grownups by going on too long, such as "Ninety-nine Bottles of Beer on the Wall" or "The Song that Never Ends." They will often carry on until you are practically screaming for them to stop.

Little children love to drive the adults crazy with the tease of continually asking, "Why?" "Why does this happen, Mommy?" Even if you give a reasonably good answer and you are proud of yourself, they continue to ask, "Why?" The kids will keep this up as long as you let them, or, that is, until you distract them or change the subject.

The other single word kids love to tease with is no. "It's time for your bath." "No." "It's time to get ready for bed!" "No." This type of mild misbehavior, if seen as a form of teasing, is perceived as less aggravating by parents. When my little one does this to me, I ask her "Are you teasing me?" She admits that she is and feels guilty because teasing has a bad name with kids.

Kids absolutely thrive on the tease of annoyance. They will untie your shoes when you are not looking or hide your belongings. They will sneak extra junk food and then laugh when caught. Kids also love to ring doorbells and hide.

Children learn from adults which flaws are permissible to tease grownups about by copying them. My husband can't spell without the spelling utility on the computer, and I love to tease him about that. Spelling is the one thing I can clearly do better than he. Marissa loves to copy me when I tease her father about this. She loves to remind him that she was spelling better than he when she was in third grade. I also feel safe in teasing my husband about his hair loss because he knows I think he is so handsome. Occasionally, he will look at the thick hair of our daughters and say, "I'd kill for your hair!" The children will laugh and answer back, "Oh, Daddy, you'd kill for anybody's hair!"

Kids also love to tease their parents about their inadequacies. As the mommy in our house, I can be very controlling. I felt obligated to teach Marissa what controlling means so she will be on to me. Sometimes when I ask my teenager Marissa to do something, she smiles and says, "You're being controlling, Mom. But I'll do it." When I tell six-year-old Jenny to do something, she'll sometimes tease me with, "Give me one reason why I should!" "So I won't come get you and tickle you all over, that's why!" I tease back. Jenny laughs her little head off. The kids will also tease me about frequently losing my keys, my pocketbook and the hairbrush. It was hard to find things in our last home because it was one floor built around a large circular hallway. When I would start to search for something, Marissa would call out, "Walking around in circles again, Mom?" This drove me crazy.

Thirty-five-year-old Brenda confessed that her five-year-old son had learned how to tease by copying his father, and now she is the target of both of them. "Instead of complimenting me directly, my son will say, 'Nice shirt!' with a snort and a raise of the eyebrow. This kid is such a sponge. When he saw me trying to cream off my blond moustache, he said, 'Nice moustache, Mom!'"

Kids also love to tease grownups after the grownups criticize each other in order to rub in the insult. After I scolded my husband for not wrapping up the cheese properly, our kids started shouting in unison, "You ruined the cheese! You ruined the cheese!" This makes kids feel powerful since they are used to being on the receiving end of criticism. Kids love it when adults get into trouble as long as the trouble is not personally threatening to them.

There are obviously exceptions to those children who don't mean any harm by their teasing. There are those young children who excel in playing practical jokes on their parents, teachers and others. I should know because I married one of those practical jokers while he was still growing up.

When my husband was eight and his big brother was eleven, they were left with a new housekeeper while their young widowed mother went on a vacation to Florida. They didn't like the housekeeper who had only been with them three days when their mother left for vacation. Neither did they like being left behind.

They decided to play tricks on the housekeeper. They went to sleep and set their alarm clocks to wake them up at 3:00 A.M. They crept outside and reached up with a broomstick to bang on the housekeeper's bedroom window to wake her up. She screamed and went to the telephone in the house to call the police. The boys had rigged the nearest phone so that a cap would go off when she picked it up. She screamed again and then the boys screamed, too. She finally called the police who figured out pretty quickly that she was not in any mortal danger. The police had to telephone the boys' mother in Florida, who then had to come home because the housekeeper refused to stay with the boys any longer. Mission accomplished.

There are some children who will attempt to bully their parents. Do not allow your child to bully you. The problem will not go away by itself. The putdowns kids target towards adults will accelerate like spouse abuse. The victim of spouse abuse will often tell us that at first her husband was civil, then he progressed to name-calling and that she accepted this. Then he became pushy with a slap and then a beating. The same thing happens with kids who are abusive towards adults. Kids will cross the line, talk back and then become more abusive to the parent or teacher. Unfortunately, there seems to be a higher level of acceptance by teachers and parents of bad behavior than in past years. Parents have lost control when their children bully them, especially if the bullying by the child turns physical. There are many parents with bruises or worse inflicted on them by their children. Although it may be embarrassing and shameful to admit a loss of control over a child, parents must seek professional help immediately for their own good as well as the good of their child. The parent must realize that, if the child has lost control in his own home with people who care for him, the child will get into even more serious trouble outside the home.

# 21

## Adults Teasing Children

*Those that teach each other, love each other.*[1]

German Proverb

Almost all adults will tease children occasionally. This sort of occasional teasing can be very playful—a way to give a child love, affection and attention. Teasing can be a way to find a common ground with a child, and a way to show interest in the child and his world.

Some adults will try to display an interest in their children's toys and games by teasing. "That stuffy is mine!" says the parent. "No. It's mine!" the child insists. "Who's going to have all the fun today?" asks the parent. "Me!" proclaims the child. When the child catches on, he will respond, "You can't have any fun today! You have to go to work and make the money so we can buy toys and ice cream!" "Humph!" replies the parent in mock indignation.

What we term "reverse psychology" is actually a type of teasing we use to help children behave and to manipulate them. When my oldest was four years old and tried to play hide-and-

seek in the department stores, nothing worked better than calling out, "Bye, Marissa! We'll see you again some day, I hope!"
She'd come running every time. With my youngest child, Jenny,
if you wanted a hug or a kiss and she refused, all you had to say
was, "Don't kiss me and don't hug me. I don't like kisses anyway." It worked every time.

Sometimes reverse psychology enables adults to trick children. I still feel very guilty for the time I teased Jenny by trick-
ing her while we played cards. We played "Crazy 8's" and Jenny
got lucky and picked up an eight from the deck. "Please don't
change it to spades!" I pleaded. Jenny fell for it hook, line and
sinker. She changed it to spades. I unloaded my spade and won
the game. Poor Jenny! She got really mad at me and left the
room. She refused to play with her big bully mother anymore. I
knew I was wrong. The therapist in me recognized that my poor
daughter might never trust me or any other grownup again.
Thankfully, things smoothed over.

Of course, the same kind of teasing strategies will not
have a positive outcome with every child. Each parent must find
out what works for each of his own children. Each child will
respond to the tease of a particular grownup in a different way.
Many factors come into play here such as, the age and sex of the
child, the child's birth order in the family, the state of the relationship with the adult, as well as what occurred that day in addition to the teasing. In our family, I notice that Jenny responds
better to her father's teasing than our oldest daughter at Jenny's
age. This may simply be due to their personalities or temperament, but I believe that their birth order may have a greater influence. When my oldest was six years old, there were no other
children in the house, and the only person who teased her was
her father. My youngest has had a totally different family experience because of her older sister who sometimes teases her. She is
more used to teasing and other types of conflict than was her
older sister and so she is better equipped to handle them.

When parents encourage a child's belief in Santa Claus or

# Adults Teasing Children

the Tooth Fairy, this is one of the most benign forms of teasing. We are teasing the child with the lie in order to aid in the continuation of the child's innocence. Innocence is a belief in magic, that life is fair and we will always be rewarded for being good. Sometimes we encourage a child to believe in Santa because we need to believe in something ourselves. When Jenny was five, we took her to see the new version of *Miracle on 34th Street*. Just before the movie started, Jenny announced to the rest of her family (and all the children sitting around us) that there was no such thing as Santa Claus, that Santa Claus was really your parents who buy you presents. I was saddened by this because I was not yet ready to give up Santa Claus myself! When I was a child, my Jewish parents celebrated Chanukah and also gave us Christmas stockings, so we have done the same with our children. I love helping Jenny write letters to Santa and setting out the food for him. By the end of the movie, Jenny was almost a believer again. After she saw Tim Allen's version of *Santa Clause*, she decided there was a Santa Claus after all. Whew! Saved by Hollywood!

The Tooth Fairy is almost as much fun as Santa Claus. We tease Jenny that the tooth fairy leaves the most money for the first tooth that falls out of a child's mouth (two dollars), and it is downhill after that.

In our house, little children are told that kisses from mommies make children big and sugar makes them little. Is this lying to a child? I prefer to say it is teasing to get the desired response—more interest in affection and less interest in eating candy.

In order to let Jenny know how special she is and how much I appreciate her, I will ask her once in awhile to please not get any bigger. "Jenny, please stay six years old forever! Six-year-olds are the cutest, most wonderful children in the world." She will inevitably respond, "Mommy, stop teasing me. You know I have to grow. Besides, you said the same thing to me when I was five and Marissa said you say the same thing to her every year of her life!" I hate kids who are smarter than I am! Don't you?

Teasing can also be just a funny way to play. When five-year-old Sam and his friends ask Sam's mother, "What's for lunch?" she will reply, "Elephant stew!" The children enjoy the element of surprise and then they realize that she was only teasing. I'll ask Jenny what she would like to drink with lunch. "Water. I mean . . . water," she'll respond. "Jenny," I tease, "Is water-I-mean-water better than regular water?" My reward is a hysterical giggle.

When one lets a child win the game this is another form of teasing, but the tease is usually meant with love. You race down the street huffing and puffing, and your little child beats you every time! Your child is ecstatic! He feels strong and powerful. You deliberately make a wrong move in checkers, and your kid double jumps you with glee!

Like some adults, some children love to be scared, especially by a loving parent. Sometimes parents and their kids will play hide-and-seek and then jump out and scare each other. Children especially love the tease of scary stories that give them goose bumps. They prefer a controlled scare where they know for sure that the characters will get out of danger in the end. It helps if there are good adults in the stories and not just villains. Obviously, children may be traumatized by a frightening book, movie or television program and may suffer nightmares and insecurities as a result. Parents must try to be aware of what their children watch. Take the fears of your children seriously. When Jenny was five we had to walk out of *The Pagemaster* movie. She was too scared. Jenny commented, "There should be a sign that says you have to be bigger than five years old to see this movie!"

Sometimes my teenage daughter's room begins to resemble the set of the play *Live Like Pigs*. If I am in a good mood, I might say, "Your room couldn't possibly be this messy. I must be imagining it, right?" "Right, mom!" is her guaranteed and grateful response and then she hurriedly straightens it up. My teasing approach gets the point across while defusing the situation. Please don't ask me what I say about her mess when I'm not in a good mood. The same approach works with other types of behavior. "No children of mine would fight like that. I must be imagining this!" This will often get them laughing instead of fighting.

There are other ways of defusing a situation where a child may be making demands by using teasing. Eve shared, "Sometimes first thing in the morning my son will say, 'Mom, can you get me that? Can you buy me this?' So at 8:00 A.M. I'll say, 'I'll go get it right now. Do you want me to go out and get it now?' My son is still in his pajamas. 'Mom, you're teasing me!' It is my way of sending a message without sending it in a sharp way."

Sometimes I tease Jenny to try to cheer her up. Small children always bump into things, like the rear view mirrors attached to cars. If Jenny cries after a bump, I might say, "I have an idea! Let's have a bumping contest. I bet you'd win!" Or, "How about having a contest to see who has the most black and blue marks on their legs. Do you think you'd win?" "Of course!" she replies in a fit of giggles.

Parents do have to be careful that by teasing their children they are not unwittingly setting their kids up for tortuous teasing by other kids. "Did someone mention nicknames? . . . I am convinced that my own Inner Child will never recover from the fact that my parents unwittingly gave me a nickname that subjected me to such relentless teasing through my teens that even now, years after the word has passed from general use, I cannot, in this public space, bring myself to reveal it. I suspect that virtually everyone was saddled with some similar defect that other children—who have radar for such things—could exploit for their own merrymaking."[2]

What should be off-limits in teasing children is teasing the child about any very sensitive area, such as his or her sex. A short-haired little girl dressed in jeans might look like a little boy to a casual stranger. If the stranger addresses her as a boy and the child corrects the stranger and the stranger insists in a teasing way that she is a boy and hurts the child's feelings, serious harm can be done to the child.

Another very sensitive area most children do not like to be teased about is their age-related habits, such as bed-wetting, thumb-sucking and temper tantrums. If you accuse the child of being a baby because of these habits, your words may backfire. When you tell her she is a baby, she may feel sad, angry and insecure and may wet the bed even more, need the comfort of her thumb even more, or want to scream even more. Try to say, "'I think you can do better' rather than 'How could you be such a baby?'"[3]

Parents also have to be careful about teasing in front of their children's friends. Thirty-five-year-old Sally reminisces, "It was sometimes very embarrassing for me to have a father who was such a tease. Take the situation where my dad would take me and my friends out for ice cream. When the person sitting next to my dad wasn't looking, Dad would grab her dish of ice cream and hide it on his lap. He thought this was hysterically funny, but his behavior seemed very immature and embarrassing to me. I know he was just trying to find a way to connect, to be included. Thankfully, he stopped doing this as I got older or I would have been afraid that my friends would have thought he was flirting with them! I know my father got his teasing from his father, but that didn't make it any easier."

There are many adults whose sole way of relating to children is by teasing them. I call these people Chronics. People become Chronics for many reasons. I believe most Chronics are actually afraid of children in the same way that some people become anxious around unpredictable, energetic cats who leap about a room. Chronics are afraid of the demands and reactions of little people, afraid of saying or doing the wrong thing. They cannot imagine communicating with children as one would communicate with adults, so they tease them. It is their way of making a connection to children.

Chances are, Chronics were teased continually themselves when they were children, thus, they repeat the pattern. They may never have actually engaged in adult-child conversations in their lives because they never learned how to talk with children, or if they did, may have long since forgotten. It may be that Chronics have long forgotten their own childhoods as well, or at least have forgotten that youngsters have feelings and insecurities, too—just like adults.

Some Chronics tease children because they wouldn't dare pick on anybody their own size! If teasing is a way to communicate in a dominant way, what could be simpler than teasing a little kid? Some people do unleash their pent up aggressions in this manner. This is the grownup version of being a bully.

Some Chronics will tease little children to impress the audience surrounding them. When I was little, the old joke was, "What color is your father's blue necktie?" Invariably, the little boy would proudly answer, "Red!" The grownups would laugh and the child would be confused and sad. Jokes made at the expense of children cause children to think that the people are laughing at them because they are stupid—not because they are so cute.

Teasing can also be a positive way of giving adults an insight to kids, a way to be on their wavelength without causing the adults to feel they are intruding into their children's group. In trying to stimulate a conversation between herself and a group of little boys in her carpool, Josey will use teasing to establish rapport. "When my son climbs into the car with his friends, to get the conversation going, I'll say something exaggerated like 'Did you just sit and stare at the ceiling all day?' This puts them off guard. They find themselves interested in talking where they wouldn't normally. Or I'll say, 'You didn't do anything? You just stayed in your room all day. Boy, that's a really crazy way to spend the day!' It's a handle, a way of connecting without being heavy, withing being too interrogative. I feel exaggeration is a form of teasing."

Josey, the mother of a son, insisted that, "Boys are more reluctant to talk about their day than girls. You have to tease more with boys to get them to talk." This sounds like the origins of sexism. This may be how the tradition of teasing gets passed down through families via the male children. Parents may not believe their sons capable of "straight talk." As all mothers of daughters can tell you, it is no easier to talk to female children. I figured out that what was needed were questions that could not be answered by one word, or a yes or a no. (See Chapter 5: Flirting.)

Some parents really do believe that it is necessary to prepare children for the hard times in life by teasing them at home. They believe that when children get to school and get teased, it will seem like no big deal. Working class mothers in a recent study made a point of teasing their children. "The kids were growing up in a tough community," Dr. Peggy Miller of the University of Illinois explained, "where defending yourself was a key to survival."[4]

Unfortunately, the plan to toughen up kids to face the outside world can backfire, and the child can think, "There is just no place for me to go that's safe." Sara Stiansen Mahoney writes, "An adult's idea of gentle teasing often feels like humiliation to a young child. And 'emotional toughening' makes about as much sense as pushing your child around to prepare her for schoolyard bullies."[5] It is best to treat each child on an individual basis.

Parents often use teasing to teach children the nuances of language, says Dr. Peggy Miller. Those who engage their toddlers in a mock chase, saying, "I'm gonna get you!" are inadvertently teaching their children that tone of voice and facial expression are important clues to meaning. Such teasing has very positive social value.[6]

Warm, affectionate teasing can become part of the ritual of a family and even help to define a family. A young mother

# Adults Teasing Children

named Betty shares, "When my son goes to bed, I tell him, 'I have something to tell you! I love you more than all the trucks in front of our house. I love you more than all the sand at'—and then my son interrupts with, 'Cape Cod!' I feel we are playing at teasing with these remarks because our game is repetitive and personal." Every family has their own teasing rituals. Think about yours. Record them in a journal for your children to read when they grow up. This kind of loving teasing is what memories are made of.

# 22

## The Recovering Tease

*Dear, damned, distracting town, farewell:*
*Thy fools no more I'll tease;*
*This year in peace ye critics dwell;*
*Ye harlots, sleep at ease.*[1]

Alexander Pope, *A Farewell to London*

Verbal teasing becomes a bad habit when it interferes with the formation of positive relationships at home, at work and at play. Because teasing makes people feel powerful and in control, the habit can easily become addictive if the teaser lacks power and control in other important areas of her life. Teasing becomes a compulsive addiction if the person becomes a slave to her teasing and uses teasing as a mood changer—to the point where all of her relationships revolve around the vicious circle of teasing communication.

Since teasing promises a short cut to intimacy, it will always appeal to people who have problems handling intimacy. In order to recover from the teasing compulsion, a person has to be willing to explore her feelings about intimacy to try and make conscious either her discomfort with intimacy, her avoidance of

# The Recovering Tease

it, her lack of understanding of intimacy, and/or her admitted total lack of experience with it.

Any exploration of unconscious motivations may be painful as one needs to strip away at least some of one's defenses in order to ask oneself:

"Why can't I tell my wife I love her without making a joke out of it?"

"Why can't I have a discussion about world events with my brother instead of our constantly joking around and teasing each other?"

"Why can't I communicate with my young children in a straightforward manner instead of teasing them to no end?"

"Why can't I watch a love story in the movie theater without cracking jokes for everyone to hear?"

"Why do I tease my secretary when I know she doesn't appreciate my humor?"

I believe that teasing is abundant because it is very difficult for people to be honest about their desires and their imperfections. It is hard to believe that anyone could have unconditional love for us if they really knew us as well as we know ourselves, that we choose to hide behind teasing rather than risk the loss of love or potential love.

It is easy to say that compulsive teasers are immature people, however, I really do not believe that is always the case. Some teasers hold incredibly responsible positions, from being surgeons to chief executive officers of large corporations, where a great many people depend on them. Perhaps it would be safer to say that teasers have a tendency to be silly or are fun-loving creatures. Teasers make a choice to avoid intimacy in favor of lighthearted communication.

Why would anyone avoid intimacy? Intimacy is a risk-taking proposition. If I love you and you don't love me, I'm unhappy. If you love me and I don't love you, then you're unhappy and then you'll be mad at me and then I'll be unhappy. If I love you and you love me, then I will be committed to a long relationship that may bring some discomfort and increased responsibilities at which times I'll be unhappy. No matter what happens, there are risks.

Some people feel that you have to experience pain to feel pleasure. Others would disagree. Perhaps they have already felt pain and they don't feel pleasure is worth it. This is a choice that every individual must make for herself. There is really no right answer here.

Just as a gambler will stop gambling when he has to, rather than when he wants to, a compulsive teaser may be willing to modify her teasing habits when she has to, rather than because she wants to. If the teaser's family and colleagues at work and at play complain frequently enough, the teaser may have the motivation to make some changes in her behavior.

One cannot help but admire the honesty of a person in recovery from any addiction, whether it be alcoholism or teasing. In many ways it's harder to admit you were sick than it is to be sick. To admit a problem also requires acceptance and forgiveness of oneself for being human which is the opposite of striving for perfection. Recovery also requires a complete change in lifestyle and an attempt at honesty and responsibility without blaming others for our problems. Recovery means rebuilding life without being locked into previous attitudes and behavior which encourage compulsive behavior.

A thirty-year-old Englishman confessed to me that he had a problem with intimacy. John said it was the fault of his mother who had never given him a kiss in his whole life. While I'm certain John's mother had a profound influence on his life, once he had made this idea conscious, he could no longer justify being a slave to his history. Okay, so Mama made life difficult, but where do you go from here?

No discussion of recovery makes any sense without a discussion of relapse. Because no one is perfect, relapse is part of recovery. We are going to fail sometimes because we're human

# The Recovering Tease

and because we are susceptible to being teased by our addictions and by teasing communications. It is harder to stay off of an addiction than it is to get off of an addiction. It is the tease of teasing, the temptation, that is the problem. As Oscar Wilde once said, "I can resist anything except temptation."[2]

The biggest mistake people make in recovery is to assume that after a brief time free from their addiction that they are cured. If they think they are cured, then they let down their guard and leave themselves wide open to their favorite tease once again.

In *The Courage to Change*, author Dennis Wholey's words apply just as well to recovering teasers. He says, "What is recovery from alcoholism or drug addiction? It's three things: honesty, sharing, and love. These deal with repeoplization, and to recover from alcoholism and other drug addictions you have to trust people, be honest with people, share with people, and love people. That will get you away from chemical dependence and give you personal accountability."[3]

In order to check the spread of addiction in our society, we have to begin with ourselves. We must examine our own values and beliefs that leave us susceptible to those who would tease us and tempt us with the promise of a quick fix to our problems. Only with self-confidence, self-esteem and true intimacy is it possible to be comfortable in our own bodies and accepting of our own strengths and forgiving of our weaknesses. The answer is found inside each of us.

Perhaps this book will foster an awareness about people who suffer from compulsive teasing. At that point, perhaps we shall see the development of the first Teasers Anonymous meeting, a new twelve-step program. Should this occur, I would give it my blessing and support. As I discuss in my earlier book, *I'm Grieving as Fast as I Can: How to Help Young Widows and Widowers Cope and Heal*,[4] support groups give their members permission for intimacy with one another. This intimacy is generally what those who attend are lacking in their lives. In order to bond completely with another human being, it is often necessary to share a specific goal or suffer from the same plight, such as to overcome an addiction of some sort or to readjust after a trauma, such as a loss. I feel support groups and twelve-step programs offer real intimacy and support from real people.

When the teasing stops, real communication begins. A chance at genuine intimacy occurs. Other problems may start to correct themselves and become resolved. As Joey from Gamblers Anonymous insisted, "When you stop gambling, you do change over time. Every situation in my life when I didn't gamble got resolved. Take the mask off. Just be there. Sure I'm a nicer guy when I am not gambling, but kindness is not the most important thing. The most important thing is not to gamble. We come to change by not putting gambling first." The same could be said for any addiction.

Members of Teasers Anonymous will learn not to deny that their compulsive teasing is an addiction. They would learn not to minimize their addiction by saying, "It's not that bad." Members would obviously be unable to avoid the subject altogether as that would be the purpose of their meeting. However, they would learn to stop blaming others, either for stupidly setting themselves up for a tease, or allowing the teasing. They would cease to rationalize and intellectualize by saying they know others who are worse teasers than they are.

Members of Teasers Anonymous would learn that the urge for a good tease will pass in about twenty minutes. Cravings to tease occur from exposure to people, places, things, as well as feelings and memories the teaser previously associated with teasing. These cravings can be so painful to the recovering teaser that in extreme cases he may change his job, leave his partner and move to a different place in order to avoid relapse. All recovering teasers should learn to expect intense cravings so they can change their old way of responding to them.

The most important thing members of Teasers Anonymous would learn is that abstinence is not the same as recovery. "In the absence of active, concrete prevention efforts, a tendency to relapse emerges automatically. . . . Relapse starts when you stuff uncomfortable feelings or deny stressful circumstances in your life, return to addictive thinking, stop taking actions to cope effectively with problems, stop getting support, use another mood changer, place yourself in a high-risk situation, and so on. Picking up your drug is actually the end point of the relapse, not the beginning."[5]

Members of Teasers Anonymous would learn that being in a bad mood is a great tease to relapse. If you are feeling bad about yourself or your situation, it is very tempting to want to cure that problem in a hurry and participate in a tease again for a quick fix. Negative moods include anger, depression, boredom, loneliness, depression, anxiety, feelings of rejection and loss, and sexual frustration. If possible, the teaser should learn to substitute positive thinking for his negative moods with the help of the twelve step program.

Teasers have to be strong not to be teased back into their teasing addiction. There are many teases which interfere with recovery. Feeling cocky is a tease. Recovering addicts assume that since they have been clean, in this case tease-free, for a while, that they have their addiction thing mastered. It is easy for recoverers to feel safe exposing themselves once again to a favorite poison. The recovering tease who accepts such invitations is denying his wish to end the addiction and doesn't want to assume responsibility for his teasing behavior. Denial is the biggest tease and precedes relapse.

For some, a good tease is a rare effort probably inspired by some naive person who left himself wide open and the teaser couldn't resist taking the plunge. For others, teasing is a hobby. For still others, people teasing is an addictive compulsion. These people are never cured. One tease and the disease starts all over again.

# *Appendix*

RESOURCES FOR TEASING IN CHILDREN'S LITERATURE

The following is a resource list for parents, teachers, counselors, and librarians. These are children's storybooks which have been written to help children better understand teasers as well as themselves.

Berenstein S., and Berenstein, J. The Berenstein *Bears and the Bully*. New York: Random House, 1993.
Sister bear is helped by her brother when she is bullied.

Billington, Elizabeth T. *Part-time Boy*. New York: Frederick Warne & Co., 1980.
A shy child learns to understand himself, learn about animals and make friends with the help of a caring neighbor.

Bosch, C. *Bully on the Bus*. Seattle: Parenting Press, 1988.
Different strategies for handling the bully on the bus.

# Appendix

Bottner, Barbara. *Bootsie Barker Bites*. New York: G.P.
Putnam's Sons, 1992.
Bootsie, a bully who claims to be a dinosaur, threatens to
eat Charlene alive. Charlene learns to defend herself and
scares Bootsie by telling him that she is a paleontologist
who hunts for dinosaur bones.

Brown, Marc. *Arthur's Eyes*. Boston: Little, Brown & Co., 1979.
Arthur gets new eyeglasses and is teased by his friends
until he proves to them that he can now see well enough
to be the best basket shooter on the team.

Caple, Kathy. *The Biggest Nose*. Boston: Houghton Mifflin Co.,
1985.
Two hippos and an alligator tease Eleanor the Elephant·
about the size of her nose until Eleanor becomes assertive.

Carlson, N. *Loudmouth George and The Sixth Grade Bully*.
New York: Puffin Books, 1983.
A big kid tries to steal George's lunch.

Carlson, Nancy. *Arnie and the New Kid*. New York: Viking,
1990.
Philip is an animal kid in a wheelchair and Arnie teases
him. Finally Arnie discovers that you can be different
and still be friends.

Cole, Joanna. *Don't Call Me Names*. New York: Random
House, 1990.
A frog named Nell gets teased by a fox and a pig named
Mike and Joe. Nell dresses up in a monster costume and
forgets to be scared of the bullies.

Coombs, K. *Beating Bully O'Brien*. New York: Avon Books, 1992.
A girl who is being bullied at home bullies a fifth grade boy.

# Teasing

Crary, E. *My Name Is Not Dummy*. Seattle: Parenting Press, 1983.
How to cope with put-downs.

Delaney, Ned. *Two Strikes Four Eyes*. Boston: Houghton Mifflin Co., 1976.
Toby is a mouse who won't put his glasses on because his friends tease him. Finally he puts them on and bats in two runs.

dePaola, T. *Oliver Button Is a Sissy*. New York: Harcourt Brace Jovanovich, 1979.
A young boy is put-down for being different.

Estes, Eleanor. *The Hundred Dresses*. New York: Harcourt, Brace & World, Inc., 1944.
This is the classic story of Wanda Petronski, the girl with the funny last name from the poor part of town who is teased. Her family moves away to avoid discrimination, and Wanda's classmates feel guilty.

Gardner, R.A. *Dr. Gardner's Stories About the Real World*. Englewood Cliffs, New Jersey: Prentice-Hall, 1992.
A little boy learns to understand himself and his problems when he learns to listen.

Greene, Constance C. *The Ears of Louis*. New York: Viking Press, 1974.
Louis is teased about his big ears and learns to tease back.

Griff, Patricia Reilly. *The Beast in Ms. Rooney's Room*. New York: Dell Publishing, 1984.
A little boy who must repeat second grade is teased by his friends and his big sister for being dumb. He develops

self-confidence and makes new friends with the help of a
dedicated teacher.

Henkes, K. *Chrysanthemum*. New York: Greenwillow Books,
1991.
A kindergarten mouse is teased because she has a funny
name.

Honeycutt, Natalie. *The Fourth-Grade Four*. New York: Henry
Holt and Company, 1989.
Alex has to wear glasses and is teased by Billy who was
left back in first grade.

Naylor, Phyllis Reynolds. *Jennifer Jean, the Cross-Eyed Queen*.
Minneapolis: Carolrhoda Books, Inc., 1994.
A preschool child whose eyes are crossed gets teased by
her friends. By the time she enters school her eyes have
been straightened by treatment and she meets a male
child who also got his eyes straightened.

Naylor, Phyllis Reynolds. *King of the Playground*. New York:
Aladdin Books, Macmillan Publishing Co., 1994.
Sammy says he's King of the Playground, and he won't
let Kevin play. Kevin's dad helps out, and the boys
become friends.

Naylor, Phyllis. *Reluctantly Alice*. New York: Atheneum, 1991.
A seventh grade girl is made fun of by another girl. The
bullying stops after the girls get to know each other by
working together on a project.

Orgel, Doris. *Nobodies and Somebodies*. New York: Viking,
1991.
A fifth grade club excludes others including a new girl
and a girl who stutters.

# Teasing

Park, Barbara. *The Kid in the Red Jacket.* New York: Alfred A.
Knopf, 1987.
This story makes fun of kids who don't have friends
their own age and so play with little kids. Fifth grade boy
has a difficult time accepting the friendship of a first
grade girl.

Petty K., and Firmin, C. *Being Bullied.* New York: Baron's
Books, 1991.
A girl is bullied and teased by another girl but gets help
from her mother and her teacher.

Savitz, Harriet. *The Bullies and Me.* New York: Scholastic, 1991.
The new boy in town joins up with the bullies and tries
to understand himself.

Spinelli, Jerry. *Fourth-Grade Rats.* New York: Scholastic
Hardcover Books, 1991.
A fourth grader tries to be a bully like his friend and
learns a lesson about manhood.

Stolz, Mary. *The Bully of Barkham Street.* New York: Harper &
Row, 1967.
Does a bully care if he has any friends or not? Grades 4-6.

Waber, Bernard. *But Names Will Never Hurt Me.* Boston:
Houghton Mifflin, 1976.
It isn't easy having a name that everyone makes fun of.

Watson, Clyde. *Quips & Quirks.* New York: Thomas Y. Crowell
Co., 1975.
A collection of the names people have called each other.
Most of them are at least one hundred years old.

Wilhelm, H. *Tyrone the Horrible.* New York: Scholastic, 1988.

# Appendix

A big dinosaur picks on a little dinosaur, but the little one tricks the big one and is never bothered again.

Wood, W., and Wood A. *The Sandwich.* Toronto: Kids Can Press, 1975.
About being made fun of because of ethnic differences. The victims use cleverness and humor.

Woolley, Catherine. *Ginnie and Geneva.* New York: Morrow, 1948. Ginnie is having trouble with teasing in third grade.

Yashima, Taro. *Grow Boy.* New York: Viking Press, 1955. A shy Japanese boy is teased and isolated until he learns to share his differences and be accepted by the other children. Grades K-3.

Zolotow, Charlotte. *William's Doll.* New York: Harper & Row, 1972.
William likes to play sports but because he also wants a doll, the other kids think he is a sissy. His grandmother helps him to understand his desire for a doll. Grades K-3.

# *Teasing*

## TEASING/BULLYING SURVEY

1.  I am a girl _____; boy _____.
2.  I am in grade _____.
3.  Circle the letter of the sentence that best describes you.
    A) I am very happy at school and I'm glad I go here.
    B) I am pretty happy at school.
    C) School is all right. I don't love it or hate it.
    D) I am unhappy here at school and wish there was
    another school I could go to.
    E) I hate school. I wouldn't go to school if I didn't have to.
4.  How often do kids tease you by saying mean things to you?
    Every day _____        One or two times a week _____
    One or two times a month _____        Never _____
5.  Who says mean things the most?
    A) Popular kids _____        Unpopular kids _____
    B) Boys _____        Girls _____
6.  Which kind of teasing occurs most in your grade?
    Friendly teasing _____        Unfriendly teasing _____
7.  How many kids in your grade tease on a regular basis
    (most of the time)?
    _____ kids
8.  Where and when do kids tease most?
    When there are no teachers around _____
    In class _____
    During lunch _____
    On buses _____
    In the corridors _____
    In after school clubs _____
9.  What are most kids teased about?

    _____

    _____

10. Why do kids tease other kids?

    _____

    _____

11. What should be done about kids who tease in a mean way?

_____

_____

12. How do you stop teasing you don't like?

_____

_____

13. Do you ever tease other kids?
    Never _____         Sometimes _____
    Once a week _____    Once a month _____
14. Why do you tease other kids?

_____

_____

15. How often are you by yourself at recess?
    Every day _____ Once a week _____ Once a month _____
16. How often do you eat by yourself in the cafeteria?
    Every day _____ Once a week _____ Once a month _____
17. What does being 'cool' mean?

_____

_____

18. Do teachers help if you complain about being teased?
    Yes _____    No _____    Sometimes _____
19. Who teases most in your family?_____
20. How often do kids bully you by doing mean things to you, like trying to push you around, or hit you or strike you, or threaten you or steal your stuff?
    Every day _____ One or two times a week _____
    One or two times a month _____ One or two times a year _____
    Never _____
21. If you were bullied this year, did you tell anybody?
    No _____ Yes _____ I told my parent _____
    I told a teacher _____ I told a brother or sister _____
    I told a friend _____ I told someone not mentioned above _____
22. If you told someone you were bullied this year, did anybody try to help you? Yes _____ No _____

# *Teasing*

Explain:_____

_____

23. Do you see other kids being bullied? No _____ Yes _____
Explain:_____

_____

24. How often do you bully another by physically pushing or
    hitting or striking or stealing?
    Every day _____ One or two times a week _____
    One or two times a month _____ Never _____
25. How many bullies are there in your grade at school? _____

Remarks:

_____

_____

_____

_____

_____

_____

_____

_____

# Notes

## CHAPTER 1—WHAT IS TEASING?

1. William Shakespeare, "The Taming of the Shrew" in *Complete Works of William Shakespeare*, ed. by William George Clark and William Aldis Wright (New York: Grosset & Dunlap, 1911), pp .290-291.
2. *The Barnhart Dictionary of Etymology* (New York: The H.W. Wilson Co., 1988), p. 1119.
3. *Webster's New Collegiate Dictionary* (Springfield, Massachusetts: G. & C. Merriam Co. Publishers, 1956), p. 871.
4. *The New Shorter Oxford English Dictionary* (Oxford: Clarendon Press, 1993), p. 3233.
5. *Dictionary of American Slang* (New York: Thomas Crowell Co., 1975), p. 538.
6. "Groom with a View," *People*, May 23, 1994, p. 871.

## CHAPTER 2—WHY TEASE?

1. Margaret Atwood, *Cat's Eye* (New York: Bantam Books, 1989), pp. 251-52.
2. John Sedgwick, "What a Tease," *Boston Magazine*, October 1993, p. 65.
3. D.C. Dinkmeyer and J.J. Miro, *Group Counseling: Theory and Practice* (Itasca, Illinois: F.E. Peacock Publishers, 1979), p. 233.
4. Mark Antsey, "Scapegoating in Groups: Some Theoretical Perspectives and a Case Record of Intervention," *Social Work with Groups*, (The Haworth Press), Vol. 5(3), Fall 1982, p. 51.
5. "Just Teasing," *American Health*, July/August 1993, pp. 66-68.
6. Ibid.
7. Ibid.

# Teasing

CHAPTER 3—COMPULSIVE TEASING

1. Scott Smith, *A Simple Plan* (1993: St. Martin's Press), p. 364.
2. J.I. Rodale, *The Synonym Finder* (New York: Warner Books, 1978), p. 594.
3. Mark Antsey, "Scapegoating in Groups: Some Theoretical Perspectives and a Case Record of Intervention," *Social Work with Groups*, (The Haworth Press), Vol. 5(3), Fall 1982, p. 51.
4. *Scarlett*, exec. prod. Robert Halmi, CBS-TV, November 13, 15, 16, 17, 1994.

CHAPTER 4—THE PERSONALITIES OF TEASERS

1. L.M. Montgomery, *Anne of Green Gables* (London: George C. Harrap & Co., 1925), p. 130.
2. *Roseanne*, Paramount, Fox Television, January 1995.
3. *Hook*, dir. Steven Spielberg, (Columbia Tri-Star Home Video, 1992.)
4. Lea Pulkkinen, *Offensive and Defensive Aggression in Humans: a Longitudinal Perspective* (Jyvaskyla, Finland: University of Finland, 1987), p. 209.

CHAPTER 5—FLIRTING

1. Lynn Luria-Sukenick, "Do You Know the Facts of Life? (Quiz)" in *Touching Fire: Erotic Writings by Women*, ed. Louise Thornton, Jan Sturtevant and Amber Coverdale Sumrall (New York: Carroll & Graf Publishers Inc., 1989), p. 178.
2. *Tootsie*, screenplay by Larry Gelbart and Murray Schisgal (Columbia Pictures Industries, Inc., 1982).
3. Susan Rabin, *How to Attract Anyone, Anytime, Anyplace: The Smart Guide to Flirting* (New York: A Plume Book, 1993), p. 94.
4. Sydney Biddle Barrows and Ellis Weiner, *Mayflower Manners* (New York: Doubleday, 1990), pp. 105-106.
5. H.L. Mencken in *Columbia Dictionary of Quotations*, ed. Robert Andrews (New York: Columbia University Press, 1993), p. 337.
6. Alexandra Penney, *How to Keep Your Man Monogamous* (New York: Bantam, 1989), pp. 35-36.
7. Susan Rabin, p. 48.
8. Joyce Jillson, *The Fine Art of Flirting* (New York: Cornerstone Library, 1984), p. 49.

# Notes

9. Sue Fenton, "The 10 Top Flirting Tricks a Woman Uses to Snare a Man," *The National Enquirer*, December 13, 1994, p. 44.

10. Joyce Jillson, p. 118.

11. Susan Rabin, p. 46.

12. Joyce Jillson, p. 101.

13. Jan Gelman, *Marci's Secret Book of Flirting* (New York: Alfred A. Knopf, 1990), pp. 62-64.

14. Susan Rabin, p. 51.

15. Joyce Jillson, p. 63.

16. Susan Rabin, pp. 55-57.

17. Georgette Mosbacher, "How to Get the Man You Want," *Cosmopolitan*, September 1993, pp. 146-152.

18. Joyce Jillson, p. 71.

19. Susan Rabin, p. 139.

20. Lona O'Connor, "Confidential: The In-Flight Flirting File," *Cosmopolitan*, December 1989, pp. 112-114.

21. Joyce Jillson, p. 75.

22. Antoine de Saint-Exupery, in *Columbia Dictionary of Quotations*, ed. Robert Andrews (New York: Columbia University Press, 1993), p. 337.

23. Sydney Biddle Barrows, p. 106.

### CHAPTER 6—SEXUAL TEASING

1. Carl Hiaasen, *Strip Tease* (New York: Warner Books, 1993), p. 292-294.

2. Anne Rice, *Exit to Eden* (New York: Dell Publishing, 1985), p. 89.

3. Bernie Zilbergeld, *The New Male Sexuality* (New York: Bantam Books, 1992), p. 79.

4. Alexandra Penney, *How to Keep Your Man Monogamous* (New York: Bantam, 1989), p. 51.

5. Philip Elmer-Dewitt, "Now for the Truth about Americans and Sex," *Time*, October 17, 1994, p. 64.

### CHAPTER 7—TEASING AT THE WORKPLACE

1. Peggy Anderson, *Nurse* (1979; New York: A Berkley Book, 1979), p. 14.

2. Ibid., p. 122.

3. Carl Hiaasen, *Tourist Season* (New York: Warner Books,

1986), p. 6.

4. Lisa Davis and Ken Jennings, "Employee Horseplay and Likely Managerial Overreaction," *Labor Law Journal*, April 1989, p. 248.

5. Ibid., p. 248.

6. Ibid., p. 249.

7. Ibid., p. 252.

8. "Just Teasing," *American Health*, July/August 1993, p. 68.

9. Ibid., pp. 66-67.

CHAPTER 8—THE MALE ASPECTS OF TEASING

1. Margaret Atwood, *Cat's Eye* (New York: Bantam Books, 1989), p. 50.

2. "Just Teasing," *American Health*, July/August 1993, pp. 67-68.

3. John Friel, *The Grown-Up Man* (Deerfield Beach, Florida: Health Communications, Inc., 1991), p. 68.

4. "Just Teasing," *American Health*, July/August 1993, p. 68.

5. John Sedgwick, "What a Tease," *Boston Magazine*, October 1993.

6. Carl Hiaasen, *Skin Tight* (New York: Fawcett Crest, 1990), p. 66.

7. *Webster's Collegiate Thesaurus* (Springfield, Massachusetts: Merriam-Webster, Inc., 1976), p. 820.

8. *Dictionary of American Slang*, eds. Harold Wentworth and Stuart Flexner, (New York: Thomas Y. Crowell Co., 1960), p. 538.

9. *The New Shorter Oxford English Dictionary* (Oxford: Clarendon Press, 1993), p. 3233.

10. Helen G. Lerner, *Dance of Anger* (New York: Harper & Row, 1985), p.2.

CHAPTER 9—SEXUAL HARASSMENT

1. Michael Crichton, *Disclosure* (New York: Knopf, 1993), pp. 112-113.

2. C.A. Beier and Marcia Greenberger, "Understanding Harassment" in *Sexual Harassment: How to Develop and Implement Effective Policies* (Washington, D.C.: National Association of Manufacturers, 1987), pp. 1-5.

# Notes

3. Ibid.

4. Ibid.

5. *Stop Sexual Harassment*, Capital Cities/ABC in cooperation with American Women in Radio and Television, Inc. and the American Library Association, 1992, pp.1-3.

6. "It's Not Just Teasing," *U.S. News & World Report*, December 6, 1993, pp. 73-77.

7. C.A. Beier., pp.1-5.

8. Jonathan A. Segal, "The Defenselessness of Sexual Harassment" in *Sexual Harassment: How to Develop and Implement Effective Policies* (Washington, D.C.: National Association of Manufacturers, 1987), p. 31.

9. Linda R. Singer and Joanne L. Hustead, "Preventing Sexual Harassment" in *Sexual Harassment: How to Develop and Implement Effective Policies* (Washington, D.C.: National Association of Manufacturers, 1987), pp. 13-18.

10. Marian Horoskip, "Sexual Harassment," *Dance Magazine*, April 1993, pp. 62-63.

11. *Stop Sexual Harassment*, pp. 1-3.

12. "A Rub, a Grab, a Feel. Is This Really Happening?" *Glamour*. February 1993, p. 75.

13. "It's Not Just Teasing," pp. 73-77.

14. Ruth Shalit, "Romper Room," *New Republic*, March 29, 1993, pp. 13-15.

15. "Sexual Harassment," *Ladies Home Journal*, September 1993, pp. 112-118.

16. "Coming Unhinged Over Hand-Holding Ban," *Boston Globe*, January 21, 1995, p. 9.

17. Ruth Shalit, pp.13-15.

## CHAPTER 10—GOSSIP IS A TEASE

1. Sydney Biddle Barrows and Ellis Weiner, *Mayflower Manners* (New York: Doubleday, 1990), p. 166.

2. Blaise Pascal in *Columbia Dictionary of Quotations*, ed. Robert Andrews (New York: Columbia University Press, 1993), p. 379.

3. Clyde Watson, *Quips & Quirks* (New York: Thomas Y. Crowell Co., 1975), p. 27.

4. Sydney Biddle Barrows, pp. 172-173.

5. Erasmus Desiderius in *Columbia Dictionary of Quotations* ed.

Robert Andrews (New York: Columbia University Press, 1993), p. 379.

6. Patricia Meter Spacks, *Gossip* (New York: Alfred A. Knopf, 1985), p. 123.

7. Ibid., p. 90.

8. Ibid., p. 13.

9. Sydney Biddle Barrows, pp. 167-168.

10. Patricia Meter Spacks, p. 117.

11. Ibid., p. 67.

12. Ibid., p. 68

13. Sydney Biddle Barrows, p. 180.

CHAPTER 11—TEASING, PERFECTION AND THE ADDICTIONS

1. Gelsey Kirkland with Greg Lawrence, *Dancing on My Grave* (1986; New York: Jove Books, 1987), p. 23.

2. Carl Jung in *Columbia Dictionary of Quotations*, ed. Robert Andrews (New York: Columbia University Press, 1993), p. 13.

3. Arnold Washton and Donna Boundy, *Willpower Is Not Enough: Understanding and Recovering from Addictions of Every Kind* (New York: Harper & Row, 1989), p. 16.

4. Jill Smolowe, "Intimate Strangers," *Time*, Spring 1995, pp. 20-21.

5. Arnold Washton, pp. 197-199.

6. Janet E. Damon, *Shopaholics: Serious Help for Addicted Spenders* (Los Angeles: Price Stern Sloan, 1988), p. 37.

7. Ibid., p. 50.

8. Arnold M. Washton, p. 133.

9. Janet E. Damon, p. 39.

10. Ibid., p. 19.

11. Ibid., pp. 64-65.

12. Ibid., p. 83.

13. Ibid., p. 206.

14. Gelsey Kirkland, pp. 56-57.

15. Stanton Peele and Archie Brodsky, *The Truth About Addiction and Recovery* (New York: Simon & Schuster, 1992), p. 109.

16. Janice Keller Phelps and Alan E. Nourse, *The Hidden Addiction and How to Get Free* (Boston: Little, Brown & Co., 1986), pp. 26-27.

17. *Diagnostic & Statistical Manual of Mental Disorders*, 4th ed., (Washington, D.C., American Psychiatric Association, 1994), p. 616.

18. Mary Heineman, *Losing Your Shirt* (Minneapolis:

# Notes

CompCare Publishers, 1992), p. 20.

19. *Handbook of Pathological Gambling*, ed. Thomas Galski (Springfield, Illinois: Charles C. Thomas, 1987), p 62.

20. Mary Heineman, p. 46.

21. Ibid., p. xix.

22. Linda Berman, *Behind the 8-Ball: A Guide for Families of Gamblers* (New York: Simon & Schuster; a Fireside/Parkside Recovery Book, 1992), p. 30.

23. Henry Lesieur, Ph.D., *Women Who Gamble Too Much* (New York, National Council on Problem Gambling, 1993), p. 3.

24. Linda Berman, p. 32.

25. Mary Heineman, p. 121.

26. "Not Just a Game," *Focus Magazine* in *Philadelphia's Independent Business Weekly*, May 16, 1990.

27. Mary Heineman, p. xxi.

28. Patrick Carnes, *Out of the Shadows: Understanding Sexual Addiction*, 2d ed. (Minneapolis: CompCare Publishers, 1992), pp. 10-16.

29. *An Introduction to Sex and Love Addicts Anonymous* (Boston, The Augustine Fellowship, 1985), p. 4.

30. Patrick Carnes, p. 39.

31. Ibid., p. 104.

32. Ibid., p. 107.

33. Stanton Peele, p. 99.

34. Liz Hodgkinson, *Addictions: What They Are and Why They Happen: How to Help* (New York: Thorsons Publishing Group, 1986), p. 199.

35. Ibid., p. 123.

36. "Caffeine Addiction, Study Finds," *Boston Globe*, October 5, 1994, p. 10.

37. Ian Shoales, "Wake Up and Find the Coffee," *Boston Globe*, December 29, 1994, p. 13.

38. Joe Rhodes, "One Cup at a Time," *Boston Globe*, February 4, 1995.

39. Dennis Wholey, *The Courage to Change* (Boston: Houghton Mifflin Co., 1984), p. 5.

40. Liz Hodgkinson, p. 80.

41. Ibid., pp. 25-26.

42. Ibid., pp. 34-35.

43. Gelsey Kirkland, p. 282.

44. Liz Hodgkinson, pp. 41-42.

45. Stanton Peele, p. 93.

### CHAPTER 12—MONEY IS A TEASE

1. Hermann Hesse, *Demian* (1965; New York: Bantam Books, 1968), pp. 19-20.
2. Philip Elmer-Dewitt, "Now for the Truth about Americans and Sex," *Time*, October 17, 1994, p. 64.
3. Marc Shell, *Money, Language, and Thought* (Baltimore: Johns Hopkins University Press, 1982), pp. 5-6.
4. Ibid., p. 19.
5. Ibid., p. 108.

### CHAPTER 13— SUSPENSE IS A TEASE

1. Susan Hill, *Mrs. De Winter* (New York: Avon Books, 1993), p. 341.
2. *New Collegiate Dictionary of The American Heritage Dictionary of the English Language* (Boston: Houghton Mifflin Co., 1981), p. 1296.
3. Bill Pronzini, "The Element of Surprise" in *Writing Suspense & Mystery Fiction*, ed. A.S. Burack (Boston: The Writer, Inc., 1977), p. 178.
4. F.A. Rockwell, "Fiction Openings: Five Musts," *The Writer*, January 21, 1992, p. 21.
5. Heidi Vanderbilt, "How to Put Suspense in Your Story," *The Writer*, January 1991, p. 20.
6. Dean Koontz, *Mr. Murder* (New York: Berkley Books, 1993), p. 44.
7. Patricia Highsmith, Plotting & Writing Suspense Fiction (Boston: The Writer, Inc., 1981), p. 56.
8. Marilyn Stasio, "Under the Spell of Scary Stuff," *New York Times Book Review*, June 9, 1991, p. 53.
9. Charlotte Armstrong, "The Three Basics of Suspense" in *Writing Suspense & Mystery Fiction*, ed. A.S. Burack (Boston: The Writer, Inc., 1977), p. 10.
10. Cecilia Bartholomew, "The Man in the Closet" in *Writing Suspense & Mystery Fiction*, ed. A.S. Burack (Boston: The Writer, Inc., 1977), p. 26.

# Notes

## CHAPTER 14—COPING WITH ADULT TEASING

1. Lillian Helman, *Pentimento*, from *The Crown Treasury of Relevant Quotations*, by Edward F. Murphy (New York, Crown Publishers, Inc., 1978), p. 132.

## CHAPTER 15—SOLUTIONS FOR PARENTS AND TEACHERS

1. *The Broken Toy*, writ. and dir. Thomas Brown, Summerhill Presentations with Domino's Pizza of Zanesville and Newark, New Jersey, 1993.
2. *No More Teasing*, exec. prod. Jean Robbins, Sunburst Publications, Inc., Pleasantville, New York, 1995.
3. *The Broken Toy*.
4. Richard J. Hazler, John H. Hoover and Ronald Oliver, "What Do Kids Say About Bullying?" *Education Digest*, March 1993.
5. *No More Teasing*.
6. "What Bullying Does to Kids," *Learning*, February 1994, p.39.
7. Ibid., p. 39.
8. Jane Marks, "Our Daughter Is So Meek," *Parents Magazine*, December 9, 1992, pp. 50-56.
9. "Battling with a Bully," *Essence*, September 1994, p. 112.
10. Laura Rhizor, "Taking in Teasing," *L.A. Parent Magazine*, July 1994, pp. 38-39, 92-93.
11. Lawrence Kutner. "Mom . . . The Kids Don't Like Me!" *Redbook*, July 1991, p. 48.
12. Grace Hechinger, *How to Raise a Street Smart Child*, (New York: Facts on File Publications, 1984), p. 119.
13. Ibid., p. 121.
14. Marilyn Elias, "Push Comes to Shove," *U.S.A. Today*, 4th ed., January 25, 1995, p. 5D.
15. Richard J. Hazler, p. 17.
16. *No More Teasing*.
17. "Bullying Breeds Violence," Learning, February 1994, p. 39.
18. *Education Reform Act, Questions and Answers on School Councils*, (Boston, Massachusetts Department of Education, Updated October 1994), p. 12.
19. Pamela Siegle and Gayle Macklem, informational packet on *The Reach Out to Schools: Social Competency Program* (Wellesley, Massachusetts: The Stone Center, Wellesley College, 1994).

CHAPTER 16—HELPING CHILDREN COPE WITH TEASING

1. Beverly Cleary, *Ramona the Pest*, Illustrated by Louis Darling (New York, William Morrow & Co., 1968), p. 162.
2. "As They Grow," *Parents Magazine*, June 1994, p. 98.
3. "Hit Me Please," *Psychology Today*, July 1994, p. 15.
4. *No More Teasing*, exec. prod. Jean Robbins, Sunburst Publications, Inc., Pleasantville, New York, 1995.
5. Richard J. Hazler, John H. Hoover and Ronald Oliver, "What Do Kids Say About Bullying?" *Education Digest*, March 1993, p. 18.
6. Andrew O'Hagan, "Growing Up Nasty," *Harper's Magazine*, November 14, 1994, p. 45.
7. Richard J. Hazler, p. 18.
8. Marilyn Elias, "Push Comes to Shove," *U.S.A. Today*, January 4, 1995, p. 39.
9. "What Bullying Does to Kids," Learning, February 1994.
10. Heidi B. Perlman, "Newton 9-year-old Teaches Wellesley Kids Lessons in Life," *Newton Graphic*, January 19, 1995, p. 9.
11. Richard J. Hazler, p. 17.
12. Dorothy M. Ross and Sheila A. Ross, "Teaching the Child with Leukemia to Cope with Teasing," *Issues in Comprehensive Pediatric Nursing*, Vol. 7:59-66, 1989.

CHAPTER 17—HELP FOR BULLIES

1. Judy Blume, *Blubber*, (Scarsdale, NY, Bradbury Press, 1974), p. 89.
2. Richard J. Hazler, John H. Hoover and Ronald Oliver, "What Do Kids Say About Bullying?" *Education Digest*, March 1993, p. 16.
3. Good Housekeeping and the National PTA, "Bumps, Bruises and Bullies," *Good Housekeeping*, October 1993, pp. 194-196.
4. Richard J. Hazler, p. 18.
5. Laura Rhizor, "Taking in Teasing," *L.A. Parent Magazine*, July 1994, p. 48.
6. Lawrence Kutner. "Mom . . . The Kids Don't Like Me!" *Redbook*, July 1991, p. 48.
7. Marilyn Elias, "Push Comes to Shove," *U.S.A. Today*, January 4, 1995, p. 5D.
8. Andrew O'Hagan, "Growing Up Nasty," *Harper's Magazine*,

# *Notes*

November 14, 1994, p. 45.

9. Lea Pulkkinen, *Offensive and Defensive Aggression in Humans:* a Longitudinal Perspective (Jyvaskyla, Finland: University of Finland, 1987), p. 197.

10. Nancy Gibbs, "Death and Deceit," *Time*, November 14, 1994, p. 45.

11. *Turning Point*, Boston: Channel 5, December 14, 1994.

12. "Another Japanese Boy, Called Bullying Victim, Kills Himself," *Boston Globe*, December 14, 1994, p. 21.

13. *Good Housekeeping*, October 1993, p. 194.

14. *Andover Townsman*, January 12, 1995, p. 11.

15. *Good Housekeeping*, October 1993.

## CHAPTER 18—SIBLING TEASING

1. Charlotte Bronte, J*ane Eyre* (New York: Beekman Publishers, Inc., 1980), pp 5-6.

2. Adele Faber and Elaine Mazlish, *Siblings Without Rivalry* (New York: Avon Books, 1987), p. 147.

3. Ibid., p.127

4. Sarah Stiansen Mahoney, "Seven Things You Should Never Say to Your Kids," *Redbook*, October 1994, pp. 190, 194.

5. Adele Faber, p. 89.

6. Ibid., p. 148.

7. Janet Bode, *Truce: Ending the Sibling War* (New York: Franklin Watts, 1991), p. 92.

8. Adele Faber, p. 153.

9. "When the Bully is Your Brother," *American Health Magazine*, September, 1993, p. 84.

## CHAPTER 19—CHILDREN WITH DISABILITIES AND TEASING

1. William Bell, *The Cripple's Club* (Toronto, Canada, Irwin Publishing, 1988), p. 13.

2. *Understanding Handicaps*, 3d ed. (Newtonville, Massachusetts: Understanding Handicaps of Newton, Inc., 1994).

3. "Heads of the Class," *People*, February 2, 1995.

4. Dorothy M. Ross and Sheila A. Ross, "Teaching the Child with Leukemia to Cope with Teasing," *Issues in Comprehensive Pediatric Nursing*, Vol. 7, 1984, pp. 60-61.

5. Dorothy M. Ross, p. 61.

6. Ibid., p. 62.

7. Ibid., p. 62.

8. Ibid., p. 63.

9. Ibid., p. 64.

10. Thomas J. Carroll, *Blindness: What It Is, What It Does and How to Live with It* (Boston: Little, Brown & Co., 1961), pp. 14-80.

CHAPTER 20—CHILDREN TEASING ADULTS

1. Carroll, Lewis in *Bartlett's Familiar Quotations*, 16th ed., ed. Justin Kaplan (Boston: Little, Brown & Co., 1992), p. 517.

CHAPTER 21—ADULTS TEASING CHILDREN

1. German Proverb, from *A New Dictionary of Quotations on Historical Principles from Ancient and Modern Sources* (New York, Alfred A. Knopf, 1977), p. 1182.

2. John Sedgwick, "What a Tease," *Boston Magazine*, October 1993, p. 66.

3. Sarah Stiansen Mahoney, "Seven Things You Should Never Say to Your Kids," *Redbook*, October 1994, p. 194.

4. "Just Teasing," *American Health*, July/August 1993, pp. 66-68.

5. Sarah Stiansen Mahoney, pp. 190, 194.

6. "Just Teasing," p. 66.

CHAPTER 22—THE RECOVERING TEASE

1. Alexander Pope, *A Farewell to London*, from *Dictionary of Quotations* by Bergen Evans (New York, Delacorte Press, 1968), p. 225.

2. Oscar Wilde in *Columbia Dictionary of Quotations*, ed. Robert Andrews (New York: Columbia University Press, 1993), p. 901.

3. Dennis Wholey, *The Courage to Change* (Boston: Houghton Mifflin Co., 1984), p. 22.

4. Linda Feinberg. *I'm Grieving As Fast As I Can: How Young Widows and Widowers Can Cope and Heal.* (Far Hills, New Jersey: New Horizon Press, 1994), p. 136.

5. Arnold Washton and Donna Boundy, *Willpower Is Not Enough: Understanding and Recovering from Addictions of Every Kind* (New York: Harper & Row, 1989), pp. 197-199.